Postmodern Praxis in Literature

Books by Jagdish Batra

Indian English Fiction (2001-2020): History and Reflections (2021)

Studies in Fiction, Feminism, Diaspora: India and Beyond (2017)

Postcolonial Literature Today (2015). Co-edited with Prof. Alan Johnson, Idaho State University, USA)

A New Approach to Literary Theory and Criticism (2014). Co-authored with Dr. R.S. Malik

21st Century Indian Novel in English: Emerging Issues and Challenges (2012)

Form and Style in Indian English Fiction (2011)

Jhumpa Lahiri's The Namesake*: A Critical Study* (2010)

T.S. Eliot: A Deconstructive Reading (2010)

Rohinton Mistry: Identity, Values and other Sociological Concerns (2008)

Rotaract Handbook (1983) Co-authored with PDG Shamsher Jung Bahadur Rana

Books by Bimlesh K. Singh

Harold Pinter: A Critical Study 2016

Interact in English Vols. I, II & III (2017-2019) Co-authored with Dr. Himanshu Sharma

Postmodern Praxis in Literature

Edited by
Jagdish Batra
Bimlesh K. Singh

Prestige Books International
New Delhi

Published by
Prestige Books International
New Delhi 110 060
prestigebooks@gmail.com
Phone: 9818755529

Associate Office
P.O. Box 2250
Sydney 2001
Australia

ISBN: 978-81-956029-0-2

Cover picture

The book cover is reproduced from a painting by Ms. Renu Batra, an amateur artist. The theme of postmodernism is represented through various streaks with blurred boundaries. Besides, the bright colours represent popular fiction riding high while serious literature is denoted by muted colours.

Printed in India

Contents

One of the basic rules of the universe is that nothing is perfect. Perfection simply does not exist . . . without imperfection, neither you nor I would exist.

Stephen Hawking

Om Puurnnam-Adah Puurnnam-Idam, Puurnnaat-Puurnnam-Udacyate;
Puurnnasya Puurnnam-Aadaaya, Puurnnam-Eva-Avashissyate.
(That divinity is perfect and this creation is perfect. Having given away perfect, divinity still remains perfect)

Isha Upanishad

Preface

The present book is a compilation of selected research papers presented at the 7th JGU International Literary Conference organized in July 2021 by the English Literary Society of O.P. Jindal Global University, Sonipat, India, on the theme of "Postmodernism: Time for Reappraisal."

The authors of the papers in the present anthology, apart from taking up the philosophical and theoretical aspects of Postmodernism, have deliberated on how it functions in the field of literature. Both the thematic and the stylistic aspects of literature, mainly fiction, have been studied, citing examples from acclaimed texts which have gained popularity in the contemporary world. In sync with the postmodern ethos, there are write-ups dealing, apart from literature, with music and movies also. Of the themes touched, one can notice LGBT, digital media, Dalit, dystopia, terror; and styles like magic realism, diary, interactive fiction, etc.

The writers whose works have been taken up for the study of postmodern elements befittingly belong to various corners of the world besides India. Thus, we find writers from UK, USA, Canada, Italy, Japan, France, Sweden, Algeria and so on. Even though locational as also national identities in these postmodern times are unstable, we still are curious about these aspects and try to locate cultural elements relevant to location. Also these writers belong to different historical timeframes. Thus, we have Chitra Banerjee Divakaruni's *The Forest of Enchantment* published in 2021 jostling with Shakespeare's *The Merchant of Venice* that was written in the last decade of 16th century.

Most of the articles come from the pens of budding scholars and display, therefore, the freshness of newer themes. We have contributors from different corners of India, right from Shillong, Meghalaya to Jaipur, Rajasthan and from Kollam, Kerala to Dharamkot, Punjab. Besides, there are contributors from other countries like U.S.A., Russia and Algeria also. The papers also show the use of different approaches in discussing, analyzing and deconstructing the chosen topics. We hope that this anthology will be helpful to students and researchers studying English literature in various Indian universities.

Although we have tried our best to edit the papers carefully, yet in a work of this type in which several writers have contributed, an occasional mistake here or there could be spotted, for which we beg to be excused. Finally, let us express our gratitude to the contributors of this book. Our heartful thanks to the publishers, M/s Prestige Books International, New Delhi, who have brought out the publication in a beautiful format. Our special thanks to Prof. R.K. Dhawan and Prof. Suman Bala for their wholehearted guidance and support in executing this project.

JAGDISH BATRA
BIMLESH K. SINGH

Introduction

Although the term 'postmodern' was used as early as 1947, yet it was around 1990s that the wave of post-modernity actually threatened to take over the world. Referring to the "time-space compression" that was happening, Doreen Massey, a critic, in her book *Space, Place and Gender*, spoke of "annihilation of space by time" and commented about the "use in literature of terms and phrases such as speed-up, global village, overcoming spatial barriers, the disruption of horizons, and so forth." She rued that the globalized marketplace was devouring the traditional business all over: "The sense of dislocation which some feel at the sight of a once well-known local street now lined with a succession of cultural imports—the pizzeria, the kebab house, the branch of the middle-eastern bank (sic)" (147). We saw this happen in India also. All this was helped greatly by the improved means of transportation and communication. The concurrent information revolution too helped usher in a new wave—not only of ideas but also of white-collar workforce (read IT professionals) who crossed oceans looking for greener pastures. In fact, postmodernity had already metamorphosed into a philosophy of postmodernism.

Soon postmodernity metamorphosed into a postmodern philosophy and was called postmodernism. Despite its glaring contradictions, Postmodernism continues to be valued as a cultural theory with the teachers and students in universities all over the academe spending much time on unravelling the complex warp and woof of this construct which many refuse to believe as a theory. The surprising aspect of it is that even though articulated first as a descriptive paradigm to denote the bypassing of Modernism in a historical timeframe, it soon got accepted as a prescriptive matrix in various disciplines like arts, architecture, sociology, politics, economics, philosophy, literature, etc.

The purpose of this section of the book is not to attempt a detailed account of postmodernism—that will require another book-length of space. However, it would be in the fitness of things to have a cursory view of Postmodernism that is variously referred to as a philosophy, approach, condition, theory and what not. Further, without indulging in hair-splitting with regard to the distinction between post-structuralism and postmodernism, or for that matter, exploring the grey area between modernism and postmodernism, we take stock of the broad features of postmodernism.

The first and foremost assault of postmodernism was on grand narratives as also on authority and tradition. While the conventional wisdom aspired to comprehend absolute truth, postmodernism has shunned all such search for absolutism, finding the search to be next to impossible. So, it favours relativism. Afterall, Derrida, the high priest of Deconstruction started his academic crusade with a challenge to the logocentric bias of western metaphysics. The age we live in is post-truth era which delineation is the reiteration of Lyotard's celebration of the failure of representation of reality. Virtual reality has taken over and all of us are getting sucked into the virtual world as foreseen by Baudrillard. Life on virtual platforms is getting to be more real than real life.

In such a scenario, the self faces dilemma with regard to its manifestation because the language has been shown to be a play of twin-forked sign which fails to appropriate meaning. Even if it could represent anything, there is the notion of discourse as stipulated by Foucault. Discourse controls our thinking and it is itself controlled by the powers-that-be. But then this leads to Catch-22 situation. If we cannot think independently, how can the theorist transcend this limitation and give us new ideas? Maybe the philosopher can do so and the thesis of discourse holds good only for the commoners. But again, the postmodernist aspires to bring the marginalized to the mainstream—will this action be hedged in so far as intellectual agency is concerned? There are a lot of questions that remain unanswered, and the only answer is that there can't be any answer. Remember George Bernard Shaw's golden rule mentioned in "The Revolutionist's Handbook" appended to his masterpiece *Man and Superman:* "The golden rule is that there are no golden rules."

However, despite the volatility of sign, literature still continues to be written and read in these postmodern times. The communication channels as well continue to work effectively. That's a relief, indeed! There are of course, some stylistic markers, mainly of indeterminate nature, that are linked to postmodern philosophy. There would be no hard and fast principles, so we have multiple registers and endings of narratives, experiments in narrative technique like magic realism, intertextuality, and so on.

Beyond literature, other disciplines too bear the brunt of postmodernism. Architecture was the first field, we are told, where the postmodern edifice in brick and mortar was raised by Charles Jencks. Then we had it in painting and arts and music. History got dislocated because the distinction between fact and fiction was found to be blurred. Talking of the social scene, we are told that postmodernism celebrates difference, diversity, eccentricity, novelty, eclecticism, hybridism, etc. etc. There are some positives though. With the assault on the logos, the margins have gained. There is recognition of the sidelined people, races, epistemologies, etc. So, LGBT is now no longer the neglected fringe. There is more talk about the tribal communities. One hopes the outreach to them is not to find new market for the mass production of consumer items!

Postmodernism would not brook the high moral tone of the old order. After all, the western states swearing by Christianity had gone to war, enslaved people around the world and wreaked havoc on earth. Even the much-touted democratic order had been challenged by Marxism. Postmodernism will not side with tradition and its high attendant notions of purity and authenticity, the conventional forms of social life, etc. So, the scriptures and hallowed texts of yore get treated as just texts. The 'text' itself envelopes all representations, whether in letter or in paint or in stone or on screen and so on!

The moral values of yore lost the base of religion and the omnipotent God. The only god that provides sanction now to values is Mammon in the globalized world with powerful MNCs—the emerging new ruling dispensation (or is it old; remember East India Company!) that would control our minds and produce alpha, beta, gamma races on conveyer belts as Aldous Huxley envisaged and as clones get replicated and life gets manufactured in labs, we shudder to think of the arrival of a despot to control the world! A dreadful scenario indeed with no agency or values or God, but Ford of *Brave New World*! Or it could be a dictator wielding the power of science to advantage? No, we are not thinking of Xi Jinping. They say it is the conflation of economy and culture like other epistemological categories getting conflated with the disappearance of false dividing lines. But it is economics that reigns supreme and its accomplice science marches on despite its condemnation by the Postmoderns for false appropriation of truth and reason.

There are, for sure, many contradictions in postmodernism. The biggest poser is if we discard essentialism, then how come postmodern condition is universal? It is like applying Lyotard's rejection of metanarrative challenging the postmodernism as a grand narrative!

Postmodernists seem stuck in the maze of their own making. Take nation, for example. Marx had envisioned disappearance of nation which woefully did not happen except that some communist states got fragmented while others disowned Marxism or created their own version of it. Postmodernism looked at nation as an imagined community. It was going to be a globalized world after all, and with over-vocal concern of the Postmodern for the peripheral, the local too crept into the field of consideration. The concoction of local and global was prepared bypassing the intervening structure of nation. But the nation refused to surrender; even got stronger when Jihadist terror struck and thereafter Corona swept the world! Howsoever nasty the picture of dystopia created out of nation be, there is no possibility of a Marxian or postmodern utopia wherein you obliterate the boundaries of nation. This aspect of Postmodernism has been criticized by the renowned scholar Rajiv Malhotra as an attempt to fragment the third world "in an intellectually deep and fashionable manner." In a talk on Postmodernism, he mentions that whereas this philosophy is cocooned in certain academic and pop culture circles and has failed to get mainstreamed in America, in the third world, intellectuals have become "a franchise to reproduce for local consumption." (Source: https://www.youtube.com/watch?v=dwjTOg-fyVq0)

II

Coming to the contents of this anthology, we find it a matter of satisfaction that these touch upon many aspects of the postmodern including postmodernity and postmodernism. We begin with the transcripted speech of the Chief Guest, renowned Indologist and committed public intellectual Sh. Rajiv Malhotra, founder of the Infinity Foundation, USA. His keynote address at the inaugural ceremony of the 7th JGU International Literary Conference held the audience spellbound. His take on artificial intelligence in these postmodern times was something that is not normally discussed in literary circles, but which indeed should be our concern. His lecture was thought-provoking which delivered a timely warning about the imminent threat posed to our civilizational values by A.I. To pass comments on his scholarship would be the proverbial "showing the earthen lamp to the sun."

The papers presented at the Conference are taken up next. We have a brilliant paper linking globalization and postmodernism to world literature by Abhinaba Chatterjee. The writer muses on the capitalistic nature of globalization which is impacting culture, and the question that bothers him is whether this will lead to homogenization or retain scope for separate identity. In this context, politics of the day appears to cast shadow on literary studies too. The identity of world literature with questions raised on the extremely important act of translation becomes an important issue.

In her scholarly article "Situating Feminism within the Modernist vs. Postmodernist Debate," Dr. S. Chitra from the Royal University of Bhutan avers that until the Modernist period, the attempts of feminist theories and perspectives had been to analyze women's oppression and think of ways towards women's liberation. While the Modernist feminism conceived various theories, postmodernism deconstructed them to find that the "universal subject of 'Enlightenment modernism' and feminism, in theory and practice, are far from being 'transcendent' and 'ungendered'" as these tend to essentialize women's condition which is differently perceived and felt in various societies. Since inherent contradictions thwart the attempts to categorize feminism as modernist or postmodernist, contemporary feminism, therefore, is ambivalent with the traits of plurality, multiplicity and difference marking it.

The paper by Abigail Fracia Lapang Sunn impressively traces the Kafkaesque elements in *The Strange Library*, a novel by the well-known Japanese novelist Haruki Murakami and compares these to similar items in a story captioned "The Augustine Ant" by the Italian writer Italo Calvino. The postmodern angle is brought forth by the ludicrous juxtaposition of the commonplace with the marvelous in the magic realist mode as also the iconic motifs of dismantling of grand narratives, fragmentation, open ending, minimalism, etc.

In his interesting essay "Why Publish or Perish? Re-reading of a report on knowledge," Umesh Patra brings out impressively the anxieties of a beginner in academia and relating Lyotard's postulate, comments on the current craze in India to somehow create knowledge because there is ample scope to subsume all types of writings under the shibboleth of knowledge. From Barthes' notion of death of the author, the writer takes it not to the birth of the reader but of the publisher which is indeed a sad reality that will resonate in every academic's heart. Also he compares the present trend of multiple platforms for the publication of research papers with Lyotard's idea of 'paralogy' and states that "In the absence of a sole truth, a transcendental signified, the proliferation of these numerous research papers could also be seen as language games between tricksters." That scenario is certainly undesirable.

Antara Biswas along with her guide Dr Rashmi Gaur takes up women's struggle for liberation in the novel *The Girl with the Dragon Tattoo* by the Swede novelist Stieg Larsson. Lisbeth Salander's bodily experience is sought to be related to socio-cultural environment, particularly the crime situation. The notion of subversion is underlined through the role that the trendy tattooing plays in these postmodern times. Against this backdrop, the protagonist emerges as a social alien and the normally neglected fashion trend of tattooing becomes symbolic of a rape survivor's quality of life.

The paper "Fluidity of Fiction and Non-Fiction: A Postmodernist Reading of *The Diary of Cotton Mather* (1702-1724)" by the Russian scholar Dr Violetta Trofimova employs the perspective of the Italian philosopher Umberto Eco toward appreciating the non- fictional piece by Cotton Mather. Through the technique, the critic conveys the idea that the literary texts are "open, internally dynamic and psychologically engaged fields" while employing the multidimensional space of semiosis. Dr. Trofimova, an expert on the 18th century English literature, discusses the selected work as a Postmodern text blurring the boundaries of fiction and non- fiction.

Mahima Kashyap, in her paper, explores the roots of terrorism in our times on the bases of memoirs of Mark Rudd and Abdullah Anas. The researcher seeks to evaluate the process through which the Western hegemony of discourse tends to limit the implications of the term "terrorism." She highlights the rise of infamous terrorist organizations in the totalitarian nature of the American as well as the European discourse on nation. At the same time, she emphasizes that the term "Jihad" is often misrepresented in the contemporary discourse with a view to establishing it as a holy cause.

R. Jaya Pratha's paper focusses on paranoia in the dystopian societies of George Orwell's *Nineteen Eighty-Four* and Margaret Atwood's *Oryx and Crake.* The researcher seeks to represent the psychological battle being fought by the characters of the novels against the backdrop of manipulation of media. In such a dystopian setting, the endless existential crisis of the populace under the totalitarian regime is delineated in Orwell's novel. Likewise, in *Oryx and Crake*, Atwood exposes the possibility of future apocalypse through the ecological destruction.

The Tamil writer Bama Faustina Soosairaj, popularly known as Bama, is an icon of Dalit literature. Scholar S. Smruthi, in her paper, carries out a postmodern reading of Bama's much acclaimed work *Sangati*. It is an astute attempt at subverting the Eurocentric schema of a typical plot. The writer aims at dismantling the hierarchy in literature, extirpating the dichotomy of the unrefined and the elitist writings. The unconventional raw language employed by the writer defies the conventional vocabulary, grammar and other dominant aspects of literature. The paper deconstructs the hegemonic/ monological truth and reveals a new kind of narrative.

The Algerian scholar Serir Lina in her paper titled "Dystopian Writings in Postmodern Literature" critically studies dystopia in the light of Postmodernism. The researcher employs the uncontrolled surge of the disillusionment issuing from the Post-World

War II scenario. Due to the rapid changes in socio-political dynamics, the value systems have been questioned and have given rise to complex perspectives like Deconstruction and distrust of grand narratives. The coming into being of the 'Dystopian' society is the natural corollary of the pervasive breakdown which the researcher has noticed in works like George Orwell's novel *Nineteen Eighty-Four*. Foucault's power dynamics has been applied to unravel the enigmatic interplay of the power variants at work.

Scholar Vinita Nair working with her guide Dr Mekhala Venkatesh explores in the paper titled "The Postmodernist Nature of the New Wave of Interactive Fiction on Television," the genre of Interactive Fiction. For this purpose, the paper critically looks at the television serial *Bandersnatch* and underlines the distinctive features of the genre. It would seem that both postmodernism and interactive fiction interface in many aspects of thematic treatment. The researchers talk about the common denominators like multiple narratives, uncertainty, freedom of treatment, etc. Interactive Fiction is represented as open space where users have control over story lines as well as endings, employing second person's point of view wherein the readers assume the role of the protagonist and determine the course of action.

Pratibha Nehra has taken up for study renowned author Chitra Banerjee Divakaruni's *The Forest of Enchantment* wherein Sita's disapproval of Ram's action, particularly, in sending her back to the woods on account of a dhobi's complaint has been underlined. The researcher must be commended for impressively applying the feminist approach which holds Ram guilty of oppressing a woman—his legally wedded wife. The critique sharpens the edge built in by Divakaruni.

Mahesh Dattani, well-known Indian playwright and first winner of Sahitya Akademi award for plays written in English has touched upon subjects which postmodernist thought has highlighted. Aarti Duhan has taken up Dattani's latest play "The Big

Fat City" to focus on the lifestyle influenced by the glitz and glamour of Mumbai life which puts all considerations of values on the backburner. Issues like live-in relationships, LGBT issues, drug mafia etc. demand our attention. It is a caustic comment on the middle class that aspires after material advancement in these postmodern times and cares two hoots for values.

Scholar Ravita has explored the issue of double displacement of Afro-Asian community in their new homeland Canada as depicted in acclaimed novelist M.G. Vassanji's *No New Land.* The movement across political boundaries and oceans has gathered speed in postmodern times. This one, however, is a forced migration that brings with it the consequent problems like culture shock, maladjustment, discrimination, etc. While postmodernism celebrates global citizenship, the middle class has problems coping with the demands of the new age. The novel also focusses on the renewed nationalistic fervour in Africa.

Aparna Ajith's paper captioned "The (Postmodern) Story of Jyoti Vishwanath" deals with a story by Chandrika Balan who writes under the pen name Chandramathi and is a frontline contemporary Malayalam writer. The paper focusses on the postmodern thematic and stylistic elements present in the short story which has characters who are familiar with the spirit of the age. The duplicity of Vishwanath with regard to practicing postmodern feminism while at the same time Jyoti's problems experienced in being a postmodern woman in the contemporary Indian scenario are effectively brought out.

In the paper captioned "Hierarchy of Digital Media Discourse in India: Dalit Perspective," researcher Jai Kumar expresses concern over the hegemonisation of digital media in the Indian Dalit context. Referring to the Dalit thinkers Ambedkar, Jyotirao and Savitribai Phule, the social structure as well as the caste system have been pinpointed as the root cause of the hierarchy in the society in general and media, in particular, wherein Jay Kumar locates an elitist tendency impacting adversely the interests of the subaltern and downtrodden. It would seem that the preoccupation with the Dalit standpoint affects the objectivity of the discourse analysis, but then, the researcher argues that the causes and concerns advocated by the Dalit writers epitomize the human concern.

Neelam Yadav's paper ''Death and Magic Realism in Murakami Haruki's "New York Mining Disaster" discusses the implications of surrealism in elucidating the theme of death in the Japanese author's story. The treatment in the story is postmodern in its emphasis on the elements of uncertainty, mystery and suspense interwoven in the fabric of the text. Like Rushdie and Ghosh, Haruki communicates the usual fact of death through the unconventional techniques of uncanny and fluidity in a complex storyline.

Aparna Bhatt's paper "Feminist Dystopian Imagination in the Postmodern Fiction" deals with the predicament of the female dystopia in the male - dominated utopian world with reference to two novels by contemporary American authors, viz., Christina Dalcher's *Vox* and Jennie Malamed's *Gather the Daughters* to show how the women have been robbed of their basic human rights of equality, freedom and individuality at both social and linguistic levels. The scholar has made apt use of both the historical and cultural allusions to validate her standpoint and to deconstruct myths.

The paper "Reading Hyperreality and Cultural Consumerism in the two Songs "Go West" and "Californication" by Lalthazami and Dr Smarika Pareek demystifies the American Dream as represented through the songs. Referring to the Baudrillard's notion of Hyperspace, the writers pinpoint pastiche, hyperreality, parody and a kind of hanging between illusion and reality as symbolizing the American society. They point out that the stereotypes and fashion of pop songs are dexterously employed as advertising agencies tend to confuse the masses and valorize the vested interests of a select few.

In their paper "Predicament of the Homosexuals: Study of Mahesh Dattani's select plays," Dr Prerna Srivastava and Dr

Sangeetha Noval discuss the existential crisis of the homosexuals. Not only the theme but also the dramatic technique employed by the playwright is postmodern. Focussing their searchlight on the three plays" "On a Muggy Night in Mumbai," "Bravely Fought the Queen" and "Do the Needful," the writers deconstruct the stereotypical attitude of the Indian society towards the LGBT community which, despite the recent Supreme Court verdict legitimizing homosexuality, needs to undergo change.

In the article captioned "Postcolonial Feminist Poetry in India: A Pleasant Protest," Dr. Poonam Dwivedi compares the stand of postmodernism as evidenced in postmodernity vis-à-vis postcolonialism and chooses to dwell on the postcolonial poetry written by women poets. In her signature poetic prose, she gives vent to the revolutionary sentiments of women which have been feeling tormented under the yoke of patriarchy in our society. She quotes lines from the poems of Kamla Das, Sarojini Naidu and her own poems to underline the ideas. Her clarion call to society to awaken to the predicament of women is indeed significant, for there just can't be a better world without women's equal and just participation in it

Dr. Priyanka Lamba in her paper captioned "Resisting Authority in *The Merchant of Venice*: A View of Shylock" deconstructs the famous play by Shakespeare. Applying current spectrum of theories to works of bygone era is always a challenge and is fraught with risks. However, Dr Lamba comes out of the ordeal unscathed. In this, she applies various postmodern theories and approaches like Deconstruction, New Historicism and Cultural Criticism. Help comes from the realization that many issues of Shakespeare's time are still around like racism, capitalism, sexism and marginalization of the Other.

The compilation concludes with a postscript by Prof. Jagdish Batra wherein he muses on the Indian perspective and points out the areas of similarity and difference between Indian poetics and postmodernism. His argument is that when postmodern ethos, on the face of it at least, accords recognition to all the "other" categories of humanity and knowledge, and when postcolonialism lays stress on re-discovering the suppressed epistemologies, it is in the fitness of things that Indian poetics should get its due. It is interesting to note the similarities between the two, even as there are bound to be points of contention.

In conclusion, it can be said that the contributors to this volume have touched upon almost all aspects of postmodernism while dealing with various literary texts or musings on theoretical bases. Thus, we find papers on globalization, dystopia, media, narrative strategies, terrorism, consumerism, hyperreality, retellings, LGBT community, diaspora, interactive fiction, Dalit cause, "knowledge" profusion, Indian perspective, etc. All this indeed has added to the worth of this project and the editors are beholden to the contributors for it.

Editors

Artificial Intelligence and Postmodernism Hijacking Your Freedom[1]

RAJIV MALHOTRA
Infinity Foundation, USA

I want to make my talk provocative. I want to provoke the young scholars and also the more experienced persons here with some fresh ideas. The field of literary theory, critical theory, postmodernism—all the different aspects of literary theory are being shaken up in a way that has not happened for the last several decades—since this field emerged—and this is being shaken up by artificial intelligence. It's being shaken up in such a serious way and yet hardly anyone in the field of postmodernism or literary theory or any of these related areas seems to be aware of this big tsunami that is coming. It's not coming thirty years later or hundred years later, and I will tell you what's happening.

Artificial Intelligence: it has been developing algorithms which learn on their own. They learn what you read, what you like, what you don't like; they can mimic you, so they can talk like you. Algorithms are being used to generate text. So the question is: who is deconstructing that? How do you deconstruct text when the agency is not a human agency? The agency that's developing it, you can't say this is brahmanical voice or this is whatever voice or something. You cannot deconstruct using the kind of vocabulary and the kind of tools that the people in theory are used to,

---

1 The article is the transcript of the inaugural keynote address delivered by the renowned public intellectual Sh. Rajiv Malhotra at the 7th JGU International Literary Conference held on July 23-25, 2021 at O.P. Jindal Global University, India, on the theme: "Postmodernism: Time for Reappraisal."

what you've been raised on, what you are being taught, none of those are going to be valid, none of those apply because now you're deconstructing a text whose author is not a human author. So what are you going to do? How are you going to locate this algorithm in the space that you know gender space or whatever space that you've been taught, because this is an algorithm. It's not even a human. It is not conscious.

Now let me explain to you what is going on. First I'll tell you, then I'll give you the implications. There are chat bots, chat bots which are computer programs that are mimicking humans and answering questions, engaged in debate, supporting somebody, opposing somebody. A large percentage of these automated chat bots that the Google and the Facebook and a whole lot of private companies are throwing out in the social media. They're actually just algorithms, very intelligent algorithms that are constantly becoming smarter and smarter based on the feedback. The algorithms are being used to write emails without human involvement, write editorials. There was a competition recently where people in the AI field were invited to have their algorithms compose an editorial, an editorial of 800 words on some topic. And so this algorithm went searching the entire internet for that topic, picking up what's the latest news. The topic could be, you know, what's happening in the second wave or third wave in coronavirus, it could be something about trade war with China, it could be something about what's happening in Kashmir, whatever the topic is, it's able to compile information, figure out what's going on, construct a very well written, good English with lot of logic, with a flow, something that is so interesting that human beings, human editors in various newspapers and magazines when they are given these editorials some of them written by machines, some of them composed by human beings and they're asked to evaluate what they think of this. They are not able to tell the difference. They are not able to tell these two are from a machine or these three are from a machine.

Algorithms are also able to compose music. Same story, there have been contests where algorithmically generated music is being seen as "hey! This is pretty good" and "we can't tell the difference." So you see what is happening is algorithms are composing using natural language processing, NLP, which is a huge topic in computer science, the understanding of natural language. So how to understand human language and being able to tell the motive of a piece that you are reading is this motive, you know, good, bad, left wing, right wing, is it for, against a topic. There's something called sentiment analysis which looks at the sentiments. It's all algorithms evaluating millions of messages that are out there to see what is the sentiment on a given topic, what is the sentiment on the CAA issue that's going on, while there are riots and there are farmer riots going on somewhere, what is the sentiment on that. So the algorithms rather than humans are the agencies evaluating the discourse, deconstructing the discourse.

Forget us deconstructing the algorithm, right now, the algorithm is deconstructing our narratives. So these algorithms are behaving more and more like human agency in the analysis of narratives, in deconstructing narratives and in coming up with new narratives. So it's not only a participant in terms of evaluating and intervening with the discourse but also putting its own discourse into the mix. Now here is an interesting point, a lot of people are mixed up and muddled and confused including some AI people because they think that since machines are not conscious, they are not able to do these things. But let me tell you, deconstruction of our human discourse has nothing to do with whether these machines are conscious. They are not conscious and they are not going to become conscious, but still natural language processing is a field in Computer Science which is advanced to the point where it's able to make algorithms behave in this manner. So, the first point I want to make is, algorithms have arrived as discourse participants. They'll argue with you, they'll deconstruct you, they'll block you, they have they're more authority than you and I have because all these social media are being driven by algorithms. Don't think that Mark Zuckerberg is sitting there, deciding what to think and who to block. It's not human beings. They've turned loose algorithms, given some general rules to these algorithms, general policies, general biases, general preferences, and the algorithms then go and implement this on a very large scale. After all, there are billions of people, sending billions of messages. It is humanly impossible to manage and control all that and yet it is being controlled. The social media discourse is being controlled with certain agendas, with certain things allowed, certain things encouraged, certain things not encouraged. If I put out a video with a certain message and I use the word COVID or I use the word caste or I use the word Kashmir or Modi or Trump or China, there are all these algorithms they look up whatever what is this guy saying, is he for this is, against that and then there are rules on what will they allow, what they will not allow, who will be shadowed, who will be blocked, who will get a warning.

So the dominant discourse and the new deep structures, the deep structures are not the old structures that you know this is gender structure, this is a structure about you know postcolonial and what not, the algorithms are creating new structures about social justice, about climate change, about human rights. So the discussion on these topics is shifting away from the kind of things that all of you are used to reading and a whole new kind of discourse which is machine generated is taking over. This is a very important thing for the profession that all of the scholars here are in. If you know the history a new world view called humanism emerged many generations ago in Europe and humanism was a big revolution in thought and one of the offshoots of humanism was liberalism. Now, humanism itself is being attacked by AI and I won't go into that here because that's a huge topic on its own but in my book on AI, I have talked about all these things. I have written a recent book called *Artificial Intelligence and the Future of Power*. Those who are interested can, it's been out for several weeks. . . . AI is a product of liberalism by the way. AI is a product of materialism, liberalism, and AI is now threatening its own origin. It's threatening the very humanism which gave birth to it. This is a very interesting topic which is for those who want to go even deeper. Now the elephant in the room is how do you deconstruct an algorithm? You know, we are used to deconstructing human discourse but how do you deconstruct an algorithm? How do you even know how this algorithm is working? How do you attribute motive to this algorithm? This is very interesting point that you have to use.

So now, let's look at how do these algorithms learn. A child is trained by the environment it's being brought up in by the kind of reading material, by the kind of you know narratives that the child is exposed to. A student, even a human being keeps learning based on whatever discourse you are given and you as postmodernists know there is no such thing as neutral, everything has a bias because the people who generate it have a bias. So somebody may say this is the absolute grand narrative but that's not true. That grand narrative includes in it a point of view, a particular built, a particular bias in it. Similarly, in the case of AI, the algorithms are not something that a programmer puts together, the algorithm learns by processing examples, examples, and examples. So, whatever data is being fed to train the algorithm gives it the bias. Now, let me just tell you this, in a Hindu *gurukulam*, he'll have a certain point of view. Suppose a child is raised in a Muslim *madrasa*, he'll have a certain point of view, different one. Suppose a child is raised in a Catholic school, he will have a different point of view. Suppose he's raised in a Maoist, Marxist training camp, he'll have a different point of view. Everybody knows that. So now if you take these texts, you will also have that point of view. If you take the entire library of madrasas and use that to train algorithms they will have that point of view. That's how algorithms are. If you train them on the text of the Vedic tradition, all the commentaries and all the analysis, they'll have a certain algorithm, they will have a certain point of view. So like that I could go on giving you examples that there is no such thing as a neutral algorithm.

So, first thing I said that algorithms are taking over more and more of the text business, not only evaluating but also producing new text, passing commentary, evaluating, judging, and more and more editors and think tanks are using it, and certainly social media is using it, certainly politicians are using it. That is one point. Second point is that these algorithms are not neutral. Now they will tell you that this is a very neutral algorithm and it's going to block you if you say bad things but who decides what are bad things. They will say that, they have terms like violating social norms. So you are being blocked for violating social norms. Well, who decides what are social norms? According to, you know, YouTube anytime, I put out a video promoting Ayurveda as a potential for COVID treatment, they would send me a warning message and this would be an algorithm telling me that this is being flagged as violating rules on things like that. So, they consider Ayurveda to be biased and Allopathy to be normal. Now, this is somebody's point of view. . . . So, this algorithm is becoming a big boss even inside these big companies, even their own employees cannot override the algorithms. So, this is a very serious situation for anybody and I'm surprised that the people in literary theory and critical theory have not discovered this and they have not made a noise about it because your whole purpose is to look for biases and look for how to deconstruct narratives and figure out what's hidden in hidden messages in them, hidden points of view that are not normal.

So what is happening is, there's a pyramid of power where at the top are people who control these algorithms, who have points of view. I asked some Google people because they are generating a next generation engine that'll compete with GPT3 which is one of these things that an organization puts together, it's very famous and it's able to understand text and it has done this by reading and being trained on, you know, millions and millions of pages of various kinds of writings. So everybody's competing against GPT3. China has announced something which is going to be much bigger than GPT3, many more, much bigger vocabulary much more content China is doing. Google has announced its own. Google brain that is called. Microsoft has something. You know Facebook has something. All these guys, all the digital giants are racing to compete against GPT3. So when you ask people, when I ask the Google people how are you training the algorithm when it comes to something like Indian culture, Indian civilization and the answer is, oh! There is a large body of academic works. So I said academic works written by whom. And so when they showed me those are exactly the people I'm fighting and arguing with all the time. They are biased. They're colonized. They have what I call Hinduphobia. They are involved in what I call breaking India and so their texts are the legitimate texts in the eyes of the western academy. That is the text that is illegitimate. Those are the texts that are quoted by the newspapers in the international press. So now what you'll find is, all of this hinduphobia and breaking India forces and the kind of stuff that people like me are fighting, I in particular for four decades, all of that kind of bias is now going to come in the form of algorithms. This is a serious matter.

A lot of them are training their algorithms using Wikipedia but Wikipedia is not a kind of an absolute neutral source. Wikipedia has its biases. The Wikipedia entry on me is biased because when I challenge something they don't accept my word. They've accepted somebody else's word because everybody is allowed to participate but you are rated in terms of your ranking. Different people have different ranking. A person of higher rank can overrule what you've written because whatever you edit you put in, a person of higher ranking in the Wikipedia scheme can overwrite it. So it's again a system of power. There is a hierarchy of power. It is not a democracy like people think. There is a hierarchy of power within Wikipedia. Even one of the founders of Wikipedia whom I know well, in interviews with me, has said that. So where do you get text that is neutral? Well, you cannot get text that's neutral. Whatever text you get has some kind of bias in it and so that's the bias that goes into the algorithms which are being trained using such texts.

Now there is a movement in the US which is trying to fight this algorithmic bias. Blacks have complained that algorithms are biased racially and the reason is that many of these algorithms have been trained on texts and on history of law and crime and all of that which is biased because blacks are stereotyped in those texts, they are considered inferior, they are more likely to have violence and be criminals according to those texts. That kind of big data and the algorithms have taken over that bias. Feminists have argued that these algorithms have gender bias. LGBTQ people are fighting, some of them litigating against bias. So the biases of these algorithms are not something novel. I'm just bringing it in a different context. There are different groups, different human rights groups and different public interest groups that are already fighting the digital giants, taking them to court saying that their algorithms are biased and hence, all the stuff they put out and how they filter out news and what they consider to be right, wrong and all that, is being evaluated and adjudicated by biased algorithms. So there is this whole field called demanding transparency of algorithms, demanding that there'll be accountability of algorithms.

Then the question is who are you gonna sue? The owner of the algorithm? He may say, "I didn't do this. I'm not a biased person." The point is that it's your algorithm. In the defense of the algorithm people, [we can say] the developer really does not know how the bias came in. If I'll just write an algorithm and tell it to learn through experience and the experience it's having maybe in a community where one point of view is dominant and so the algorithm picks it up. If I turn my algorithm loose in a certain type of community and I said, go learn from them, listen to what they're saying and learn, learn, learn the way, you know child learns by listening, this algorithm will not be a neutral algorithm because the views and the tilt in that community will be assimilated into that algorithm's own mindset.

So the problem that India faces as a result of this is very unique. So far I've told you what is generally a problem, nothing to do with India in particular. People in the United States and Europe are who are at the cutting edge of AI, are in dialogue, I am a part of that group, in dialogue with people in literary theory and critical theory to see how does it revolutionize critical theory. What I'm now talking about is going to become very common knowledge, commonly talked about in future conferences. AI as a voice, as a development voice in narrative and a critical voice in controlling narratives because the AI is owned by these very big giants and the AI is their weapon, and this is in the hands of people with an agenda. They are all—whether it's a Bill Gates or Eric Schmidt who is a very, nationalistic American, more nationalistic beyond left or right. There are strong left-wing, you know, thinkers in this field and they have a lot of investments in algorithms. There are strong Christians, there is a whole community called Christianity and AI, and I'm participating in that. There is a whole community called AI and faith. The latest issue of New York Times magazine, the article was on, you know, on AI and God. I mean what they were talking about is faith. How does AI interact with Islamic point of view, Christian point of view, you know Jewish point of view? The Vedic point of view has not been represented there and that is where I come in. I'm trying to get in and represent a Vedic point of view that we have a lot to say about AI and its biases and we need a seat at the table also.

But the problem I'm facing is that in India you do not have people interested in this topic. You do not have people who even know about this topic. I mean they're very dubious, some people think this must be some kind of a conspiracy theory this guy is talking about. They're not taking the matter seriously and that's a concern of mine. So to conclude what I want to say is this India has not invested, neither at the government level nor industry nor academic. The computer industry, the AI industry has not invested in creating its own equivalent of GPT3 which would give us an engine that is based on natural language processing, that has our point of view, that has studied all our texts all our shastras. It has also looked at all the other philosophies and all the other points of view in the world but looked at it from our point of view. We don't have such a machine, so we cannot sort of say that somebody else's algorithms have a problem and ours are superior in managing the discourse because we don't have such a capability. What India is, where is India headed in this? This is not a pleasant message to give, but it has to be given, especially since you are in this business of theory and looking beneath the surface and interpreting things. I have to give you this message and the message is this—westerners mainly United States and also to some extent Europe are perfecting these algorithms that are controlling the social media and controlling the discourse and politics and what not and these algorithms that they are controlling have some biases, that are very sort of western oriented biases.

You might say that these algorithms are tools of colonization. So AI is recolonizing the world intellectually. Artificial Intelligence and the recolonization of the world is a big topic in my book. I have chapters on this book so you can read it. I have chapters on the return of the East India company because the East India company was a private company like Google is a private company and many of these are private companies but they got huge amount of power because they understand all your secrets, they have been listening to you, they have your data, they have your private data, and the machine learning is figuring you out. It's saying that this guy is vulnerable to this, he likes these things, he dislikes these things, he's ideologically this way, politically that way, these are the ways that he's compromised, these are the skeletons in the closet that could be exposed to bring him down. I mean the algorithms know a whole lot about you. In some ways they know even what you do unconsciously which you may not be aware of yourself. Certainly, the algorithms know more about you than your friends, relatives, even your very close, those who are very close to you. So with algorithms able to keep track of billions of people and figure them out and manipulate them, it's a very dangerous world that we're entering and India does not have its own investment.

India does not have its own investment in anything similar to GPT3, even though it's based on natural language processing and natural language processing started out with the study of Panini, Panini's Sanskrit grammar. Twenty-five years ago, my friends in the Sanskrit department at JNU, the Sanskrit department Delhi University, in Varanasi, and all these kind of places, in Pondicherry, were being flown to all the conferences on natural language processing because the Computer Science people wanted to learn the whole NLP field, they wanted to learn, you know, Panini and how to use that grammar to translate languages, translate from one language to another. So the field of Computer Science benefited a lot from Indian thought in the early days and then it went beyond. It went beyond on its own and now it's pretty much free to go and keep extrapolating and expanding on its own, very rapidly. But India has been left behind. Some Indians, in an individual capacity, helped all this but they are left behind. A very large percentage of AI researchers in the world are Indians but in a personal capacity. They're not doing anything for India. . . . That intellectual property belongs to Google or it belongs to Microsoft or it belongs to Apple or whoever, it belongs to somebody else. It does not belong to India. . . . So what's happening is that all this technology is being imported into India and Indians are getting colonized. So the next generation of postmodernists, people who are post-colonialists, people who are into gender studies, people who are into social justice, human rights, the next generation of such people are going to be trained by and they're going to be taught how to use algorithms how to evaluate algorithms they will learn all the things that I'm telling you.

But those things which they will be taught will be with a bias. We'll be with the western bias because that's where these things are being developed so you know if you look at who developed, who developed Postcolonial Studies, where did you know this whole idea of Orientalism and then postcolonial studies and then subaltern studies and gender studies, then postmodernism all these—what I call five waves—the five waves of critical theory applied to a literary theory, applied to India and Indian culture, are the five waves of Indology. I have written on five waves of Indology, written works and given lectures and all that on it. Indians are basically just regurgitating, parroting, what they read from foreign writers, foreign thinkers. So foreigners are the theory *walas*. They are the ones who come up with all these different kinds of theories that you read and the Indians are basically data *walas*. We supply case studies, we supply examples, we supply, "sir, in my neighborhood this happened, they abuse this woman, they abuse this caste *wala.*" I'll fill it, supply it as my case study, maybe, I'll be sent on a plane ticket to somewhere in a conference. So basically Indians in the field of literary theory and critical theory, postmodernism, postcolonial etc. are applying western models to Indian cases, Indian examples, Indian case studies, but we are not creating our own theories and now with the advent of algorithms and AI, the same thing is happening. These algorithms with their biases are being brought into India and Indians are absorbing them and assimilating them. I won't name names but big companies, big government people are involved in this, in the sense of importing these ideas in the name of progress, in the name of "hey! You know we are becoming very world-class because we've now got this collaboration with Google" not realizing that what we are really doing is inviting the East India Company to come in and set up shop here. That's what is going on.

So this is a very provocative statement I'm making that the AI is using postmodernism, critical theory, all these things as a window to get in and bring with it all the biases and it's a tsunami that's sweeping and a lot of the young people in this field are mesmerized but this is going to recolonize India. And therefore, my talk is more like hey guys let's wake up and do something! I've written a whole book on it. I'm willing to give workshops talk about it, have q and a's and I've had about fifty of these, you know, discussions and q and a's in the last five or six months, I would say and I'm willing to do more. I'll stop there. I just want to provoke some young people so they can look into it and hope we can create a kind of Made in India AI with Made in India algorithms. Indian, if there are going to be biases, we might as well have our biases because everybody has their biases. The Chinese have got their China biases. There is no deconstruction of China's grand narrative they are putting their whole Chinese grand narrative into AI and implementing it, not only on Chinese society but also exporting it to Africa and exporting it to various other countries that they're trying to colonize. So India has to become a player. The future of the people in the theory business in general is huge because either you'll get colonized and it'll be bad for India because you'll become the colonizers of the whole lot of Indians through all these theories that you bring in or you could be home team that counters it. You are educated, you know all this stuff, you know the game and AI could be an opportunity for us to turn things around because it's still very new and if we learn this and train our young people in this we may have a made in India position to counter all this and become a true *vishwaguru* that we think we are. I want to thank the university. You're a great university. The mere fact that you are having conferences on very broad, big topics like this provocative topics is a good sign and I'm glad I got this opportunity to do it, to speak to, especially your young people. Thank you very much. Namaste to all of you.

Postmodernism, Globalisation and World Literature

ABHINABA CHATTERJEE
Research Scholar, Gurukul Kangri University, Haridwar

It is a universally acknowledged fact that we live in a post-modern globalized world, characterised by the dominance of a global capitalist economic system. The latter has resulted in a shift from the primacy of the nation state by transnational corporations and organizations, adversely affecting the local cultures and traditions by a global culture. Something is successful, so other authors begin to imitate it—or, more accurately, something is successful, so publishers and film producers begin to pour money into projects (novels, screenplays) that seem to share the crucial, profit-generating quality. The resulting uniformity is a matter of topic, theme, style, narrative structure—not a specific plot or particular moments of dialogue. For example, it is commonplace to remark that the financial and critical success of *Midnight's Children* prompted publishers to recruit Indian authors, prompted Indian authors to write in English, fostered the spread of certain stylistic techniques and 'postmodern' approaches to writing 'postcolonial' novels, and so on. Indeed, even *Midnight's Children* is a peculiar example. The general point here is that the globalization of political economy tends to foster a sort of global literature and culture: a 'world literature,' in one sense of the phrase.

The term 'globalisation,' like postmodernism, has been a notoriously difficult term to define. Notwithstanding the same, all definitions of 'globalisation' mention border crossing as a fundamental characteristic of the process. On the one hand, postmodernism was still an exclusive myth for intellectuals, globalisation seems to possess planetary powers of delusion. On the other hand, like postmodernism, globalisation has been considered as an abstract concept, all the more so as its *pathos* refers to the temporal ecstasy of the future. That is why globalising cannot have a definite objective, but it is assumed that it marks a radical break with the past (modernity as unconditional technical progress), which puts a question mark over the relation towards Other and implies the levelling of differences.

Postmodernity opens up new possibilities and even new political functions of literature and literary criticism today that might seem quixotic at best. While freeing us from the illusions of modernity of having a rigid identity it also opens a Pandora's Box of such a degree of heterogeneity that it seems to be impossible to have an identity, whether racial, cultural or sexual, especially in so far as the process of globalization at various levels contributes to the 'circulation' of cultural identities.

World Literature and Translation

It is at this juncture that I would like to introduce the term 'world literature' as advocated by David Damrosch. Damrosch defines the term 'world literature' in his 2003 book *What Is World Literature?* As "all literary works that circulate beyond their culture of origin, either in translation or in their original language." This does *not* mean all literature ever created: some stays within the culture and language that produced it, and never leaves. In other words, *World Literature* is the interaction between the various language literatures and thus inevitably invokes translation as border-crossing. Damrosch's definition of *World Literature* refers to instances of influences such as that of Russian novels on English literature, an interpretation of the translations of Lebanese poetry by Japanese critics and the like. The phenomenon of World

Literature, thus, can almost always be seen as a process of interpretation and (mis)understanding.

The postmodern impulse can be used in the creation of the 'World Literature' from two different perspectives—one from that of the reader and the other from that of the language. From the perspective of the reader, to create a 'World Literature' would imply crossing the political boundaries and reading the texts of other languages in 'original.' Thus, from the perspective of the reader, the reader will have to be familiarized in all the languages to be able to read them in original. Now, this is almost an impossible venture. Hence, according to Damrosch, rises the significance of the process of translation. In the absence of the process of translation, world literature ceases to be a reality due non-accessibility of the heterogeneous language-literature. Moreover, according to Damrosch, it is the very fact that the translation and the original text can be subjected to an aesthetic transformation what is in itself an inherent feature of the literary fact. There is no denying that if the role of cross-cultural communication is played inadequately or unsatisfactorily, the circulation of national literatures is impeded to become world literature. The process of translation considers individual context dimensions, cross-cultural interpretations and forms of mediations and provokes further needs for investigation. In each of the translation processes, the capitalist emphasis of location, time and need plays an important role in rendering the heterogeneity of the source text. The quality, or rather acceptability, of translation for the purpose of enabling the circulation of literary texts across national boundaries is determined by the world capitalist system. Thus the appreciation and acceptability of the 'Other' is determined by the governing principles of capitalist system which shapes the concept and the very idea of the 'Target Text' (TT) into the source culture. Thus, while Toury (1995) insists on 'value free' norms in the process of translation, Venuti believes that "Toury's method . . . must still turn to cultural theory in order to assess the significance of the data, to analyze the norms. Norms may be in the first instance linguistic or literary, but they will also include a diverse range of domestic values, beliefs, and social representations which carry ideological force in serving the interests of specific groups. And they are always housed in the social institutions where translations arc produced and enlisted in cultural and political agendas." (29)

The consequences of this turn of the translation studies and practices, that are putatively so characteristic of postmodernity, and at a further remove, for the question of identity, cannot be separated from the process known as globalization which, as Suárez-Orozco and Qin-Hilliard (1) point out, 'defines our era.' As David Kellner points out, "globalization . . . highlight the emergence of a new transnational ruling elite and the universalisation of consumerism" (3).

Capitalism and Identity Formation

In the context of world literature, it is important to note that several contemporary voices have warned against the negative consequences of providing students access to world literature only through translations, considering the fact that translation is, in practice, a one way phenomenon, thereby creating not only a homogenizing effect, blurring the distinctiveness of individual languages, literatures and cultures, but also promoting a form of capitalism that will eventually result in economic and cultural imperialism. Indeed, as Dorothy Figueira argues that the world of 'World Literature' is a "rather imperialistic vision of a world to be packaged and consumed in English, the ever-increasing hegemonic language of academe." (Figueira 42). Gayatri Spivak discusses the ideological implications of translating the literature of the Third World to hegemonic languages. She argues that while there is no doubt about the 'democracy of the majority' in which one must speak to be heard, the process of translation inevitably involves some loss of 'rhetorical silences' which she illustrates in the translations of Mahasweta Devi's *Stanadayini*. In her own words: "In the act of wholesale translation into English there can be a betrayal of the democratic ideal into the law of the strongest. . . . This happens when all the literature of the Third World gets translated into a sort of with-it translates, so that the literature by a woman in Palestine begins to resemble, in the feel of its prose, something by a man in Taiwan" (Spivak 1993: 182).

It is precisely at this juncture that Emily Apter introduces the term 'untranslatability,' which is in sync with the translation methodology advocated by Gayatri Spivak in that it retains the 'rhetorical silences' in the source text. Despite the retention of the 'untranslatable,' the 'Target Text' evolves as a promoter of the 'hybrid' identity that so characterises the postmodern literature and culture. The dialectic relationship between the national and the cultural identities posited as a result of the advent of postmodernism can be studied, as Theo D'haen says, under two hypotheses. Firstly, the relationship between the shape postmodernism assumes in a given culture and the culture's national narrative may well be as 'deconstructive' as happens to be the case in the original American context, and as extrapolated from there into a 'universal' characteristic of 'postmodernism' but need not necessarily be so. Here, postmodern identities, as promoted through the postmodern and postcolonial translation strategies in world literature, are becoming more homogeneous or uniform, and not—as the advent of postmodernity seemed initially to promise—more diverse. Secondly, one might posit that in certain contexts, postmodernism, while still reacting to Enlightenment thinking as embodied in a specific 'national narrative,' may well take a 're-constructive' rather than a 'deconstructive' turn. It is via the detour of the postcolonial call for postmodern independence from universal postmodernism that we have arrived at a comparable call on behalf of Western literatures. Steger (2003: 75) aptly suggests, however, that the crucial question is whether all these powerful homogenizing forces are capable of eradicating the cultural diversity in the world. Clearly, some of the pessimistic theorists of globalization believe that this is the case, while many of their more 'optimistic' counterparts do not seem to care much about diversity. As for myself, I tend to agree with a third group of interpreters who, pointing to evidence of new cultural forms making their appearance across the globe, claim that these "arise precisely in the interaction between homogenizing globalizing forces and local cultural practices" (Steger 2003: 75).

Considering that translation is a political act, driven by the ideologies of capitalist economic system with its impact on the world literature, there is an ambivalence of the postmodern valorization of 'difference' in the face of this mono-dimensional manipulation of identity (which subverts authentic differences in favour of a more fundamental, capitalist-induced homogeneity). Read in conjunction with Theo D'haen's two hypotheses, as stated above, it would seem that opposing tendencies are active in the postmodern condition—the homogenizing globalisation with the evolution of hybrid identities by means of postmodern translation practices as envisaged in Damrosch's World Literature. A brief consideration—given the vast area of research implicated by it—of what 'identity' means is called for here; that is, how an individual's identity is acquired, and what its structural characteristics are. Among the various possibilities concerning identity are that it could be considered unitary, dualistic or multidimensional, stable or dynamic. If the latter, could one still legitimately speak of 'identity'?

If information is acknowledged to be the basic raw material of the new global economy and significant economic gains are to be made from the production of goods with a high cognitive content, then not only is language a key factor in the expression of that information but language also represents a crucial means of accessing the information. An important consequence of translation is that speakers of different languages seek to translate themselves into the language perceived to have the greatest information-density. This is the translation movement that results in a language perceived as information-poor gradually being abandoned for a language deemed to be information-rich, thereby making the translation a unidirectional phenomenon. In a fundamental sense, what is repeatedly at stake in the relation between the phenomenon of globalization and translation practices is a tension between what might be loosely labelled centrifugal and centripetal forms of globalization. On the one hand, there is the centripetal form, the notion of globalization as homogenization—implying imperialism, subjection, hegemony, Westernization or Americanization. On the other hand, there is the centrifugal form, suggesting globalization as resulting in interdependence, interpenetration, hybridity, syncretism, creolization and crossover. Thus, we can see translation as the *sine qua non* of the cultural dominance and an agent of centripetal globalization if we consider that the capitalist economic interest in the Hollywood films would lose their global market in the absence of the translation services rendered by the dubbers and subtitlers. Conversely, translation can be seen as the quintessential expression of centrifugal globalization if we reflect that it is translation which alone allows speakers of a language under threat to be able to communicate through translation into the language of the majority. That we are familiar with the identities as reflected in the literature of the Aboriginals of Australia, the Maoris of New Zealand and the Dalits of India, is largely due to the accommodative capacity of the translation.

Notwithstanding the above, the identities of the Aboriginals, the Maoris or the Dalits, who, according to Spivak, were 'Subalterns,' have not started to 'speak,' perhaps in the way and in the language in which they would have loved to speak. In this sense, the identities that are rendered in their literature (in translation, that is, in English which is not their mother's tongue), are not their 'original.' Their speech is not their own but as defined by their colonisers and are published by the colonisers only to subvert and alter their identities. This happens to be the colonial version of the 'postmodern' identity. In this kind of translated version, these literatures contribute to the canon of 'World Literature' as, according to Damrosch, these literatures have crossed the boundaries of their cultural existence.

Conclusion

As an active agency of the phenomenon of world literature as defined by Damrosch, translation puts the criterion of identity in flux. A person's understanding of the self is wrapped up in language. If one adopts the language of an Other, then primary elements of a person's roots (tied to place and time) are cast in doubt, thereby rendering them 'postmodern' in its colonial sense. Advocates of translation studies contributing to the canon of 'World Literature' claim that border crossing is only possible if the language, literature and culture of the 'Other' is accessible to them in terms of categories that can be identified by the people of the target language and culture. "Language effects on cognition are context-bound and transient, revealing unprecedented levels of malleability in human cognition." Thus, in speaking in the language of the Other, the mind begins to think in the structures and rules of that language, which reflect the culture to which the language is bound. The more you write in Tagalog, for example, the more Filipino you "become." Thus, globalization, as an offshoot of postmodernism, impacts the translation process, creating the concept of 'world literature' and impacting the 'identity' formation.

Works Cited

Apter, Emily. *Against World Literature: On the Politics of Untranslatability*, Verso, London, New York, 2013.

Arac, Jonathan, ed. *Postmodernism and Politics*, Manchester University Press, 1986.

D'haen Theo and Pieter Vermeulen, ed. *Cultural Identity and Postmodern Writing*, Rodopi, Amsterdam, New York, 2005.

Damrosch, David. *What is World Literature*? Princeton University Press, Princeton & Oxford, 2003.

Figueira, Dorothy *"Salut au Monde": The World as Envisioned by World Literature*, pp. 41-52 in "Contextualizing World Literature," Jean Bessiere & Gerald Gillespie, ed. Peter Lang, Berlin, New York, Oxford, Wien, 2015.

Kellner, Douglas. *Dialectics of Globalisation: From Theory to Practice*, pp. 3-29 in "Postmodernism in a Global Perspective," Samir Dasgupta & Peter Kivisto, Sage, Delhi, 2014.

Maurya, Vibha, ed. *Postmodernism: A Discussion*, Kalinga, Delhi 1994

Spivak, Gayatri Chakravorty. *The Politics of Translation*, pp. 179-200 in "Outside in the Teaching Machine," Routledge, New York & London, 1993.

Stegar, M.B. *Globalization: A Very Short Introduction*, OUP, Oxford, 2003.

Suarez-Orozco, M.M. & D. Baolian Qin-Hilliard, ed. *Globalization. Culture and education in the New Millennium*. Berkeley: The University of California Press, 2003.

Toury, Giddeons. *Descriptive Translation Studies and Beyond*, John Benjamins, Amsterdam & New York, 1995

Venuti, Lawrence. *The Scandals of Translation: Towards an ethics of difference*, Routledge, London & New York, 1998

Situating Feminism within the Modernist vs. Postmodernist Debate

S. CHITRA
Yonphula Centenary College, Royal University of Bhutan

The problem that lay buried and unspoken for many years in the minds of women, has been described by Friedan: "It was a strange stirring, a sense of dissatisfaction, a yearning that women suffered. . . . Each suburban wife struggled with it alone. As she made the beds, shopped for groceries, matched slipover material, ate peanut butter sandwiches with her children . . . lay beside her husband at night—She was afraid to ask the silent question—'is this all?" (15) The name of the problem is male supremacy, patriarchal ideology and social constructivism. The notion of dominant—dominated binary, has constructed a world in which, "women possess only one-hundredth of the wealth and do two-thirds of the work for only one-tenth of the wages; whereas men monopolize public power in government, law, industry, commerce, science, culture, education and religion; wherein discrimination on the basis of gender is grievously the most socially accepted form of oppression.' (Thompson 16; Faludi 397). Male supremacy being the oldest form of domination, according to Weiner (24), "all other forms of exploitation and oppression are extensions of male supremacy." That's the reason, in the class and racial oppression, women are doubly subjugated and twice marginalized.

The words that express women's condition, one of inequality, oppression, subordination, have their implications and each describes its own version of the problem. Anne Phillips writes: "Inequality notes that women are denied what is granted to men; oppression carries with it a sense of weight pressing down due to the anomalies of female exclusion, perpetuated by the burden of ideological forces—all the norms combined to 'keep women in their place.'" The term 'subordination,' though not mutually exclusive, identifies the agents in the process of crushing the identity of women. Women's condition described by these terms somehow has been linked to the biological difference—of male and female sexes—based on which the archetypal gender roles were constructed by society and enforced on women as stereotyped patriarchal norms.

The term feminism derived from the Latin 'Femina' meaning 'Woman' initially meant 'having the quality of females' and came into use in the 1890s as an idea on sexual equality. Prior to it 'womanism' stood for issues of sex equality. Nineteenth century usage of the term 'The Woman Question' signaled its interest in the condition of women as a feminist consciousness than denote feminism as a political movement, as conceived of today.

Waves of Feminist Movements

In every era, from Sappho in the 7th century B.C., through to the middle-ages, the modern and postmodern period, there has been an unrelenting feminist presence in history despite patriarchal attempts to control it. According to Cott, the first wave feminism that dates from the nineteenth century and extends into the first two decades of the twentieth century comprised more focused campaigns for 'women's rights' equivalent to those that men enjoyed on legal, political, economic, civic grounds. It focused on gender equity through anti-discriminatory legislation.

The Second wave feminism emerging from the late 1960s onwards was born in USA out of the political 'new Left' that included broad-ranging pronouncements and activities and moved toward self-determination to liberate women from the age-old shackles of structures, conventions and attitudes enforced in the name of custom. The understanding that feminism as a social and political movement, aimed at changing the existing power relations between women and men, is because, in societies which divide the sexes into different cultural, economic or political spheres, 'women are less valued than men.' The second wave feminism usually referred to describe the Post-1968 Women's Liberation Movement, was marked by the publication of theoretical works such as Kate Millet's *Sexual Politics* and Shulamith Firestone's *The Dialectic of Sex* (both 1970), marked as the 'texts of revolution.' Young refers to this woman-centered approach as 'gynocentric feminism.' With these texts, emerged the second wave of sexual revolution, for both Millett and Firestone identified feminism as 'theoretical' standpoint with the women's movement as 'political practice,' because, theory and politics are interdependent for feminism.

Until the Modernist Period, the attempts of feminist theories and perspectives had been to describe women's oppression and explain its cause and consequences, including the strategies towards women's liberation. As the books by Millett and Firestone make it clear, following the modernist tenets, feminist politics has engaged with issues of culture and representation, which are the very objects of postmodernists' critique. Postmodernism, characterized by a change of attitudes, represents a cultural break with modernism. However, as part of the modernist project, the 'metanarratives' of 'Enlightenment modernism' represented 'woman' as a cultural construction of femininity, an insignificant object of desire, incapable of speaking in her own voice even within her cultural domain, which has inevitably reduced her to the status of object, from which feminism attempted to emancipate the female gender and transform women's position from the state of 'object' to that of a 'knowing subject.' It is in the emancipatory metanarratives of 'Enlightenment modernism,' in other words, it is in the modernist promise of liberation and social reconstruction, that many feminist theorists of the second wave positioned themselves.

To realize their aim of attaining equality by changing the existing power-relations between the sexes, feminists adopted the means of 'theory and praxis.' From the theoretical end, 'knowledge' is sought as a means to liberation and in the part of practice, through 'consciousness raising' and 'communal self-analysis,' an insight into the operations of male power was to be achieved with a resultant 'feminist enlightenment.' In the view of early feminism, the idea of 'feminist enlightenment' prevailed as a claim for 'equality' through women's inclusion in the spheres of rational thought and intellectual discourses, from which she has been systematically excluded by the structured principles of patriarchy. As Simone de Beauvoir pointed out in 1949, woman's representation as "Other' was to confirm man's identity as Self, as rational thinking being, based on which the 'sexual politics' of dualism was constructed and gender binaries were generated: Male/female, self/other, rational/irrational, subject/object so on and so forth. De Beauvoir critiqued this gender binary, which is formulated on the idea of 'thinking by means of oppositions,' in which one term of the opposition must always be devalued. This critique of 'binarism' has been fundamental to feminist thought.

The concept of Self, Beauvoir writes, can be produced only in opposition to that of not-self; that is, to constitute himself as subject, man has constructed woman as 'Other.' She is the incidental, the inessential as opposed to the essential. He is the Subject, he is the Absolute—She is the 'Other.' From this discussion, one could gather that the premise of 'Enlightenment modernism' and 'Feminist enlightenment' are not different. The idea of 'grand narratives,' attaining the absolute, the essential by reversing the existing social binaries has been rejected by the postmodernist thought with the apprehension that modernist tenets will be yet another social constructivist trap for feminism. The argument is that, by way of inclusion, women would find themselves only within the framework of 'masculine' logic, as surrogate men. That is to say, women will attain 'equality' in terms of 'sameness,' not 'difference,' not specifically as 'women.' Here, the postmodern idea is that the universal subject of 'Enlightenment modernism' and feminism, in theory and practice, are far from being 'transcendent' and 'ungendered.' In the words of Sue Thornham, the position of feminism as an offshoot of 'Enlightenment modernism' can be summed up as: "Feminist theory cannot 'both' claim, that, knowledge and the self are constituted within history and culture and that feminist theory speaks on behalf of a universalized 'woman'" (101).

Rather, the third wave feminism proposes to embrace differences between women and accept a position of partial knowledge(s). The present 'third phase' examines differences between women, concentrating on the diversity and variety of women's lives. This standpoint is gaining attention due to the diverse oppressive experiences of women depending on their location and its cultural practices. For instance, Daly's "Gyn / Ecology: The Meta-ethics of Radical Feminism," analyzed a range of oppressive practices such as Indian Sati, Chinese foot binding, African genital mutilation, European witch burning and so on as examples of universal existence of 'planetary patriarchy.'" (Jordan & Weedon 545).

On the other hand, the task of synthesizing the various strands of feminist theory seems to have been assumed by Socialist Feminists, with a focus on unity and integration, by integrating all aspects of women's lives to produce a unified feminist theory, one that is fixed, stable and universal. But such an attempt to find integration and to establish a single feminist standpoint, representative of how women experience the world, have not gone unchallenged. Postmodern feminists consider the whole enterprise as "yet another Phallocentric thought, typical of male thinking to seek the one, true feminist story of reality. For Postmodern Feminists such a synthesis is neither feasible nor desirable, because, women's experience differ across class, race and culture as well as the 'One and True' are philosophical myths that have been employed to bring into submission the differences that best describe the human condition." (Tong 7)

As a result, mainstream feminism seems to be dubious in maintaining a seemingly 'innocent' collusion with patriarchal and modernist tenets in the form of binarism, a stable universal idea that precipitated the reactionary shift to the postmodern feminist moment. With this understanding, the feminist thought begins to 'move away' from its origins of 'Enlightenment modernism' toward the postmodernist thought. It is a move away from the critique of 'binarism,' which was fundamental to feminist thought that universalizes women's experiences incommensurably without any difference. In modernist terms, sexual/biological difference constitutes gender discrimination. But, if universalized, this term of difference is only one which is not the only fundamental constitutive element of our identity. If so, then the modernist project of feminism will be "just another . . . totalizing fiction or totalizing experience" of women in general, that need to be deconstructed to embrace differences. In other words, it is true, the experiences of women are necessarily different from those of men, but more than that the question of 'women's condition' is not universal. With myriads of women living in widely different historical realities of class, race and culture, their gender experiences too differ immensely, which need to be counted upon.

Jane Flax argues that feminist theories, "like other forms of postmodernism, should encourage us to tolerate and interpret ambivalence, ambiguity and multiplicity, as well as to expose the roots of our needs for imposing order and structure no matter how arbitrary and oppressive these needs may be." (27) In this argument, postmodernism becomes a sort of corrective to feminism's universalizing tendency by avoiding the analysis of grand causes of women's oppression and replaces unitary conceptions of 'woman' and female identity with 'plural and complexly structured conceptions of social identity, treating gender as one relevant strand among others, attending to class, race, ethnicity, age and sexual orientation.' In Postmodernist feminism, sexual difference is no longer seen as a fundamental organizing category, but is replaced by the concept of multiple and shifting differences.

Postmodern Feminism

The major concern raised by Postmodern feminists is that feminism in trying to explain the reason behind women's oppression, tend to imitate the traditional assumptions of truth and reality, which is rejected outright by Postmodernism. Rehabilitation of 'Phallogocentric' thought is also excluded by Postmodernism. This particular postmodern thought fuels Contemporary Feminism with the traits of plurality, multiplicity and difference. By revolting against the austere autonomy of high modernism, the stance of Post modernism toward cultural tradition is one of irreverent pastiche. Against the modernist belief in absolute truths, rationality and linear progress, Postmodernism is "based on plurality of spaces and temporalities. It is a network of heterogenous intermedia, not a homogenous epoch or movement and much less a unique life or artistic style." (Gardiner 96); its priorities are fragmentation, indetermination, polymorphic correlations (Foucault), the belief that universal history cannot exist and mistrust of any totalizing discourse. As Eagleton says, we are now in the process of awakening from the nightmare of modernity, with its manipulative reason and fetish of the totality, into the laid-back pluralism of the Postmodern, that heterogenous range of life styles and language games which has renounced the nostalgic urge to legitimate itself.

The term 'Postmodern Feminism' gained popularity with writers such as Helene Cixous, Luce Irigaray and Julia Kristeva who had in common not just their 'Frenchness' but a philosophical perspective, shared by Postmodern philosophers Jacques Derrida and Jacques Lacan. Like Derrida, the postmodern feminists are 'deconstructionists,' who tend to illuminate "the internal contradictions of apparently coherent systems of thought." Contrary to feminists' preoccupation with the socio-historical realities of women's experiences, a typical characteristic of postmodern French feminists is their emphasis on the primacy of theory over politics. The roots of postmodern feminism can be traced to the seminal work of Simone de Beauvoir who questioned the position of woman being 'the Second Sex': 'Why is woman the 'second sex'? In Postmodern terms, 'Why is woman, 'the Other'?. Postmodern feminists have revolutionized de Beauvoir's concept of Otherness by interpreting the condition of 'Otherness' as a means to empower women, whereby women vocally and vociferously criticize the imposed norms and values of patriarchy. Thus, in Postmodern view, 'Otherness' is more than an oppressed, inferior condition; it is a way of being, thinking and speaking that celebrates openness, plurality, diversity, difference and contradiction. Contradiction is an inherent interplay of Postmodernism. For example, the prefix 'Post' refers to the paradoxical dependence on (or) independence of, what has gone before in time. Its aim is neither dialectic nor a totalitarian coherent unification, but rather to question, to set forth a series of problems, to achieve a new intellectual energy, which in turn could be subverted. For instance, Linda Hutcheon, who initially prefers not to identify feminism with Postmodernism, later admits that the usage of irony and parody in feminist texts to subvert the patriarchal universe are typically postmodern. Thus, one of the essential resources of Postmodernism is parody because it incorporates what it actually defies.

In Hutcheon's view, Postmodernism is a movement characterized by the use and abuse, construction and deconstruction, creation and subversion of those very concepts which it confronts. Particularly, this characteristic of contradiction and paradox, the capacity for duplicity and dialogue, makes it a political movement.

The main aim of Postmodernism is to dismantle some of the outstanding absolute features of life, to make it clear that there are a number of entities that which we call 'natural' are in fact, 'cultural' and are edifices founded upon social conventions.

French vs. British/American Feminisms

Essentially, 'while the British and American was empirical, the French was theoretical; where the American and British were staunch believers in the authority of experience, the latter questioned not only the category of experience, but even that of the "experiencer," the female subject herself. This ongoing theoretical diversity has strengthened the potency of feminism by not only shattering the core of male constructed worldview but, with Postmodern Feminism, has brought in a revolutionary challenge against naturalized ideological perspectives opposing the essentialist, masculinist rationality of Modernist feminism; This is so because, Dualism, the root of Enlightenment thought, is a product of the fundamental polarity, the sexual distinction between male and female, reducing woman to a man's opposite, his 'other.' In each of the dualisms which support Enlightenment thought: rational / irrational, subject / object, culture / nature, the male is associated with the privileged first element and the female with the dis-privileged second. According to Derrida, "the leading terms are accorded primacy; their partners are represented as weaker or derivative; yet the first terms depend on and derive their meaning from the second to such an extent that the secondary terms can be seen as generative of the definition of the first terms." (Selden 219).

But, Contemporary Feminists agenda is to reveal its gendered character. Postmodern feminism encourages women's experiential diversity that has urged a re-evaluation of the fundamental, basic tenets that shaped modernist thought. This theoretical challenge has created a tension and the resultant tension between 'modernism and post-modernism' remains unresolved without a precise definition of either of them or the exact periodization of postmodernism. However, following Nietzsche, Postmodernism 'questions' the foundationalism and absolutism of modernism's emancipatory impulse and proposes a 'non-dualistic, non-unitary' approach to knowledge.

On the other hand, though Feminism is linked to Postmodernism for the reasons cited earlier, that is to say, the aim of Postmodernism and feminism had been to dismantle the so-called 'natural' but the culturally constructed social conventions of gender roles. But, at the same time, Feminism is also an ally of Modernism with its roots in liberal humanism, a movement that remains as one of the objects of the postmodernist challenge. Here, the contention is that, modernist aspects such as liberalism and emancipation are very much part of contemporary feminist position, that it can only inevitably perpetuate the dualism than its dissolution. Therefore, radical feminists believe that even if these polarities are maintained, it should be in 'inverse order': valuing the feminine more highly than the masculine.

Such 'inherent contradictions' thwart the attempts to categorize Feminism as 'modernist or postmodernist.' The problem is that many feminists while identifying Enlightenment dualisms and thereby privileging the male, refuse the postmodern recommendation of their dissolution, preferring the reversal of dualism, thus privileging the female characteristics over male. As far as the 'Enlightenment dualism' is concerned, Post-moderns see it as an error but the feminists define the dualism as 'gendered,' thus making the two movements complementary.

In this situation, the notion of post-feminism, a term originated in popular journalism of the 1980s, was seen as heralding a celebration of difference, personal liberation and play, performed primarily through processes of consumption, a kind of release from the narrow preoccupations of feminism. Post-feminism also proposed to be both a continuation and a critique of second-wave feminism incorporates feminism's goal of 'equality' while embracing the pluralism and diversity, the typical characteristics of postmodernism. Therefore, to apply feminism metaphor to describe postmodernism, it would "look like a tapestry composed of threads of many different hues than one woven in a single colour.'

Works Cited

Friedan, Betty. *The Feminine Mystique.* W.W. Norton & Company INC. 1963.

Cott, Nancy, F. *The Grounding of Modern Feminism.* Vail-Ballou. 1989. Literariness.org

Faludi, Susan. "Blame it on Feminism." In: Andersen, M.L. & Hill Collins, P. (Eds.). *Race, Class and Gender*. Wadsworth. 1995.

Flax, Jane. "Women Do Theory." In Pearsall, M (Ed.). *Women and Values: Readings in Recent Feminist Philosophy.* Wadsworth. 1992.

Gardiner, Michael. "A Postmodern Utopia? Heller and Feher's Critique of Messianic Marxism." *Utopian Studies. Vol. 8, no.1, 1997, pp.89-122.* https://www.jstor.org/stable/20719608.

Jordan, Glenn & Weedon, Chris. Class, Gender, Race and the Postmodern World. Wiley-Blackwell. 1995.

Phillips, Anne. "LSE Commission on Gender, Inequality and Power." *Blog BPP Team*, Dec. 19, 2015. https://blogs.lse.ac.uk/

Selden, Raman, Widdowson, P. & Brooker, P. A Reader's Guide to Contemporary Literary Theory. Pearson. 2005.

Thompson, Jane, L. *Learning Liberation: Women's Response to Men's Education.* Croom Helm. 1983.

Thornham, S. "Postconstructionist, 'New' Material Feminisms: Bleaking Feminist Waves," *New Reproductive Technologies & Disembodiment: Feminist and Material Resolutions*. Routledge. 2016.

Tong, Rosemarie. *Feminist Thought: A Comprehensive Reader.* Routledge. 1989.

Weiner, Gaby. *Feminism in Education: An Introduction.* Open University Press. 1994.

The Kafkaesque in Postmodern Narration: A Comparative Study of Murakami and Calvino

ABIGAIL FRACIA LAPANG SUNN
Research Scholar, North Eastern Hill University, Shillong

Haruki Murakami was born in Kyoto, Japan on 12 January 1949. At the age of two, his family moved to Kobe, a city bustling with foreigners. This exposure to foreign influences shaped his sensibility, which is much pronounced in his writing. Murakami identified himself with the world outside of Japan, a world he knew through Jazz records and Hollywood movies. As for his style of writing, Murakami prefers the Surrealist style. These are stories where "abnormal things happen to normal people." Murakami's fiction often explores the themes of the complexities in relationships, the circular nature of time, separation, sex, self-discovery, western influences in Japan, violence, and the aftermath of World War II. Heavily influenced by Kafka, Murakami often renders the "Kafkaesque" themes of alienation and isolation in his work. Though Murakami writes in a style unfamiliar and very much detached from traditional Japanese writers,' he is deeply committed to Japan and claims that his novels "are about Japan, about the Japanese people, their life, who they are, where they are going and why they are here."

He is often preoccupied with his protagonist's search for self-identity and uses magical realism as a mechanism that portrays the protagonist's unconsciousness. Murakami's earlier novels that are filled with illustrations of global cultural commodities, his treatment of history, and his protagonists' sense of alienation may well fall under the postmodern genre.

Among his most famous works are *Kaze no uta o kike* (*Hear the Wind Sing*, 1979), which won the Gunzō Shinjin Bungaku-shō (The Gunzō New Writer's Literary Award) in 1979, *Nejimakidori kuronikuru* (*The Wind-up Bird Chronicle*, 1995) and a collection of short stories entitled *Kami no kodomotachi wa mina odoru* (After the Quake, 2002). Matthew Carl Stretcher, a Professor at Winona State University, had much to say about criticisms thrown at Murakami's art: "Many established critics were nonplussed from the beginning by his new style, or rather non-style, which signalled a rejection of the Modernist urge toward literary language, and some found his prose lacking in depth. Others found his characters' disaffected urban lifestyle too detached for their taste. Murakami was just a little too 'cool' for their comfort and failed to measure up to standards of intellectual social critique that had marked Japan's great writers since the 1960s. . . . He did not match any of the familiar "types" of contemporary Japanese literature. His writing style was odd and his fictional world was bizarre." (16)

Murakami's stories are woven around the isolated protagonist who finds himself/herself in a series of adventures and misadventures, which culminates in his/her journey through self-discovery. Murakami's novels have gained popularity all over the globe as they deal with universal themes of love, loss, hope, and self-determination.

One of the most important literary figures of Italian literature in the 20th century, Italo Calvino is an Italian journalist, short-story writer, novelist, publisher, and critic born on October 15, 1923 in Cuba and died on September 19, 1985, Siena, Italy. He is often described as "an intellectual, a critic and a creative writer" (Lauretis 97). His novel *The Path to the Nest of Spiders*, which came out in 1947, was inspired by his participation in the Italian

Resistance during World War II; it also marks the threshold of his literary career. *The Ancestor's Trilogy*, famously known as *The Italian Trilogy (The Cloven Viscount* (1952), *The Baron in the Trees* (1957), *The Non-existent Knight* (1959) "reveals Calvino's shift from the neorealistic to the fantastic" (Tinkler 68). Calvino's best-known work *If on a Winter's Night a Traveller* 1979 is a "novel written about itself. Its main character is a reader who sets out in the first chapter to read Italo Calvino's new novel *If on a winter's night a traveller*" (Morse 111).

Calvino's whimsical stories and allegorical fantasies make him one of Italy's genius storytellers and because he combined the folktale style with scientific discoveries, he is regarded as one of the most innovative novelists of the 20th century. There is undoubtedly no single term to define Calvino's output for his oeuvre, which ranges from Hemingwayesque neorealistic stories of war in the 1940s to fantasy in the 1950s, then science fiction in the 1960s and experimental projects of the 1970s. His essays are also important as they illuminate his vision for writing for example one of his famous essays "Why read the Classics?" discusses different definitions of what it means to read a classic and what we get out of it. Calvino defines a classic as a work that is never finished saying what it has to say which implicitly suggests that we as readers mature and become more capable of reading beyond simply the surface of a text.

The New York Times describes Calvino as follows: "Mr. Calvino was attracted to folk tales, knights and chivalry, social allegories and legends for our time: Fabulous and comic memory chips, slightly askew, seemed to be imbedded in his unprogrammed mind. His characters defied the malaise of daily life in the modern world" (Mitgang). His technique of writing was to start with a certain image. Methodical in his writing, his novels are well structured with a language that is not only technical and scientific but also poetic.

The Texts

One morning, Joseph K was falsely accused and arrested for some crime he knew for a fact he did not commit. This begins the novel *The Trial* written by Franz Kafka, a prominent literary and philosophical writer known for his uniquely dark, disorienting, and surreal style of writing. The protagonist of the novel, K is arrested and then made to go through a complexing and overwhelming situation where he never understands the reason for his arrest or the nature of the judicial proceedings even until the end of the novel. This type of scenario is emblematic of Kafka's work, so much so that a new word came into existence that describes a genre of thinking and writing, which involves similar scenarios that are frustrating and unnecessarily complicated—Kafkaesque. In a 1991 interview, Kafka's biographer Frederick R. Karl defined the term this way: "What's Kafkaesque is when you enter a surreal world in which all your control patterns, all your plans, the whole way in which you have configured your own behaviour, begins to fall to pieces, when you find yourself against a force that does not lend itself to the way you perceive the world. You don't give up, you don't lie down and die. What you do is struggle against this with all of your equipment, with whatever you have. But of course you don't stand a chance. That's Kafkaesque." (Edwards)

Kafka's works are drawn, in part, from his own miserable experience working as an insurance clerk who is unpaid and overworked, and thus deal with mundane and absurd aspects of modern bureaucracy. His protagonists are mostly office workers struggling through a web of obstacles to achieve their goals. This web of obstacles turns out to be so illogical that success seems to be pointless. In another novel, *Metamorphosis*, the protagonist Gregor Samsa awakens one morning only to find himself turned into an insect with no explanation of how or why. His primary concern, however, is how to get to work on time, how to deal with his strict boss, and how to provide for his inconsiderate and needy family, all these tasks to impossible to perform as he is now a mere insect. The protagonists in Kafka's works are faced with some sudden absurd circumstances with no real explanation as to how they got there and how to overcome obstacles presented to them and get back to normal. The crux of Kafka's work tends towards the confrontation with the absurd- a conflict in which a character's efforts, reasoning, and sense of the world converge with inescapable elements of meaninglessness where success is unattainable and, in the end, pointless. However, despite the despairing circumstances, Kafka's characters do not give up trying to work their way out of the senselessness, even though losing is inevitable.

The Italian Kafkaesque

Italian authors such as Italo Calvino, Italo Svevo, Susanna Tamaro, Tommaso Landolfi, Elsa Morante, Massimo Bontempelli, and Dino Buzzati, imbue Kafka qualities, both thematic and stylistic, in their work. From the use of animal imagery and oppressive spaces to representations of crises, alienation, and repressive bourgeois relations, the disparate themes of Kafka's fiction are reflected throughout modern Italian literature.

"My author is Kafka," Calvino once told an interviewer when asked about his influences, and his presence permeates Calvino's work including stories like "The Argentine Ant" and "Implosion." Calvino's favourite book is indeed a work by Kafka, *Amerika.*

Reading a Calvino story takes one on an adventure to foreign lands. With the sense of expectation, he inspires and the temperance with an atmosphere of melancholic pessimism, the stories invite nothing short of admiration. Terror is also one of the many images that recur in a significant minority of his works an example of which being "The Argentine Ant" (1953).

"The Argentine Ant," published in a collection *The Watcher and the Other Stories* 1971 tells of a young man who, with his wife and child, moves to the Italian coast as recommended by Uncle Augusto who claims that this place offers an enjoyable and excellent lifestyle with work opportunities. What Uncle Augusto fails to mention, however, is the overwhelming presence of familiarity. The young man narrates the story as he describes his experiences in a modest house, he rents from Signora Mauro. In the first night at their new home, the couple experience the terror of ant infestation as everything in the house- their beds, their kitchen, their furniture etc., is overrun with ants. They consult their friendly neighbour, the Reginaudos, as well as a local innovator, the eccentric Captain Brauni, for insights on how to rid their home of these ants. These well-meaning neighbours offer temporary solutions to their shared problem of ant infestation. Soon arrives the "ant man" at the narrator's place, who looks like an ant himself, to alleviate the problem. He coats each room with poisoned molasses in order to attract and kill the ants. His method, however, turned disastrous as ants got into the baby's ear, which in turn drives the narrator's wife crazy as she runs around in the neighbourhood vowing to track down the ant man and choke him. The wife's actions make her look deranged in front of the other neighbours; therefore, the narrator resolves to never make a fuss about the ants again. He takes his family to the seaside where they enjoy the fresh air as people work nearby and children play.

The story, in addition to dealing with several themes like marriage and the power of nature, also depicts a scenario described before as Kafkaesque. The promise of a new beginning, the sense of hope is at the heart of every Calvino story. In the story, the movement of the family to a new village enforces that theme. This dream of a new life however, turns into a nightmare as the entire locality is heavily infested with ants. American writer, Gore Vidal states that the story is, "as minatory and strange as anything by Kafka," and the way the air of threat and mystery is progressed with plain and subdued language recalls Calvino's description of Kafka "using a language so transparent that it reaches a hallucinatory level."

Characteristic of a Kafkaesque narrative, there is no explanation as to why the problem has occurred only that the protagonist has to find ways to overcome the obstacle. Similarly, in the story, no explanation is given by the narrator about the overrun of ants in the village, in each household, we just know that there is an alarming infestation of ants causing disturbance to the villagers. The narrator, though well versed in the origins of these ants, offers no concrete explanation as to why the ants have infiltrated alarmingly. He notes that by calling them Argentine ants their presence may seem more acceptable: "by calling them by the exact name I want to suggest that their presence was already expected and in a certain sense normal." (5) He seems to want to make things as normal as he wished them to be. "The invaders formed an uninterrupted veil"; they are "an enemy like fog or sand" that penetrate everything: "in every kitchen garden, in every house I sensed streams of ants climbing the walls, covering the fruit trees. . . . In the baby's room, there was a stream of ants going along the windowsill. In the kitchen, ants going around the rims-of tea cup I left in the sink, the baby's bib, and the fruits. In the garden, the sticky tree was covered with them and there must be thousands of underground nests and feeding on the thick soil and the low vegetation." (17) The narrator tries to find solutions on how to rid the house of these intruders but nothing works, success seems pointless. Throughout the story, hopelessness pervades. They are forced to come up with schemes to create areas free of ants. Food preservation becomes a tedious task: "everything had to be washed first, even the sardines in oil and the cheese, and each ant sticking to them picked off one by one." The baby's health was another pressing concern for the parents:

> It was pitiable looking for ants on that skin which reddened as soon as it was rubbed . . . examine him for any bites (luckily, there did not seem to be any), dress and feed him . . . we washed the floor, calmed the baby, and put him to sleep in the basket, isolated him all around with insect powder, and covered him with a mosquito net

> tied tight. . . . An ant had got into his ear; we could not understand at first why he cried so desperately without any apparent reason. (5)

The Ants extinguish the high expectations the couple had when they moved to a new location as they generate a feeling of intense disappointment: "We hadn't the pleasure now of feeling we were starting a new life, only a sense of dragging on into a future full of new troubles. . . . Daily life is wearing . . . it is impossible to stand still in one place; every minute either she or I jumped and said, 'ouch! They're biting,' and had to scratch ourselves and rub off the ants or put our arms and legs under the faucet'' (15)

Nuisance seems to be the 'leitmotif' of this particular Calvino text where the object of annoyance i.e., the ants cause itch, destroy food supplies, and their presence dominates and frustrates daily life. In the story, this nuisance is a shared sentiment, as the neighbours are as obsessed with ants' control as the narrator and his wife are and the task consumes all their time and resources. The women of the village are positively distraught by the ants' overwhelming presence that they organize a small protest against the inefficiency of the 'Argentine Ant Control Corporation,' the official service against the ant invasion. The story ends with no solution to the ant infested home and the narrator finds respite from this natural but frustrating occurrence when he takes his family to the seaside. "The Argentine Ant" is a masterpiece of persistent terror with absurd undertones, illustrating man's defeat to an enemy too small and ubiquitous to overcome. The definition of Kafkaesque by Friedrich Karl truly encapsulates the main idea of "The Argentine Ant."

The Japanese Kafkaesque

As mentioned before, Murakami's sensibility has been shaped by foreign influences and no doubt one of these influences was Franz Kafka: "It goes without saying that Kafka is one of my very favourite writers. However, I don't think my novels or characters are directly influenced by him. What I mean is, Kafka's fictional world is already so complete that trying to follow his steps is not just pointless, but quite risky, too. What I see myself doing, rather, is writing novels where, in my own way, I dismantle the fictional world of Kafka that itself dismantled the existing novelistic system. One could view this as a kind of homage to Kafka, I suppose." (Murakami)

Murakami's obsession with Kafka's oeuvre is reflected in his novel *Kafka on the Shore* where the protagonist renames himself, Kafka, as he decides to run away from home. The protagonists of Murakami's *Sputnik Sweetheart* and Franz Kafka's *The Castle* share the name "K." There is the short story "Samsa in Love" which is Murakami's rendition of The Metamorphosis. Haruki Murakami piques the readers' curiosity about what happens to Kafka's Gregor Samsa after he turns into an insect and is rejected by his own family. The Japanese author reverses the process of alienation to reinvent the message of this peculiar story thus renders it relatable to readers in the 21st century. Murakami also won the Franz Kafka prize in 2006.

The Strange Library, an illustrated novella by Haruki Murakami made its first appearance in 2005 in Japan. It is a curious beautiful little book about an unnamed boy, who narrates his terrorizing experience as he finds himself imprisoned in a labyrinth beneath a library. His captor is an old librarian who wants to eat his brains after he has memorized the contents of three weighty tomes on the subject of tax collection in the Ottoman Empire. The boy finds company of two other characters who are also held captive in the library: one is a man dressed in sheepskin, and the other is a mysterious and beautiful girl, who is vocally impaired and who may or may not exist, but tries her best to help the boy plan an escape from the library.

Like other works of Murakami, *The Strange Library* is surreal, it involves the presence of the other world quite detached from the real world and is separated by a door marked 107 from which the boy enters. The protagonist is a normal boy plunged into an abnormal world of the little old man who suddenly becomes tall as he threatens the boy into the reading room, then the sheepman, and the girl who "talks with her hands." Murakami said: "I think what Kafka gives us is his description of the nightmare in his creation. During his life in this world, real-life and nightmare somewhat tightly tied together. . . . Kafka successfully conveys the true horror nightmare implies, not by centralized describes the reaction of the hero, but the nightmare itself nuanced portrayal." The nightmare begins for the boy the moment he entered room 107. The boy wonders how he got into this labyrinthine nightmarish landscape when all he wanted was to borrow books from a public library. His enemy comes in the form of the old man who traps him in the reading room and forces him to memorize the books cover to cover in one month, after which the old man will eat his brain. Despite his endless protests, the boy remains entrapped in the cell dutifully reading the books all the while planning a way to escape. Kafkaesque themes of fear and menace, the inevitable and chance fate, persistent and anxiety, cowardice and tenacious pervades the book as the boy awaits freedom. The theme of menace is incorporated in certain recurrent images like the room, prison, cell, freedom, and confinement. The notion of menace in Kafka as well as Murakami implies a sense of imprisonment or entrapment of the individuals in a prison-like enclosed area, often a room that serves to epitomize the imprisonment.

Like Kafka's works, *The Strange Library* also deals with a system that punishes and tortures the petty individual who dares to question its authority. The old man represents this system that exercises power over the boy and the sheepman in the library and demand absolute compliance from them. If they attempt to defy his authority, they are disciplined and tortured and if defiance prevails, there is a hint of an incoming execution.

As in a dream, the passage of time becomes murky and the action unfolds in a sequence of increasingly disturbing images. There is no evidence that the event occurred and the boy further elaborates on this inconclusiveness in the end after his narrow escape from the clutches of the old man as he ruminates on his experience: "Did the mysterious girl and the Sheep Man really exist? How much of what I remember really happened? To be honest, I can't be certain." (73) The story ends with a sense of loneliness: "I lie here by myself in the dark at two o'clock in the morning and think about that cell in the library. About how it feels to be alone, and the depth of the darkness surrounding me. Darkness as pitch black as the night of the new moon." (76) Therefore, in the end, even though he escapes the labyrinth and the old man, the boy is left alone without a mother, without the friends he made- the sheepman and the girl. His success seems pointless in a way.

Postmodernist Perspective

Postmodernism involves not only a continuation, sometimes carried to an extreme, of the counter traditional experiments of modernism, but also diverse attempts to break away from modernist forms which had, inevitably, become in their turn conventional, as well as to overthrow the elitism of modernist "high art" by recourse for models to the "mass culture" in film, television, newspaper cartoons, and popular music. (Abrams 177)

There is a major fact stressed upon by Structuralists that to understand one thing we need to understand the exact opposite of it- Binary Opposition. For example, if we want to understand what Structuralism is we need to understand what post-Structuralism is. So also, if we want to understand Postmodernism, we need to juxtapose it with Modernism.

Postmodernism is a questioning of ideas and values associated with a form of Modernism that believes in progress and innovation. It describes the Contemporary culture or the recent culture that we have now. 20th century witnessed a movement in art, architecture, and criticism that departed from Modernism. A movement that silently and non-violently revolted against the rationality, absolutism and boundaries of Modernism. Some of the major differences between modernism and postmodernism are while the First World War influenced Modernism; the Second World War influenced Postmodernism, while Modernism believed in the universal validity of ideals and values, Postmodernism believed in the pluralism of ideas and values. While Modernists believed that, a work of art bears a universal truth or meaning, postmodernists believe that works of art are open to numerous interpretations. Modernism sees reality as the first source of experience, while Postmodernism sees virtual reality as a source of experience. Modernism has a rational and critical view of the world, Postmodernism; however, has an aesthetic and imaginative view of the world. In the modern world, we find empathy and social involvement but in the post-modern world, there is a fragmentation of social life and self-distance. Postmodernism celebrates fragmentation and disorientation. In simple terms, Post Modernism focuses on three things: 1. No absolute truth 2. No absolute meaning 3. No absolute certainty. People can interpret realities in their own ways. It includes a sceptical interpretation of culture, literature, art, philosophy, history, economics, architecture, fiction, and literary criticism.

In literature, it is characterized by a heavy reliance on techniques and literary conventions such as fragmentation, paradox, and questionable narrators, often unrealistic and impossible plots, games, parody, paranoia, dark humour, and authorial self-reference. It denotes a style that emerged after World War II- the horrors of the Holocaust, the bombing of Hiroshima and Nagasaki, events which influenced how people thought and wrote giving rise to literary forms and developments like the Theatre of the Absurd, the Beat Generation, and Magical realism. The works of Samuel Beckett often signify the significant break from modernism to postmodernism in literature. In Postmodern literary criticism, there is a shift in the authority of interpretation from the author to the reader. The reader could now rewrite, retell, and re-interpret.

An example of Murakami's proclivity for surreal stories, *The Strange Library* possesses elements of post-modern like magical realism—where we have characters "disappear into walls, take elevator to different worlds and become possessed to animals." (Musari 97) Most of his other short stories deal with everyday life, isolation, mystery, and characters living with their imagination. Italo Calvino also employs several post-modern techniques like minimalism, metafiction, pastiche, lack of a grand narrative, etc. to his stories. This paper illustrates some of the postmodern elements and narrative techniques found in the two selected short stories.

Lack of a grand narrative: One of the many elements of postmodernism that Murakami, as well as Calvino employs is the lack of a Grand Narrative, which is obvious in the selected narratives of the two writers. The two stories have nothing to do with grand ideologies like Capitalism or The Enlightenment, or Political democracy, etc. They do not portray larger-than-life heroes who go on great voyages but rather on characters that are more modest and a singular event, that adds more meaning to their individual lives. The heroes in a Murakami story are "invariably male, urbane, often unemployed, and either bored with life or caught up with little things such as food or clothing. Further, they are not at all interested in much less committed to, social or political struggles; they constitute the antipode to the protagonists of the heroic narrative." (Kawakami 309) Similarly, Calvino's characters in the story are simple, unremarkable and an ordinary couple wanting to start a new life in a new place. Since Murakami's novella is a surreal story, we do have characters that are strange and peculiar like the sheepman and the girl who is only visible to the narrator. Nonetheless, the main protagonist of the story is an ordinary boy. Murakami's story narrates a simple visit to the library that turns into a terrifying episode for a young boy but the events are never confirmed whether they are real or not. Calvino's story again takes a simple issue of ant infestation and creates a tapestry of humans confronting a hostile non-human world. The absence of a grand narrative in postmodernist literature curtails any plausible and definitive ending to the texts.

Nameless protagonists: In both of these stories, we have a nameless narrator and protagonist, which is also another postmodern narrative technique. In *The Strange Library*, this nameless narrator and the other characters' notable lack of names reinforce the main character's emptiness. As he does in many of his novels, Murakami is commenting on the emptiness and disaffection of postmodern Japanese with his use of a nameless narrator or protagonist. In Calvino's story we find while the protagonist and his wife are unnamed, the other characters he interacts with, his neighbours are all named. Names tantamount to emotional attachment or intimacy. Therefore, the most obvious reason for the use of this technique in postmodernism is to depict that the protagonist's life is empty and lacks meaning or purpose that is why he remains unnamed throughout the entire story. A name connects itself with and is part of what makes people memorable, and because these two stories are first-person narratives, the reader experiences first-hand what it is like to see the world from an obscure locale through unfocused eyes.

Minimalism: "The world is so complicated, tangled, and overloaded that to see it you must prune and prune." (Calvino 244) Literary minimalism can be characterized as a story that sticks to brevity and concision- focusing only on one incident (ant infestation), having a single setting (a Ligurian coastal village in Italy), a limited number of characters and covering a short period. The minimalist story is usually devoid of flowery, excessively descriptive language and it prioritizes brevity. Minimalist stories capture the life of unexceptional characters and typically slice of life in genre. The same can be said of Calvino's "The Argentine Ant" which is a story of a young couple renting a house in a town. The story itself begins with an abrupt introduction into facts, omitting the conventional exposition: "When we came to settle here we did not know about the ants." The plot is straightforward, simple, and not intricate portraying the challenges the characters face. Calvino refrains from using too many adjectives, adverbs, or fatuous details. The strangeness that the story renders with the abnormal infestation of ants in every household in the town turns it into a subject of nightmarish. The story is a mingling of comedy and menace.

Magic realism: The term magic realism is applied to narratives that feature super-fantastic elements. It also refers to "an extraordinary occurrence and particularly to anything spiritual or unaccountable by rational science." (Bowers 19). An attribute of magical realist texts includes the merging and juxtaposition of supernatural elements with the ordinary everyday lives of characters in a narrative- "two modes of representation that normally exist in opposition: realism and the fantastic." (Sim 161) Magical Realism makes use of mythology, fairy tales, time shifts or dream-like atmosphere and "reality is represented as having strange, mysterious, or magical qualities." (Mason 191) This co-relation between realism and fantasy is obvious in *The Strange Library* where a boy finds himself trapped in a jail cell somewhere in a public library by an old man who eats brains. Other fantastical elements include the sheepman, the pretty girl who is invisible to everyone except the boy and who eventually turns into the boy's pet starling. The dream-like quality of the story, which ends in the boy's questions about whether the events at the library happened or not also enforces this element. He, as well the readers, remain confused whether this was a dream or reality.

Open ending: Ambivalence is the hallmark of postmodernist writing achieved through open-endings that permit unguided responses by readers. Open-endings are postmodern concepts we find in the two stories. Postmodern writers usually leave their stories open-ended with no adequate finishing enabling the reader to gain more insights and meaning the more they read, that the search for meaning is never-ending. The use of Open-endings also highlights a post-modernist's aversion to cohesion and completion. It subverts the idea of "narrative closure" by evoking the possibility of multiple endings. This technique offers the text a fragmented quality by offering numerous possible outcomes. In *The Strange Library*, the very fabric of the text is fragmented by the use of illustrations. The ending of the story is in a dream-like tone that renders it unclear whether the events in the library happened or not since the boy questions: "Did the mysterious girl and the Sheep Man really exist? How much of what I remember really happened? To be honest, I can't be certain." (73) We do not know where the sheepman disappeared to after his escape with the boy from the old man's clutches. The boy's mother also suffers from a mysterious illness that may or may not be related to the library incident since many things that happened in the library seem to be connected to his home like the beautiful voiceless girl eventual transformation into his pet starling. "The Argentine Ant" ends with the couple going to the beach. Nothing is said about the ants, which were the main antagonists so to say throughout the story. Are they gone? Did the narrator and his wife find a solution to their ant problem? The ending is left to the readers to decide and imagine. Post-modernist Theorists believed that, adhering to the idea that the author is the final authority, implies that there is only one final and correct meaning to a work; which in turn reinforces the idea of a grand narrative, to which Postmodernism is firmly against. To conclude, to Postmodernists, the author's as well as the readers' interpretation of a text are equally valid.

Conclusion

This study has undertaken a postmodernist reading of *The Strange Library* by Haruki Murakami and "The Argentine Ant" by Italo Calvino by discussing different postmodern elements in each story and illuminating the Kafkaesque affinities that we find in them as they fuse "the mundane with the marvellous." In both the stories, we find the two authors have successfully woven Kafkaesque motifs into the fabric of their postmodern works. Systematic parallelism has been drawn between the world of Kafka and the fictional arena of Murakami and Calvino as they are predominantly preoccupied with the representation of situations seemingly baffling and bizarre with acute feelings dissolution and evasiveness manifested in both theme and language. The works of both writers studied are obsessed with anxieties and inner turmoil of human predicament in a world of menace and violence, operated through a powerful mechanism in which an individual is caught up and doomed to be annihilated. The analysis indicates that Calvino uses the technique of minimalism and the use of unremarkable and ordinary characters with everyday events in his story. To trace the concepts of Magic Realism, *The Strange Library* by Murakami is an excellent example with his story of an ordinary boy imprisoned in a labyrinth beneath a library by an old man who wants to eat his brains. A lack of a grand narrative is obvious in both Murakami's and Calvino's characters that are simple and low rather than complex and grand. This study, which analysed Murakami's and Calvino's short stories from the postmodernist perspective, offers us a better understanding of these two writers in the realm of short fiction.

Works Cited

Abrams, M. H. et al. *A Glossary of Literary Terms*. New York: Heinle and Henle. 1999.

Bowers, Maggie Ann. *Magical Realism*. New York: Routledge, 2004.

Calvino, Italo. "The Argentine Ant." *The Watcher and Other Stories*. Trans. Archibald Colquhoun. Massachusetts: Houghton Mifflin Harcourt, 2013.

_____. *If On a Winter's Night a Traveller.* Trans. William Weaver. New York: Harcourt Brace Jovanovich, 1981.

_____. Interview. *Italo Calvino, The Art of Fiction No. 130*. By William Weaver & Damien Pettigrew. *The Paris Review*, Fall 1994.

_____. www.theparisreview.org/interviews/2027/the-art-of-fiction-no-130-italo-calvino

Edwards, Ivana. *The Essence of 'Kafkaesque.' The New York Times.* Dec. 29, 1991. www.nytimes.com/1991/12/29/nyregion/the-essence-of-kafkaesque

Kawakami, Chiyoko. "The Unfinished Cartography: Murakami Haruki and the Postmodern Cognitive Map." *Monumenta Nipponica* 57.3 (2002): 309-37.

Lauretis, Teresa de. "Italo Calvino: In Memoriam." *Science Fiction Studies* 13:1 (1986): 97-98. www.jstor.org/stable/4239732

Mason, Fran. *Historical Dictionary of Postmodernist Literature and Theatre*. Maryland: The Scarecrow Press, 2007.

Mitgang, Herbert. "Italo Calvino, The Novelist, Dead at 61." *The New York Times*. 19 September 1985. www.nytimes.com/1985/09/19/books/italo-calvino-the-novelist-dead-at-61

Morse, John. "On Italo Calvino." *Chicago Review* 33:2 (1982): 111-14. Doi.org/10.2307/25305131.

Murakami, Haruki. *The Strange Library*. Illus. Ted Goosen. 2014.

Murakami, Haruki. "Questions for Murakami about Kafka on the Shore." *Haruki Murakami.* Penguin Random House, n.d. www.harukimurakami.com/q_and_a/questions-for-haruki-murakami-about-kafka-on-the-shore

Musari, Mark. *Today's Writers and Their Works, Haruki Murakami*. New York: Cavendish Square Publishing, 2010.

Sim, Stuart. Ed. *The Routledge Companion to Postmodernism*. New York: Routledge, 1999.

Stretcher, Matthew. *The Forbidden Worlds of Haruki Murakami.* Minneapolis: University of Minnesota Press, 2014.

Tinkler, Alan. "Italo Calvino." *Review of Contemporary Fiction* 22: 1 (2002): 68. https://www.thefreelibrary.com/Italo+Calvino.-a087460084

A Postmodern View of Mahesh Dattani's Play "The Big Fat City"

AARTI DUHAN
Research Scholar, SRM University, Sonipat

Mahesh Dattani is one of India's best and most serious contemporary playwrights writing in English. All of his plays are based on social issues. He is one of the most dynamic voices of modern Indian English Drama. He has directed many plays ranging from classical Greek to contemporary ones. Several of his plays have been turned into films also. In 1998, Dattani won the Sahitya Akademi award for his book of plays titled *Final Solutions and Other Plays.* What one loves about him is the way he brings in the dynamics of personal and moral choices while focusing on human relationships.

The main thing about Dattani is that he stands for all those who have been marginalized by society. He has taken up themes which cover a wide spectrum of social and political problems. He studies the impact of these issues and developments on the individual in a society. Asha Kuthari Chaudhuri elaborates, "He deals with sexuality and gender issues, religious tension, and workings of personal and moral choices as he explores a gamut of human relationships. From *Where There's a Will,* to the matrix of gender roles in *Dance Like a Man* and *Tara,* to *Bravely Fought the Queen* that explores the shame of the upper middle class joint family, to *Final Solutions,* a gripping and sensitive play about the Hindu - Muslim conflict, to *Do the Needful,* originally a radio play that comically talks about alternate sexual choices as do *On Muggy Night in Mumbai* and *Seven Steps Around the Fire,* to *Thirty Days in September* which looks at incest and child abuse, Dattani has never fallen short of serious issues that need to be addressed" (Chaudhuri 18-19).

Dattani is widely acknowledged for his innovative techniques in stage craft. When asked in an interview by as to where he got the inspiration to present strong characters belonging to metropolitan cities, Dattani replied, "I am an Urban person. I have a visitor's experience with rural India. So, the environment in which I can express myself is comprised entirely of the urban spaces. My art is bound to express that. My plays revolve around the urban current day India. ("Interview")

Dattani's latest play "The Big Fat City" is a black comedy. This play is a sarcastic take on the new middle class, their aspirations and their anxieties. It examines the depiction of grim and disturbing picture of Indian family life. Despite an undercurrent of comedy, this play is very thought provoking and introspective. Settling down after a few private runs of this play in Bangalore to a select audience, this is what Dattani himself told a reporter that the play is about people "stuck in the endless cycle of a metropolis that forgot to pause for breath. Lives taken over by wealth or the lack of it, technology, irrelevance of relationships—the protagonists are seen grappling with their own realities" (Nandy). His criticism of contemporary society—the upper stratum of it at least—is quite apt. The characters in the play become so greedy that they forget the societal values. Greed for power and wealth results in not only the destruction of oneself, but in the others also who are related somehow. Modern living and western thinking encourage people to break free from the shackles at familial, social and cultural norms and turn stark hypocrites who pay lip sympathy to societal ideals. Economic growth has become a measure of individual growth which even overshadows the lofty ideals. The play is a dismal and sarcastic tale of a murder and carries all the elements of high drama—love, greed, hypocrisy, artificially, jealousy, adultery, murder, violence, drugs, mafia, family honour and corruption.

Phony Lives

The story is set in a fancy Mumbai apartment (in a one BHK flat), where a couple (Niharika and Murli) invite an old friend (Sailesh) for dinner, so that they can get some financial help in clearing off their home loan. Murli's wife Niharika makes every possible effort to train Murli to convince his banker friend to help them with their EMIs (equalized monthly instalments of the loan). She repeatedly asks Murli to appear quite presentable and confident in front of Sailesh. Niharika wants Murli to impress Sailesh:

> Murli: Can't I wear my regular shirt, please?
> Niharika: Stop fidgeting with that kurti. You will tear it. No, you can't. (156)

Niharika not only puts up a mask of a successful modern woman but also compels her husband to put up another mask only to execute her plot in a successful way. In Mumbai, everyone is looking for an apartment, a role and a lover. And when they have these then they are looking for a better apartment, a better role and a better lover. Murli who has recently been fired from an MNC, is facing debts due to a loan on his newly acquired apartment. We find Murli to be less confident and desperate and in a conversation with Sailesh, he blurts out the truth of his being fired from the job: "I didn't! I was fired! I lost my job!" (164)

Niharika has invited the TV actress Lalita Jagtiani to impress Sailesh. By impressing Sailesh, they want to get their loan sanctioned only to live in the "big fat city." Sailesh, on the other hand, is himself in debt. He has come to Murli's house for some monetary help. Sailesh made some adjustments in one customer's account and now desperately needs money to manage that customer. Lalita as Lolly is recognized by Sailesh as Yamini, the character in Ekta's serial "Saas Bani Saperan." She plays the character Yamini in her past time but in present, her condition is pathetic, as she fails to grab roles in TV serials, and so she has joined theatre group. Her husband Kailash is a drunkard and her son Rahul gets high at late night parties. Hence, Lalita is in charge of earning and maintaining the family. Throughout the text, Sailesh would refer her as Yamini which quietly shows how a television identity blurs out the real identity of a person in this urban space. Lolly, like other characters, is using the façade of a popular television star to convince them about her demand in her sphere. But the text message reveals her true self that she is in dire need of a single role. In his postmodern style of stagecraft, we can read the mind of the author through his/her text messages sent through the cellphone.

> Lolly. I am doing one of those serious plays by Hamesh Dattani. There is so much more depth to that kind of work.
>
> *Lolly sends her message.*
>
> SCREEN *(from Lolly):* SORRY EKTA. BUT PLEASE, PLEASE GIVE ME A RUNNING CHARACTER IN YOUR NEW SERIAL. I REALLY DON'T WANT TO DO THAT MORBID DATTANI PLAY. I AM DESPERATE. PLEASE. (168)

Very ironically here, the real space reflects the unreal things and the virtual space reflects the real things. The use of technology to reveal their thought process and unmask the characters of their pretentions enhances the dramatic quality of the play. The audience gets familiar with what is going on inside the minds of the characters through text messages they see on the screen.

Due to her worse economic condition, Niharika rents one portion of her small apartment to Anu, a struggling TV star who comes from Haryana. Her lover Puneet always snubs her for her proximity with producers. Anu and Puneet storm into the house with their dispute and when Puneet enters Anu's room and finds out Kailash on her bed, he becomes apprehensive of an intimate relationship between Kailash and Anu. Puneet strangles him to death. Anu plans to present Kailash's murder as suicide. She convinces Niharika, Murli, and Sailesh to help her. Anu, comes out as the most grotesque and ruthless of all the characters when in order to save Puneet from being charged for Kailash's murder, she forges a plan and throws Kailash's dead body from the balcony of fourteenth floor of the apartment. Her insensitivity comes forth as she has no remorse or guilt complex for her brutal act because all this is done to get money as promised by Anu whose brother is a rich landlord and whom she has been reporting of her "success" in Bollywood.

Postmodern Materialism

The hypocrisy and naked greed of the middle class is brought of relief when Anu, whose boyfriend commits the murder, bargains with Sailesh over the money he would take to keep quiet. Anu proposes to pay them one crore to manage the situation. Lolly who was assuming to be very affluent was also in need of money. One is extremely surprised to see that she chose materialistic fulfilment, remains calm and give indifferent reaction to her husband's mysterious death as she says, "Oh, Sailesh! When I saw Kailash's body on the floor I knew he had left to make way for better things! I am so happy I don't need to feel guilty about anything." (218)

The thing that she is really worried about was the drug packet that was worth fifty lakhs, and that packet was in Kailash's pocket. She was trying to arrange cash for drug mafias. She wants to save her only child Rahul from the goondas of the underworld who have been threatening to kill him. But she was getting disappointed because she had failed to arrange the drug money. All the characters in the play used a dead body to achieve their dreams and desires. Everyone wants to fulfill their personal motifs. The characters of the play are as hollow, artificial and materialistic as the world where they exist.

Anu devices a plot to extract money from her brother Harjeet. Anu invites her brother to finance a film where she is doing a good role. She dupes her brother by pretending that she is struggling to be an actor. But she pretends that only to be with her boyfriend and to marry him. However, she fails to trick her brother Harjeet. Harjeet at the end of the play shoots both Anu and Puneet for the sake of their family's honour. Anu's life story reminds us how Indian families discriminate a girl child from a male one. Terror of patriarchal institution and honour killing, another major social cultural issue has been discussed in the play. Anu and her lover Puneet had eloped from their village to Mumbai and wished to get married, and this is the only reason that Harjeet kills both of them. Dattani makes a bold assertion about the orthodox and conservative side of society which deprives individuals of their freedom of choice. Incidentally, this theme is very prominent in many of Dattani's plays.

At the end of the play Murli and Niharika prepare themselves to go back to Murli's roots, his homeland Thirunalvelli. They could not save their own house in Mumbai. Murli is yearning to go back to his root and homeland: "I don't want this job, I don't want this city! I just want to come home." (185). Thus, the play dramatizes three murders onstage but it does not affect the flow of life of any of the characters. The characters in "The Big Fat City" compromise their ethical values and as a result forfeit their integrity. They also fail to maintain the sanctity of motherhood, marriage and friendship. The characters here are people of dead conscience who lack sensitivity towards one another. They desperately try to use one another for their personal gains. The failure of Lolly as a mother and wife, Niharika's scheme to exploit Murli's college friend to save her house, Sailesh's indulgence with Lolly and Anu's gruesome disposal of Kailash's corpse speaks volumes about the emotional and spiritual vacuity in the modern world.

"The Big Fat City" portrays the lives and emotions of middle-class people of Mumbai. However, it is not surely and solely the story of Mumbai. Any resident of metropolitan city can identify himself with that of Murli, Niharika, Sailesh, Anu and Lolly. Regarding the theme of the play, A critic rightly says: "It depicts ordinary people caught in extraordinarily situations, Each struggling to deal with their own situation in a bizarre way. It is a black comedy in the true sense of the term." (Kaur). In this city, everyone is continually thinking about oneself and by and by, self-centeredness becomes the center of this city space. The issues highlighted in the play are firmly rooted in the metropolitan city of Mumbai and reflect the city in its different shades. The necessity to focus on the conflicts in the lives of contemporary Indians arises due to the complexities in their lives. Morality, values, respect towards elders all are getting dissolved day by day. Money controls the lives of every citizen and it is the pivot of this city.

Mahesh Dattani's plays have varied content and appeal. He writes purely for the theatre and is a very conscious artist who always gives proper and elaborate stage-directions. He deals with the issue which are very much a part of the educated urban society but the people do not want to confront them. The thing that makes Dattani one of India's finest playwrights is the manner in which he speaks to the audience straight from the heart. In this play, Dattani shows us that how are greedy people are becoming in today's time. Nowadays everyone is starting to value money instead of people. These days you can buy almost anything. There are fewer realms of life in which the language of money does not speak powerfully. We now live not only in a market economy, but also in a market society.

It is not that the playwright supports all types of values upheld in society as is evident from Anu's murder by her brother. In fact, Dattani has hit out at the orthodoxy prevalent in society in many of his plays. In his play "Do the Needful," for example, he debunks certain conventions. A critic observes about it: "The sociologists believe that we accept moral principles devised by society partly because we have identified ourselves with others in society or are convinced of the desirability of such principles. We reject morality at times when it comes in conflict with something that is deeply desired by us so much so that we become ready to plough a lonely furrow. In modern times, with the surge of existentialism, individual choice and freedom have been fetishized" (Batra 188).

Conclusion

In the play "The Big Fat City," Dattani deals with such serious issues as commodification of moral and ethical values, breakdown of relationships, adverse impact of technology on human lifestyle, emotional and spiritual hollowness of man. We can easily stamp his themes and techniques postmodern because Dattani deals with the subjects relating to a society that is more riveted to a virtual mode of living that is unreal and yet becomes more real for some. This lifestyle thrives on material success in this fast-globalizing world, and takes all revered social values as flimsy and disposable, *a la* postmodern "play" (latitude) in which it is not the incapacity of the characters to come up to them, but rather the lack of awareness and the incapacity to appreciate the worth of those values. In a way, it is the celebration of this incapacity that is reflected in the smugness of almost all the characters. All this is presented to us by Dattani in a dramatic format and stagecraft which is postmodern too.

Dattani's plays are primarily performance oriented addressing bold themes and have issue pertaining to the urban-middle class Indian society. In all of them, he provokes our thinking, compels us to think afresh about the problems. He mirrors the contemporary society through short dialogues appealing directly to the heart and mind of the audience. This play "The Big Fat City" contains reality and is about current situation as we have also seen and read about such stories and blunders in our surroundings and newspapers.

Works Cited

Batra, Jagdish. "Mahesh Dattani's Do the Needful: Examining Fossilized Value System." *Recent Indian Drama in English*, Ed. R.K. Dhawan. New Delhi: Prestige International, 2010, pp. 185-195.

Chaudhuri, Asha Kuthari. *Mahesh Dattani: An Introduction.* New Delhi. Cambridge University Press, 2008.

Dattani, Mahesh. *Me and My Plays.* New Delhi: Penguin, 2014.

Kaur, Achint. Google Review of *Me and My Plays by Mahesh Dattani.* n.d. <https://books.google.co.in/books/about/Me_and_My_Plays.html?id=KitiAgAAQBAJ>

Nandy, Priyadarshini. "Mahesh Dattani in his 'Big Fat City.'" Lifestyle, *DNA*, 21 November, 2013. <https://www.dnaindia.com/lifestyle/report-mahesh-dattani-in-his-big-fat-city-1825113>

"Interview with Mahesh Dattani." *The Scholar's Avenue*, 30 Sep. 2015. <http://www.scholarsavenue.org/interviews/interview-with-mahesh-dattani/>

Postmodernism in "The (Postmodern) Story of Jyoti Vishwanath"

APARNA AJITH
Sree Narayana College for Women, Kollam

Indian writing in English has come of age. The slender sapling planted decades ago has ripened by the passage of the biological clock bestowing spectacular expectations and numerous branches have emerged hitherto. Indian English narratives hold a significant position in world literature for their powerful and pulsating receptivity. The paper attempts to look at the postmodern elements present in the short story entitled "The (Postmodern) Story of Jyoti Vishwanath." Postmodernism is an umbrella term that is extensively used in academic parlance these days. It generally refers to a socio-cultural and literary theory, and a shift in perception that has been displayed in diverse disciplines comprising the literature, social sciences, art, architecture, communication, fashion, and technology. "Postmodernism is a school of thought or a movement that took place after World War II, but it gained popularity in the 1960s and 1970s. Postmodernism is often used alternatively with post structuralism "as two perspectives from which to view the history of modern literary and cultural criticism" (Habib 246). It is characterized by broad skepticism, subjectivism, or relativism; a general suspicion of reason; and a critical understanding of the role of ideology in asserting and maintaining political and economic power. This literary movement underscores play, fragmentation, metafiction, and intertextuality. Postmodernism manifests experimentation and innovation. It is the style of the age and has become a worldwide movement in all arts and disciplines due to its permeable limits, openness, and multidimensional approach. Chandramathi's postmodern short story evinces a touch of uncommon irony, anti-realist terrain, and a metafictional approach. The story brimming with humour acts as a sharp critique of the values and behaviours of the patriarchal society.

Chandrika Balan aka Chandramathi

Dr. Chandrika Balan who writes under the pen name Chandramathi is a frontline contemporary Malayalam writer. Her characters display a receptivity that is familiar with the spirit of the age, in terms of content and form. She is an award-winning bilingual writer who holds a position of her own in the arena of contemporary Indian writing in English. She wears many hats as a fiction writer, translator, and critic in both English and Malayalam. She has published 20 books in Malayalam that comprise 10 collections of short stories including a novelette, an anthology of medieval Malayalam poetry, 2 collections of essays, two memoirs, and 5 books translated from English. . Her stories depict wide-ranging familiarities of being a woman in the contemporary era without taking any parochial or particular standpoint. Her writings manifest a passionate awareness of the gendered reality in Kerala and elsewhere and raise relevant queries regarding it. She is well acknowledged for her delineation of women characters, defying familial issues in multifarious ways. She paints her women as modern gaining strength and trying to approach their problems from a diverse angle.

Her stories have been translated into numerous Indian and foreign languages. Chandrika Balan's stories are women-centered. K. Satchidanandan, the prominent Malayalam poet and critic, in his scholarly "Introduction" to this volume has labelled her historically as a link in the chain of women's writing in Malayalam. She falls in line among a dazzling array of forerunners like Lalithambika Antharjanam, K. Saraswathi Amma, and Kamala

Das, and adores a status of eminence among her contemporaries like Sara Joseph, Gracy, Ashita, and Priya A. S. All these writers have in their unique style grappled with the concerns of women's bias and independence in a patriarchal and consumerist society that passes through the speedy advancement of the modern age such as urbanization, globalization, and westernization. *Arya and Other Stories* is the maiden volume of her self-translation of the stories marked by the audacity of their motifs and freshness of form and language. In this collection of twelve short stories, Balan renders a preview into the world of the woman in a village where feminism has reached. She explores and highlights the kind of queries a woman goes through in the present society. She employs various writing styles comprising magic realism, metafiction, irony, and postmodernism.

Storyline

"The (Postmodern) Story of Jyoti Vishwanath" was originally published in 1994 in the *Mathrubhumi* weekly, and later incorporated in Chandramathi's 1995 collection, *Aaryavartanam*. Jyoti Vishwanath's story begins with the author's words to the readers regarding the boundless freedom they enjoy in reading the story. It begins with an exciting disclaimer. "This story is purely fictitious. It has no connections whatsoever with people who are merely alive or with people who have escaped unto death. Any semblance to life, if discovered, has to be dismissed at once as a figment of fancy" (Balan 104). She has given complete freedom to her readers to finish the story in one go or as they wish. The readers can edit and rewrite the paragraph of the story as per their choice. The author is irrelevant and it's up to the readers to decipher the story according to their perceptions. Balan has her justification in giving the term 'postmodern' in brackets in the title. "As for the 'postmodern' tag in the title, the adjective has been added as a signpost to future critics who, otherwise, would attach it only to the writers of their choice" (104).

Balan expounds why she has chosen the name 'Jyoti' for her heroine after a lot of careful thought of discarding the outdated rustic names. "Our lady passed her MBBS quite honourably without paying any capitation fee, went abroad for higher studies and, like any good-looking Malayali girl who goes abroad for higher studies, returned with a husband" (104). Jyoti, 'the educated, efficient and well-experienced modern woman' was cautioned by her father, Mr. Ramanand Menon while seeing her off to the United States that she may love anyone but marry only an Indian. Balan with a tinge of sarcasm states that Jyoti deserves full marks for filial disobedience just because she took care to marry an Indian despite being in love with a Chinese, Yankee, and a Japanese. She married a Keralite who is an engineer and she works as the MD of a five-star hospital designed and built by her husband. The writer feels that names like Bhagavati or Dakshayani will never fit a resourceful woman like her Jyoti, the beautiful burning flame! Her husband has been attributed the name Vishwanath, the Lord of the Universe. Though they are husband and wife, Jyoti and Vishwanath remain different and distant in their desires and passions. Vishwanath is portrayed as a feminist whereas his wife Jyoti is not. "Unlike most other feminists, Vishwanath preached what he practiced. He did not grumble or pull a long face if his doctor-wife came home late, instead, he received her with a smile. Whenever Jyoti went out of town for medical seminars, it was Vishwanath who packed her suitcase for her" (105). By seeing Vishwanath's feminist behavior, the neighboring women who claim themselves as feminists would feel jealous. They look down upon Jyoti for her unsympathetic attitude towards their struggle for women's rights and equality. They brand Vishwanath as a hen-pecked husband who is ready to wash Jyoti's undergarments in the washing machine.

Feminist vs Anti-Feminist

The author reveals the shocking truth that Jyoti is not a feminist by narrating an incident where Jyoti shows indifference to

American feminists. "In fact on 14 May 1986, at Illinois, Jyoti had told her friend Adrian Clinton: 'I hate all feminists! Adrian's mom had been a member of the bra-burning brigade of American feminists" (105). Balan gives a fleeting reference to Kerala women who fought for the right to cover their breasts long ago. Jyoti has totally confused the story of the struggles encountered by Malayali women with her stand on feminists. Jyoti is unmindful of the rumours spread by the neighbouring women as she has no time to go behind or respond to them. She is mostly preoccupied with her job and her all-too-rare holidays are spent in the kitchen making ghee-rice for Vishwanath. He never raises any complaint even if she comes late at night. He eats his dinner warmed in the microwave oven by Santha, the maid. He reclines on the hammock in the balcony waiting for Jyoti's Contessa. They live in their own worlds.

In this context, Balan raises the question of whether this couple has any child. The author wishes to answer far away from the oft-beaten tracks of childbearing and rearing. She finally resolves it by stating that if they have no time to look after their children, there is absolutely no guarantee that their children will look after them in the old age. "So, let Jyoti and Vishwanath take a resort in the oft-heard cliché 'we cannot think of anyone coming between ourselves, even if it is our own child!" (106). The collapse of social structure, tradition, and customs is explicitly mentioned here. Postmodernism is a unique way of life and way of feeling. The series of social and cultural tendencies are disrupted or decoded in a different aspect. The author takes the right to play with the lives of the characters and their family planning.

The Big Twist

The story of Jyoti Vishwanath takes a different turn when a team of foreign doctors landed at the airport to collaborate with Jyoti in her experiments to extract an antidote for AIDS from neem or margossa. Jyoti starts devoting her days and nights working at the laboratory designed by her husband. As Jyoti is completely engrossed in her busy schedule, Vishwanath withdraws into the solitary world of his musings. Chandrika Balan discloses the fact that Vishwanath is a talented poet who has been honoured from his school days. "It is said that when the young Vishwanath had recited this poem (beginning 'O Sudha, Vasudha, darling Earth') in his booming baritone, R. Sudha Devi, the Malayalam Lecturer, had been so overcome as to forget the sanctity of the teacher-student relationship. It is also said that nothing untoward happened because of Vishwanath's restraint" (107).

Vishwanath has drenched deep in the nuances of his poetry. The author feels it is quite unfortunate that the critics never got a chance to evaluate his overflow of personal feelings.

O World, clad in beautiful white,
If you melt the heart and head as one
How far away from the Lord of the World are you!
O my seductive dream, do you know
That the Lord of the World now is
Destitute with no World of his own!

Balan albeit not certain admits that something must have happened to Vishwanath on these lonely nights. Jyoti's research is nearing fruition and somewhere in the air, she could even sense a Padmashri or Padmavibhushan.

When Jyoti comes back to Vishwanath after all her hectic work schedule, she takes a calm sleep resting her head on his chest. The writer brings an unexpected postmodern sort of twist here. "Jyoti in her dream was flying to Sweden to receive the Nobel Prize. The aeroplane suddenly hit an air pocket and Jyoti opened her eyes with a start. To her surprise, she saw Vishwanath closing the bedroom from outside" (108). Jyoti gets up slowly after her initial bafflement and starts following him. He enters the kitchen and closes the door behind him. Jyoti hears only the click of the lock from within. Chandrika Balan's modern heroine, Jyoti does not try to commit suicide or a scientific death by slicing the jugular veins. "It is interesting to speculate what Jyoti would have done, had she been a traditional wife. She could have kicked open the closed door of the kitchen. She could have rolled on the floor hysterically crying and cursing loud enough to wake all the neighbours" (108).

Jyoti is concerned about her accomplishments and the innumerable preoccupations in the years to come. She does not have time to cook sambar and aviyal, go to the market to buy fish and vegetables, fill the empty cans in the storeroom, wash the soiled clothes, manure and water to the plants in the garden, vacuum-clean the house, feed, bathe and brush two Alsatians and look after the countless lovebirds. She finds only one solution to all these: Santha, the maid who has been with them for years and is familiar with everyone's likes and dislikes. Although a lot of uneasy feelings stirred within her, she ruthlessly suppressed her momentary weakness. Jyoti concludes that it is better not to react to the problem as it is very difficult to get servants nowadays. Another one in the place of Santha would only mean time wasted in fresh training and, perhaps the reoccurrence of the same problem. Balan finds Jyoti's decision wise and practical as it is very hard to get servants these days. She concludes the story by granting readers the full liberty to rewrite the end of the story in whatever way they like.

The tenets of postmodernism are explicitly seen in the short story of Jyoti Vishwanath. The false and frenzied meaningless activities of life, materialistic approach, irony, and ambiguity of life are portrayed in the story. Chandrika Balan has made the story 'open' so that the readers can make their own connections, supply alternative meanings and provide their own interpretations. Jyoti Vishwanath's burning flame of life can be viewed from an entirely different perspective as per the whims of the readers. The chaos of an incoherent world reverberates throughout this short story. Historiographic metafiction is employed by the writer to blend fact and fiction. Megan Terry, President Clinton, and the bra-burning brigade serve as excellent instances of this. Loneliness in a jam-packed world is also a feature of postmodernism and Vishwanath is a silent sufferer of this situation.

Postmodern writers often leave their stories open-ended, without any satisfying conclusion. Postmodern stories and novels rely heavily on irony, parody, pastiche, and satire. Postmodern authors often reject the boundaries between the different genres. The postmodern texts reveal skepticism about the ability of art to create meaning, the ability of history to reveal the truth, and the ability of language to convey reality. All that skepticism led to fragmented, open-ended, self-reflexive stories that are intellectually fascinating but often difficult to grasp. The stylistic techniques of postmodernism include the frequent use of intersexuality, metafiction, temporal distortion, magical realism, faction, reader involvement, and minimalist techniques of reduction, omission, and suggestion. (Yousef, 35)

Tawfiq Yousef's views exactly underscore the crux of postmodernism in "The (Postmodern) Story of Jyoti Vishwanath." Chandrika Balan leaves the story open-ended without offering a satisfying conclusion to her readers. The story translated by the author herself from Malayalam renders a different rhythm altogether in the source language. Languages develop over time and words accrue significance. The main challenge faced by the translators is how far they can convey the same meaning without causing any damage to the subtle linguistic nuances and cultural flavour of a target language. Translation studies unite many nations; it is because when a text is translated, people can find commonalities as well as disparities between their languages and the translated text. In fact, translation shows that how language is universal rather than being regional or national. It unites two or more literature in the gamut of comparative literature. Despite all the linguistic subtleties, the story is translated in such a way that the readers can grasp the sense acceptably and comprehensively. Translation of Jyoti's story into English surmounts all linguistic, cultural, regional, and national disparities. The impeccably well translation is accepted and echoed in alien lands too.

Conclusion

The story of Jyoti Vishwanath with a pinch of symbolism written in an unconventional style is intellectually appealing to the readers though it is quite hard to comprehend. Chandrika Balan brings into open the awkward fact that even an educated and employed woman remains silent to the sudden change in the behavior of her husband. Even though Vishwanath pretends to be a feminist and behaves likes a henpecked husband, he finds solace in his private world of affairs. His pseudo feminism is ripped apart by the end of the story. Jyoti is oblivious of her womanly duties as she is engrossed in her career dreaming of a Nobel Prize. The pragmatic reality of contemporary women is far more complex and variegated than it is generally assumed. Balan tries with her postmodern narrative techniques to captivate this intricacy and diversity of female experience in her stories. Jyoti continues to haunt the psyche even after one has read the last line umpteen times and devoured the short story in its entirety. Although not progressive in the strict sense of the term, the story of Jyoti Vishwanath bespeaks the experience of being a postmodern woman in the contemporary Indian scenario.

Works Cited

Balan, Chandrika. *Arya and Other Stories*, New Delhi : Orient Blackswan, 2014.

Chandramathi. The (Postmodern) Story of Jyoti Vishwananth." *In the Shade of the Sahyadri: Selections from Malayalam Poetry, Short Fiction and Drama*, ed. Raveendran et.al. New Delhi: Oxford University Press, 2013.

Habib, M.A.R. (2011). *Literary Criticism from Plato to the Present: An introduction*. Oxford: Blackwell, 2011.

Krishnaswamy, N., John Varghese, Sunita Mishra. *Contemporary Literary Theory*, New Delhi: MacMillan, 2001.

Yousef, Tawfiq. "Modernism, Postmodernism, and Metamodernism: A Critique." *International Journal of Language and Literature* 5.1 (2017): 33-43.

Reversing the Authorisation: Tattoo and Crime as Connecting Tools in Stieg Larsson's *The Girl with the Dragon Tattoo*

ANTARA BISWAS
Research Scholar
RASHMI GAUR
IIT, Roorkee

Originally published in Swedish language in 2005, translated into English in 2008, screened in the year 2011, the global bestseller novel *The Girl with the Dragon Tattoo* is the first instalment among the millennium trilogy by Stieg Larsson that sketches a revolting beauty in presenting the female protagonist, Lisbeth Salander. Larsson has always been well venerated for his generous social works and continuous efforts to divulge the racial, misogynistic discrepancies in society. The novel, though a mystery thriller, harmoniously balances the "suspense" of the fictive plot along with the realistic portrait of contemporary Swedish society (Mehta). The patrimonial title of the novel is refurbished with the one that focuses on "The Girl" whom Mehta finds as one of the main strengths of the trilogy. Though unnamed, "the girl" proves to be the most pivotal ambassador of the novel that not only attracts the readers' attention because of the Dragon-shaped tattoo on the skin but also her unpredicted powerful femininity. There is an ever-present struggle with her individual and social identity that continues to reject her will to be closeted within the boundary of social expectation, apparently brings out the uniqueness of the character. As the title evokes, the attention to her marked body, on a deeper scale, shares an interconnected dealing with the development of bodily experience. The plot of the novel slowly unfurls how perpetrating violence paves the way to re-establish the power of authorization in Lisbeth's life. The tattoo on her skin along with the atypical delinquency celebrates her unique heroic femininity. It avails a wing of liberation from her tragic fate of a rape survivor while enabling an opportunity for the readers to trace her journey in the novel.

Transmodernism

The term transmodernism, as documented, was first coined by Spanish feminist and philosopher Rodriguez Magda in her essay, *La Sonrisa de Saturno: Hacia una teoria Transmoderna* (1989). Magda is one of the introducing ambassadors to betoken the term transmodernity as a proliferating affiliation in different aspects of life. Enrique Dussel, an Argentine-Mexican philosopher, further developed the idea of transmodernism, propounding his foundational theory of liberation with the averment of Latin-American cultural position from the "West and the rest" spectacle. The Eurocentric imposition denies the cultural and pedagogical authenticity of other cultures. Irena Ateljevic proclaims transmodernism as an "integrated approach" and a tool for "synchronicity" that is responsible for the "emerging paradigm shift" towards the socio-cultural, political, economic, and philosophical interconnectedness. To assess the novel *The Girl with the Dragon Tattoo* equivocally with Transmodernism as an annexure of global affiance, it has to be detonated that the novel has been appreciated for its worldwide expedition in "cultural assimilation," and "international political themes" (Panichi 2). It deals with the universal concerns such as women's oppression, sexual crime, and corporate politics. The fact that the novel reveals itself as universal social justice and more than just typical crime fiction makes it summon the widest range of readers from every corner of the world.

Transmodernism is considered to be an inter-subjective phenomenon that shares similar distinctive qualities to incorporate "female image" into literary narratives (Magda). Several basic key characteristics of transmodernism can be applied to engage an analysis of Lisbeth Salander's bodily experience as delineated in the novel. The fundamental themes that share common phenomena in Feminism and Transmodernism are respectively as follows: the continuous presence of hegemonic power, wrestling with the conflicts, struggling through interconnectedness, exclusion, and resistance. To include the theoretical approach of Enrique Dussel's theory of Liberation which insists on asymmetrical power of domination to marginalize the exteriors as "the other," the plot of the novel remarks on women's bodies as a product of marginalization and exploitation. Notwithstanding the imperial conditioning, the rise of the popular culture ensures "resistance through cultural creation." Besides the zeal of resistance, he also advocates to "reconstruct" the "cultural conditioning" to seek for "self-identity" which to put in a simplified notion, requires three steps of accomplishment (Dussel 29-35). The journey of restoring Lisbeth's independence in the novel is parallel to the steps what Dussel describes in his theory of liberation. Starting from the state of struggling to be fitted into social customary and to achieve the proprietorship of her own body and cultural identity, her journey includes acknowledging, validating, and revolting her unique self.

It is not very often that the literary scholarships contemplate women with tattooed skin as capacitated for motivation. Still today, Tattooed women are considerably refused to be a part of mainstream fiction. They are detained as a marginalized social abstract in the genre of crime fiction. Historically, tattooed bodies have been associated with extreme contrasting social identities; an exclusive cultural extension from the aristocrats to criminals, divine to the devil has been reflected in literature inviting attention to both the positive and negative identities. However, with the rise of the aura of whimsical fashion in the late twentieth century, tattooing as an act of body modification has become the most popular cultural phenomenon where "half of all tattoos were already being performed on women from every social class" (Kluger 7). Still, as much popularity as it celebrates; academic attention towards tattooed women in literature fails to succumb to its dynamicity to analyze a character properly. Margaret George-Cramer (2013) analyses Lisbeth's character from the perspective of the Jungian Archetype of Trickster. She has examined the life of Lisbeth as a hero's journey, extending her story as a compulsive and influencing one by projecting her as a female trickster figure. She describes how Lisbeth as an influential "survivor," inspires other women to represent themselves in life. Riedlinger (2011) uses Judith Butler's gender performativity to account Lisbeth as a bold, fiery individual subverting the gender expectation of the society. Anna Stenport and Cecilia Alm (2009) have encountered crime on female bodies and its connection to the structure of business and corporation in Swedish society. Schorn (2013) extols Lisbeth for setting an example that dispels the "rape myths" and re-establishes the empowered self through venturing "rape-revenge." The list of existing studies on the character Lisbeth formulates an interesting scope to juxtapose gender and crime by instigating an interconnection between patriarchal orchestrations of society branded with "delocalized, dehumanized, misogynistic" order and the society that encourages gender inequality by forcing women bodies to negotiate with a sexual crime. Corporate inefficiency sets the crime against suppressed women, which is why for a unique record Lisbeth attempts to administer the law by committing the same crime. The present study will attempt to connect the gap by taking a step forward to exponentially exert Lisbeth's impoverished tattooed skin as a communicative tool. The article also investigates sexual crime concerning her troubled bodily experience. Keeping the tattoo and crime as its main concern of contribution in the novel, her journey of liberation towards independence is evaluated.

Struggling Body: Struggling Culture

The human body is the source of an episodic "movement" rather than a static cultural correspondent of "materiality" (Eichberg 3). Substantially, it is a cultural production that is exercised and managed by continuous processing of socially interactive information. The apprenticeship of the Body, according to Foucault, renders as an act of continuous exercise within a socio-cultural transmission. He argues that the body is a cultural expression of generating power relation and implication "even when they use 'lenient' methods involving confinement or correction" (25). Thus, this exercise or the movement of a body as a "locus of social control" piles on a series of experiences involving individual and collaborative, continued and discontinued, common and conflicted issues (Bordo 165). This development of an experience generated from the continuous adjunction and elimination of collected information results in a complex struggle of bodily experience. Lisbeth's experience is evolved in the novel by her attempt to interconnect as well as restrain her cultural association, and therefore, derives at an insatiable social environment. Foucault puts forward that "the body and its forces" stimulate cultural distribution and (their) submission." The detailed information about Lisbeth Salander reflecting her physical appearance suggests a complete discordance with the traditional picture of a female beauty. Her short-fused hair, pierced nose and eyebrows, underdeveloped breasts, and most importantly, tattooed skin has always remained questionable to the terms of any cultural convention. She, defying any perfect paradigm to belong to, proves to be a transfusion of different cultures altogether as her facial details also trigger Asian features. Again, Lisbeth's professional superior endorses her "exceptionally decked out" while clearly emphasizing her "otherness" to the extent of exteriorizing as a "foreign alien."

The imprinted words "I AM ALSO AN ALIEN" written on her black attire reflect rigorous uncertainty confronted by her to be able to fit into the social endeavour (33). Besides, the very prominent "sullen I" on Lisbeth's face, noticed and further affirmed by Armansky, in fact, is a clear indictment of some sort of emotional disturbances which she has been fighting since her childhood. Her position in an ever-present tussle, not only with herself but also the patriarchal supremacy becomes more acute when she encounters incidents like her body being interrogated, violated, and sexually gazed at by the men who are powerfully superior in position. Her legal guardian Bjurman interferes with her body rights such as hygiene practices and piercing fashion. As a social guardian, he meddles with her legal and financial decisions. He also occupies her body as a product of his legal supremacy when he proudly declares "I am legally and financially responsible for you" (129). On her first monthly meeting, she is made strikingly uncomfortable with questions about her sex life which is again suggestive of hijacking her privacy rights.

Beyond Fragmented Body

The essence of postmodernism is pervasively dignified with the ideology that is noncommittal to the unified or an absolute blueprint of the existential truth. It has always been credited with a clear disconnect to the "coercive response" which Foucault and Lyotard's idea of postmodernism distinctly enunciates. However, the fact that the idea of "Fragmentation" does not confine itself to the compartmentalization of truth or identity but expands beyond, further illustrated by Christopher Falzon. He argues that "Fragmentation vision" is not an antithetical but a continuation to the possibility of a "complete, all-embracing world view" (3). Since the fragmentation can also distinguish an evocative extension to the presence of accumulation or entanglement, a tattooed body can be interpreted as something to be connected with the experiences one gathers. Registering a tattoo on skin is an example of creative artistry that does not simply imply the cultural abstractness of any individual. It has significance in manifold that requires special attention to be paid.

A tattoo is an artistic junction on the skin that preserves information in the form of images, narratives, or symbols. Also, the importance of tattooing may involve to "reclaim body," or "transgress gender norm" (Kang and Jhones 45). To use a particular space on a body as imprinted, it initially triggers the other spaces as unimportant and fragile, moreover, the forsaken "other." Tattoo as a sign to a particular space of a body, gives prominence and vitalize the intended space to tangle with one's bodily experience. This connectedness is formed through the act of transcription of past experience reflected on skin. Just after the realization that she has acted as nothing but a subject of submission to the sadist Bjurman, it occurred to Lisbeth as an obligatory mission to frame her mistake as a piece of permanent evidence on skin. The deliberate choice of imprinting a circular band surrounding her ankle enacts as a "reminder" that permits her for an anytime visit to the memory in particular. This also reflects the very insatiable as well as helpless state of her journey in the novel where she is torn between her true validity as an individual and the immobile controlled self. On one hand, the ring around the ankle reinforces her incarcerated self in a male dominated society, on the other; the tattoo compels to gaze back to it. Such are the other eight tattoos on her body; signifying experiences that caused her body to go through the breakdown with immense pain and suffering, resulting in a fragmented version of her. However, the broken pieces are indicative of the wholeness of her Individual experience. Lisbeth uses the tattoos on her body as a collection of scarred reminders to refrain from any further deceiving actions. In both the ways, the intention behind reconnecting to the past events is to escape the past itself.

Tattoo on her body plays an important role to intervene with the proprietorship over her bodily experience. The very decorative body also reflects her conflicted state of identity where she is torn between the sense of interconnectedness and exclusion. Lisbeth as an "alien" to the society is always restless and partially seeks acceptance. She is never interested to look for society's validation but to settle individual freedom in her life. Lisbeth's body is decorated with multiple tattoos- a wasp on her neck, a loop around her left ankle and arm, a dragon-shaped creature around her shoulder blade and more. Still, it offers a strange engagement of distraction. Lisbeth's superior Armasky does not agree to the fact that he is sensually attracted towards her because of the pierced and tattooed body. Blomkvist takes a moment to sneak at the dragon tattoo as "tattoos compel one to gaze" (Kosut 82). The dragon tattoo, being a correspondent to the disturbed or insatiable state of Lisbeth deserves a sincere enunciation. The Dragon, both in Chivalric and Christian myth is heralded as an evil spirit which, however, in the orient tradition contrived as a symbol of wisdom and strength. The semantic pattern of the mythic connotation indicates the very nature of Lisbeth as contesting and rebelling, an unconventional fusion of the contrasting whole.

Liberation through Crime

Throughout the novel, Lisbeth is depicted as a rebelling figure that reflects a constant tussle with her mental and body sagacity. Armansky, for the first time, notices her "unusual intelligence" perplexed with "some serious emotional problem," which in fact, is the result of strong offensive events from her childhood. She has become so emotionally numb that "even rape could evoke no adequate emotional response" to her. Lisbeth as a child was bullied by her fellow mates in elementary school. Later, most of her philanders sexually assaulted her with the application of extraneous force over her body. Her legal guardian, who is a sexual sadist, exploits her body considering himself not only in charge of her personal and financial engagement but also as his personal property. Bjurman rapes her brutally using all advantages he has to satisfy his intense urges. Sexual sadism, one of the "sexually related crime(s)" is known for using "power, control, and rage" to cause someone else "to feel pain, to be humiliated, or to feel unrelenting fear" (Lerner and Lerner 27).

Although fear is a common phenomenon among most Swedish women to come out of a violent relationship, Lisbeth proves to be a fearless fortitude gazing back to masculine supremacy without any hesitance (Lindgren and Renck 113). As a "legally incompetent" and "defenceless" citizen, she is left with no alternative choice to filing a report against Bjurman. Again, her prevailing legal status defines her as a "cunning and unjustifiably violent" woman and her nature as "anything but forgiving" (176). Hence, she plans to revenge back without letting Bjurman leave "unpunishable." "And what would happen if she lost the battle? Would she be institutionalized? Locked up?" (178)

Eventually, the last thing she desires for herself is to be imprisoned by male dominated forum. Her strive for the ultimate liberation from any kind of authoritative domination finally leads her to employ "rape-revenge" as a route to escape. The reason that Lisbeth stands out among the other women characters in the novel is because she has always given back what she has been treated with. Her way of gazing back is to serve platter with the same that she has been served. She chooses the path of crime while assaulting Bjurman physically just the way she was sexually abused. She attacks Bjurman with a taser, fastens him up on his bed where he had kept her in handcuffs for hours, subjects him to anal penetration with the electrodes he owns, and tattoos the words "I AM A SADIST PIG, A PIG, A PERVERT, AND A RAPIST" across his chest (205). As a result, Lisbeth secures her independence once again, defying the stereotypical feminine picturesque of non-violent, bleak rape survivors. She also damages the 'rape myths' by introducing "rape-revenge" culture in feminist narrative construction (Schorn).

Conclusion

The novel disseminates and discusses women's struggle for liberation which is widespread far beyond the border of Sweden. Sexual crime is an everyday challenge for any Swedish woman, and by portraying Lisbeth's journey as a victim, Larsson familiarizes the very "structure of society that suppresses women" (Marta). The true position of women in society and physical violence as a part of their misery is the central point of discussion in the novel. While solving the mystery of the Vanger family, Lisbeth and Blomkvist dig up a brutal case of a serial killer sexually torturing women before murdering them, which again represents the intensity of crime against women in the novel itself. But unlike other women, Lisbeth Salander is designed uniquely who is capable of struggling and moulding the respective patterns of the story of any rape survivors. Moreover, the irreversible victim phase is challenged and further repudiated by Lisbeth while protecting herself from impinging over her personal freedom. Therefore, the importance of discussing and contemplating *the quality of life* lived by a rape survivor in fiction is emphasized (Ateljevic 211).

Lisbeth's journey of re-establishing her financial and personal freedom includes the continuous process of wrestling with hegemonic power, interconnectedness and exclusion, repression, and annihilation in response to socio-cultural identity. Lisbeth as an exceptional feminine setting eliminates social "exteriority," on one hand, by defeating sexual "domination and exploitation" and on the other, by acknowledging, revolting, and liberating herself. Lisbeth's journey from a troubled soul to a reconfigured liberated self is understood with an intimate co-operation with her action related to crime and the act of tattooing. Lisbeth's tattoo as an important incarnation enunciates more than just a tool for self-reflexion. Tattoo, in fact, becomes a salient part of her revenge process. It represents the power of showcasing the truth and framing the evidence permanently on Bjurman's chest for his future reference. In this essence, it indelibly functions as a medium for both Lisbeth and Bjurman to connect their past and future, though visibly frozen on skin.

Works Cited

Ateljevic, Irena. "Visions of Transmodernity: A New Renaissance of Our Human History?" *Integral Review* 9.2 (2013): n.p.

Bordo, Susan. *Unbearable Weight*. University of California Press, 2003. *Unbearable Weight*.

Dussel, Enrique D. "Transmodernity and Interculturality: An Interpretation from the Perspective of Philosophy of Liberation." *TRANSMODERNITY: Journal of Peripheral Cultural Production of the Luso-Hispanic World*, 1 (3). (2011): 28-56. https://escholarship.org/uc/item/6591j76r

Eichberg, Henning. "How to Study Body Culture-Observing Human Practice." *International Journal of Eastern Sports & Physical* (2007): 1-12.

Falzon, Christopher. *Foucault and Social Dialogue: Beyond Fragmentation*. Taylor and Francis, 2006. *Foucault and Social Dialogue: Beyond Fragmentation*. Web.

George-cramer, Margaret. "The Feminine Trickster Archetype : Trickstar at Work in The Girl With the Dragon Tattoo." August (2013): n. pag.

Kluger, Nicolas. "Epidemiology of Tattoos in Industrialized Countries." 48 (2015): 6-20.

Kosut, Mary. "Tattoo Narratives : The Intersection of the Body , Self - Identity and Society." January 2000 (2014): n. pag.

Mehta, Sonny. "Stieg Larssson's Legacy." Bookpage; 2010. Web. <https://bookpage.com/interviews/8594-sonny-mehta-mystery-suspense#.YTFB750zbIU>

Larsson, Stieg. *The Girl with the Dragon Tattoo*. Penguin. 2015.

Lerner, K. Lee, and Brenda Wilmoth Lerner. *Crime and Punishment: Essential Primary Sources*, n.p., 2006.

Panichi, Andrea, "An analysis of the life, work, and social change created by author Stieg Larsson" (2012). *Honors College Theses*. 113.

Riedlinger, Elise. "'Somebody'd Get a Fat Lip If They Ever Called Me Pippi Longstocking': Gender, Sex and Red Hair in Stieg Larsson's." (2011): n.p.

Rodríguez Magda, R.M. "SIMONE DE BEAUVOIR, A TRANS-MODERN READING." *International Journal of Cultures and Literatures*, no. 12, Apr. 2012, pp. 157-72, https://revistascientificas.us.es/index.php/CulturasyLiteraturas/article/view/7467.

"Safe Sweden Faces up to Wave of Women's Killings." BBC News, 6 May 2021, <https://www.bbc.com/news/world-europe-56977771>

Scheffer Lindgren, Maria, and Barbro Renck. "Intimate Partner Violence and the Leaving Process: Interviews with Abused Women." *International Journal of Qualitative Studies on Health and Well-being* 3.2 (2008): 113-24.

Schorn, Johanna. "Empowerment through Violence: Feminism and the Rape-Revenge Narrative in the Girl with the Dragon Tattoo." *Gender Forum* 41 (2013): n.p.

Stenport, Anna Westerståhl, and Cecilia Ovesdotter Aim. "Corporations, Crime, and Gender Construction in Stieg Larsson's the Girl with the Dragon Tattoo: Exploring Twenty-First Century Neoliberalism in Swedish Culture." *Scandinavian Studies* 81.2 (2009): 157-78. www.jstor.org/stable/40920850

Feminist Dystopian Imagination in Postmodern Fiction

APARNA BHATT
Independent Scholar

In his 1983 essay *The Discourse of Others: Feminists and Postmodernism,* Craig Owens argues that feminism is not just "compatible with but also an instance of postmodern thought." (2) He asserts that women's experimental writing is compatible with postmodern discourse and the overthrowing of the grand narrative. Post-modernism confronts and challenges orthodoxy and in doing so it also, inadvertently, becomes a critique of patriarchal ideas. Postmodernism tries to test and push the limits—"limits of language, subjectivity, of sexual identity, and we might also add: of systematization and uniformization." (Hutcheon 249) And in doing so, it lends itself to feminism and breaks stereotypical internalized illusions.Terry Eagleton had said that postmodernism is a child of a political failure . If you cannot attack and destroy masculinism, hegemony or patriarchy in the real world, you can always subvert them in the world of literature and visual arts. The crisis that postmodernism causes the male-dominated modernist discourse also extends to the feminist need to eradicate masculine-centred discourse.

Talking about dystopian, it is often acknowledged as a common motif in postmodern literature. The works of seminal feminist dystopian writers like Margaret Atwood suggest that dystopia is caused by great authoritative power and for the most part the victims of this brute domineering power are women. Restricting female voices (both individual and collective) and controlling female bodies and sexuality are the most effective ways to dehumanize women not just in these aggressive, masculine fictional societies but also historically. Often in feminist dystopian fiction like Margaret Atwood's *The Handmaid's Tale*, female sexuality is presented as an instrument of social control and the success of the dystopian totalitarian regime/government/party depends heavily on crushing the female desires and silencing the female voices (both literally and metaphorically).

Suppressing Feminine Agency

Silence and powerlessness go hand in hand. Christina Dalcher's 2018 novel *Vox* underlines this in a compelling manner.*Vox's* premise is that a new conservative Christian government in the United States has banned women from speaking more than hundred words a day. This has been done in order to enforce male supremacy. Women of all ages and ablities are fitted with bracelets that deliver electric shocks if the word limit is violated (the shocks grow severe as the womon transgresses and if she persists in her verbal transgression, the bracelet burns her). Jean, the narrator, is a neurolinguist who was working on pioneering experiments regarding speech disorders until the new administration orders that women stay at home. Women are reduced to being silent shadows that exist and opearte only at the fringes. "I've become a woman of few words," Jean says by way of an introduction. "Tonight at supper, before I speak my final syllables of the day, Patrick reaches over and taps the silver-toned device around my left wrist.

It's a light touch, as if he were sharing the pain, or perhaps reminding me to stay quiet until the counter resets itself at midnight. This magic will happen while I sleep, and I'll begin Tuesday with a virgin slate. My daughter, Sonia's, counter will do the same. My boys do not wear word counters. Over dinner, they are all engaged in the usual chatter about school. Sonia also attends school, although she never wastes words discussing her days. At supper, between bites of a simple stew I made from memory, Patrick questions her about her progress in home economics, physical fitness, and a new course titled Simple Accounting for Households. Is she obeying the teachers? Will she earn high marks this term? He knows exactly the type of questions to ask: closed-ended, requiring only a nod or a shake of the head," she tells us (Dalcher 12). Jean's frustration at being unable to voice her thoughts and feelings is tangible. But *Vox's* most interesting element is the way it shows that how easily men can deprive even the women they love of their basic rights. Mothers, wives, daughters, sisters, lovers—none are spared by their men. The government exercises its repression not only through police and agents but also through common family men.

By silencing the literal voice—the sound produced by the vocal cords(vox)—this authoritarian regime curbs women's ability to speak up, to express themselves as human beings, to claim their rights and to control their narratives, pushing these women into oblivion. Who is heard and who is silenced is extremely important in understanding this feminist dystopian imagination of Christina Dalcher. Jean's narration demonstrates that American society under the new President and the menacing influence of the fanatic "Pure Movement" has been pulled back in time with submissive wives and daughters relegated to the private sphere and hard-working men in the public sphere, running the world in the name of righteousness and natural order. Naturally, all the female activists, gays and lesbians have been either cured or imprisoned. Women have no access to books, pens or computers. Nonverbal communication is prevented by the ubiquitous presence of the surveillance camers. Each woman judiciously utilize her 100 words a day quota. Jean observes, "The films are a distraction, the only time I hear female voices unconstrained and unlimited. Actresses are allowed a special dispensation while they're on the job. Their lines, of course, are written by men. . . . Patrick and the boys, out on the back porch close to my window, are swapping stories about school, politics, the news, while crickets buzz in the dark around our bungalow. They make so much noise, those boys and those crickets. Deafening. All my words ricochet in my head as I listen, emerge from my throat in a heavy, meaningless sigh." (Dalcher 26) Jean is a "woman of few words" but she has many plans and out of her tough will we see the birth of a resistance movement.

Vox's world is a terrifying exploration of Saint Paul's prohibition against women speaking in Church in *1 Corinthians 14:34* ,"As in all the churches of the saints, the women should keep silent in the churches. For they are not permitted to speak, but should be in submission, as the Law also says. And if they desire to learn anything, let them ask their own husbands at home; for it is improper for a woman to speak in church." (The Holy Bible 2245) Dalcher's 100-word limit a day for women accomplishes centuries of patriarchal efforts to silence women's voices, to belittle their articulations, to ignore their subjective experiences, to chastise them for talking, to quash their claims, to eliminate their stories from the dominant narrative and to ridicule their voice using gendered insults like "bitchy," "bossy," "hysterical," "nagging," etc. To that end, gossip has also been appropriated socially and culturally as a female thing by the patriarchy. The mainstream narrative is not constructed by women, it doesn's include women, it is not open to hearing the experiences and expressions of women. The majority of women's voices and narratives, which over the years have strived to locate, explicate, or even combat marginalised status of women, are always on the receiving end of the dominant patriarchal status quo.

In order to resist the status quo in the world of *Vox* , it is imperative that Jean's story must be told. Jean produces her own counter-narrative to the dominant narrative by recounting her own story in her own words and that's where subversion begins. Storytelling is used by Dalcher as an empowering medium and a tool of resistance. Jessica Senehi writes in her academic paper

Constructive Storytelling: A Peace Process that "those who generate narratives are in a position of relative control in the process of the social construction of meaning; they have narrator potency." (Senehi 43) This "narrative potency," the power to share her own narrative is pivotal to Jean's identity and her subversion in *Vox.*

Postmodern Feminist Dystopia

Pulished in 2017, *Gather the Daughters by* Jennie Melamed uses female body and female sexuality to talk about loss of identity and control in a grim patriarchal dystopian future. Women as child bearers, as child raisers and as sex objects are manipulated and subjugated in the name of a utopian present in this dystopian novel . Clearly male utopia is female dystopia.

Gather the Daughters begins with a girl being sent home from school for getting her period for the first time. This appears to be a normal instance of a biological process. However, menstruation has always been permeated with significance, and on the fictional island of *Gather the Daughters*, it indicates an instant departure from childhood (characterized by sexual abuse) and a movement towards "summer of fruition" followed by a conventional married life (characterized,once again, by severe physical and sexual abuse). This misogynist fictional island is ruled by the "Wanderers," an elite group of men who make regular trips to the "Wastelands" (the mainland, or the rest of the world). They have access to knowledge, and they also have the agency to disseminate knowledge selectively. The "Wanderers" have constructed a society with no technology (other than pen and paper), no money and some deeply disturbing sexual practices aimed at oppression of women.

This society is based on controlled breeding and ancestral worship. Girl child abuse has been legitimatized. Incest is culturally sanctioned between fathers and daughters until the girls reach puberty. Then, they are expected to become dutiful wives and breeding machines for their husbands who have complete authority over their bodies and by extension over their lives. The women stay at home, looking after food, clothing and cleanliness. Attendance at each other's childbirths is the only occasions on which they gather without a male escort. The so-called "defectives"—the elderly, babies with genetic defects due to inbreeding and women who try to resist and reclaim agency over their bodies and lives—are conveniently eliminated. In this closed culture, women are literally beaten into voiceless submission to men. For the women of this island, their sexuality, their bodies, infact their very existence is regulated by men through physical force. Vanessa sums it up when she states, "What if we didn't have to obey our fathers? That would be nice, but the truth is that we have fathers and they make us obey them—with their fists if they need to." (107)

By eliminating personal choice, by curtailing freedom and by establishing how a woman will be sexual, with whom and for what purpose, women are systematically robbed of their personhood. This is a world in which being female is so agonizing that the women share a group cry when another one of their sex is born. Melamed writes, "Laughter for a boy, tears for a girl. Everyone at the birth is supposed to weep if it's a girl, and now everyone is dutifully crying. . . . Vanessa once asked Mother why everyone cries for girls. It doesn't seem fair that boys are greeted with celebration, but that everyone cried when she came sliding into the world on a river of salt and blood. Mother told her she'd understand when she was older" (46). The female citizens of this fictional island encounter a sexist system that enforces upon them body politic. Women are expected to satisfy certain requirements in order to fulfil their destiny in this rigid, regressive society. Women are not viewed as individuals. Instead, they are collective bodies that occupy hierarchical positions below their superior male counterparts.

The story of *Gather the Daughters* is told through the perspective of a few young girls: Vanessa, Janey, Amanda and Caitlin.These girls of the community are led by Janey—who, at seventeen years, is older than most of the girls as she starves herself to delay mensturation, her body being the site of resistance in a society where every man is a rapist. Janey is so unwilling to become a woman that death appears to be an easier option. By choosing to slowly destroy her body , Janey seeks to achieve bodily autonomy. Janey does not know for how long can she keep puberty at bay but then she continues to defy patriarchal expectations by starving herself to death as she "can't imagine herself with a husband, cooking dinner, looking up into a man's face, or lying with her legs spread apart, screaming a new life into the world." (57)

Janey is a born leader, who steps up to seek the truth. She leads the uprising of the girls but the road to revolution is not a smooth one . Vanessa laments, "We have no weapons, nothing. We're like a herd of goats plotting to overthrow the humans that keep them. It's laughable. What's the point of thinking about it differently?" "Because," says Janey, "they can't stop us from thinking. They can force us to do anything they want, but they can't stop us from thinking. And maybe if we think, we'll think up a way to." (153) Led by Janey, the girls get braver, shedding their fears and apprehensions and begin to question everything around them. The more they inquire, the more they push against the babrbed boundaries that confine their bodies and souls, the more they bleed both literally and metaphorically. In the process, some break free, some choose status quo over change, some fail and some die. The cost of resistance is definitely high.

Conclusion

Vox and *Gather the Daughters* project the culmination of the feminist issues of female identity and personhood where the identities of women have been dragged down to the lowest depths of misery. When these two novels are seen through the postmodern lens, the issues of control, resistance, oppression, female sexuality, surveillance, the female body and questions about whose voice is heard and whose is stifled, whose knowledge is valorized and whose is disapproved appear to exemplify the need to interrogate as well as challenge the grand narrative. Blending of feminsim and dystopia in a postmodern landscape produces difficult and disturbing fiction that, just like postmodern thought, reacts to the narrow vision of an androcentric patriarchal idealism.

Works Cited

Dalcher, Christina. *Vox*. New York: Berkley, 2018.

Hutcheon, Linda. *A Poetics of Postmodernism : History, Theory, Fiction*. Routledge, 1988.

Melamed, Jennie. *Gather the Daughters*. New York: Little, Brown and Company, 2017.

Owens, Craig. *The Discourse of Others: Feminists and Postmodernism*. Columbia, 21 July 1983. http://www.columbia.edu/itc/barnard/arthist/wolff/pdfs/week15_owens.pdf>.

Senehi, Jessica. *Constructiv Constructive Storytelling: A Peace Process*. Vol. 9. Florida, 10 December 2002.

The Holy Bible. London: Penguin Classics, 2006.

Hierarchy of Digital Media Discourse in India: A Dalit Perspective

JAY KUMAR
Research Scholar, M.G. Central University, Motihari

In this era of technology, digital media, also called "new media," has emerged as the most crucial platform of discourse making where every individual irrespective of caste, creed, religion, and gender could participate. New formats of communication- based on the internet like chat, social media discussion platforms have created a new public space for common folks, especially the marginalized ones, to enter the world socio-political discourse affecting their lives. It has very successfully filled in the deep trench between ordinary and elites in the politics of democracy. The introduction of digital media has almost made democracy more accessible and affordable to the masses and made it even more popular and attractive than ever before.

When we talk of Dalit perspective regarding any issue, we should be very confident that it's universal. A Dalit vision is not limited to one particular community or caste, but all humanity. When a Dalit ask for equality, justice, and freedom, he/she asks for the whole human world. Whether it was Mahatma Phule, Savitribai Phule, or Ambedkar, they always worked for the welfare of society as a whole. We shouldn't mistake the upliftment of marginalized ones as the downfall of others.

The interactive feature of the "new media" allows quick and seamless communication between the common folks, public officials, and media persons, and thus reduces the gap between subjects and their leaders. Hence, it helps in establishing a more democratic and equitable society. Internet access on mobile phones has transformed elite media into people's media. The internet has made communication horizontal which is a healthy sign for any democratic society. The digital means of communication have brought more transparency, accountability, and efficiency in the working of the political structure.

Although, in theory, we claim to be a democracy, in practicality we know that we are still quite a distance away from being a democracy. The dome of democracy will only be stable and secure if all its four pillars work properly and in tandem with each other. And media is one such pillar that not only checks on the other three pillars but also provides them the strength and support to keep carrying on. In recent decades, there have been a lot of talks regarding the corruption of the fourth pillar, and thus there's a concern regarding the falling out of the dome of democracy in India. Fortunately, digital media came and got hold of the fourth pillar of the dome which was losing its balance and harmony. But, with the rise of digital media, there's also a rise in fear, particularly among those groups of people who got their voice after centuries of struggle and suffering, of losing this like the traditional media in the hands of elites. Thus, as the largest democracy of this world, it's the duty of not only the marginalized but all to protect and promote all the four pillars of democracy, especially the pillar of media.

While discussing Media Hegemony, Antonio Gramsci claims that media as a social institution has become an ideological state apparatus of the ruling class, using it to create a consensus, and thus enforce their discourse to the mass as righteous and universal. Furthermore, Michael Foucault in his essay "Discourse as Knowledge and Power" mentioned discourse as the production of knowledge through language. According to him discourse never consists of just one statement or just one action or one source of information. The same discourse that characterized a way of thinking or talking in a state of knowledge at any one time can cross a range of texts that may lead to different forms of conduct within different institutional sites within a society.

In addition, Jürgen Habermas while talking about the discourse ethics as the part of the Enlightenment Project of the political emancipation and democracy has stated that "only those norms can claim to be valid that meet (or could meet) with the approval of all affected in their capacity as participants in a practical discourse" (Cavalier 4). Besides these, Ambedkar in his most revolutionary work "*Annihilation of caste*" proclaimed that Brahmins form the intellectual class of Hindus. His views hold for other upper castes Hindus also. They have the power and thus they control the discourse of the nation as per their interest. Another major benefit of "new media" is its interactivity. By looking at the above discussion about discourse making and the vital role played by media in it, it is quite imperative to delve into the role of the most prominent media of discourse making i.e. digital media.

This paper will try to examine the present situation of digital media from the subaltern perspective, in particular from the Dalit point of view. Here, we look at how like the mainstream media digital media is being pushed to become the ideological apparatus of the dominant group in India? The discussion also focuses upon the possible threats endangering the democratic characteristics of digital media.

Media and Democracy

In an interview with BBC News in 1953, when he was asked by the interviewer, "Dr. Ambedkar do you think democracy is going to work in India?" And Ambedkar replied, "No!" He reasoned that the factor which would hinder the working of democracy in India is our social structure which is completely incompatible with parliamentary democracy (Attri). In all these years, it is the caste system that has haunted our democracy the most. It has divided Indian society into many parallels, self-contained communities that didn't allow for the conversation and negotiations necessary for a healthy democracy.

It was the media who was supposed to be the savior and promoter of spirits of Indian democracy, namely liberty, equality, fraternity, and diversity. They failed to give voice to the deprived and subalterns, especially the lower caste communities.

The empirical data of the last two decades clearly shows the situation of the upper caste hegemony in media and a lack of lower caste representation in Indian media and its associates (Mandal, "Upper caste Domination"). When Ambedkar, Phule, and Periyar stood against the suppression of Dalits, their fundamental demand was to make Dalits part of the national socio-political discourse. A nation's vision and ideology are made through discourse. So, a democratic nation should ensure the participation of every sphere of people to participate in the discourse making and thus ultimately be a part of the nation-building process. But unfortunately, Dalits and other lower castes were repeatedly denied this, and even when they were provided with a certain franchise in the political sphere, its effectiveness could be questioned.

The political arena of the nation is still headed by the believers of the caste system. The political presence of Dalits, although it is limited in nature, social democracy is still a dream for Dalits. Dalits could be anything, but the majority of the society still recognizes them through their caste mainly. Their lower caste identity couldn't be dissolved. And that's the fundamental fight of Dalit. They fight to dissolve this caste identity. And discourse making is one of the most important parts of their fight. Therefore, when the upper caste-dominated media denied them their spots in discourse right, they turned to digital media which seemed more promising and accessible to them.

It was the digital media that gave voice to the subalterns and ensured their participation in the discourse of the nation. Since, the arrival of digital platforms, many Dalit thinkers and activists has joined these platforms to put forth the stories, ideas, and vision of not only his/her own, but the whole community. Many critics call digital media the tool of segregation where different groups work on their own for the benefit of their own. But they forget the cause behind this. This is not the first time that Dalits have endeavored to get their platform to tell their own stories. In the past also, right from the times of the bhakti movement to the Independence of India, time and again they tried to tell their stories by various means, like poetry, songs, writings, etc. In the 1920s Ambedkar started *Mooknayak* for the very reason that he was denied to be heard by the media as the majority of them were owned by the upper caste and class. He later went on to publish *Bahishkrit Bharat, Janata, Samata, and Prabuddha Bharat*. Later on, another great Dalit leader Kanshiram also ran his own media house and published the newspaper titled *Bahujan Sangathak* (Mandal, "What Mooknayak").

While publishing his own media newspaper which is completely devoted to the cause of Dalits and other downtrodden communities, Ambedkar had his reasons. He said, "I know the Congress Press well. I attach no value to its criticism. It has never refuted my arguments. It knows only to criticize, rebuke, and revile me for everything I do and to misreport, misrepresent and pervert everything I say. Nothing that I do pleases the Congress Press. This animosity of the Congress Press towards me can to my mind not unfairly, be explained as a reflex of the hatred of the Hindus for the untouchables" (Mandal, "What Mooknayak"). At present times, Dalits engaging in social media discourse and other digital media channels are also forced by the elite and casteist mainstream media to segregation. They have left no space into the regular discourse, and thus they chose to create their own space and discourse as a counter to the elite and upper castes. Although Dalits lack professional media representatives, it was only filled by Dalit activists and intellectuals. They work tirelessly to realize the dream of Ambedkar's India which is more equitable, just, and humane. Dalit perspective is not based on power acquisition by themselves, but power distribution among all. Their idea of democracy is based on fundamental human rights like the right to live with dignity, right to equal opportunity, right to freedom, for all. And through their communication channels, they are promoting this very idea of democracy which once Ambedkar had inscribed in the Indian constitution.

After the arrival of digital media, Scott Grant, author of "We're All Journalists Now" was very confident of its freedom, viability, and democratic characteristics. Grant further went on to claim that in the era of technology freedom of the press now is not limited to the printing presses, but extended to the cell phones, video cameras, blogging software, and other digital news instruments (Mandal, "India's oppressed").

Crisis in Digital Media

After the detailed analysis of the historical as well as current state digital media and the media overall, three major threats are endangering the digital media democracy:

1. Lack of Representation

According to Jurgen Habermas, the basic principle of discourse ethics claims that "every subject with the competence to speak and act is allowed to take part in a discourse. Everyone is allowed to question any assertion whatsoever. Everyone is allowed to introduce any assertion into the discourse. Everyone is allowed to express his attitudes, desires, and needs. No speaker may be prevented by internal or external coercion" (Mandal, "Upper caste Domination").

While talking about the ideas of Jyotirao Phule in the context of Brahmin caste domination in Sarvajanik Sabha, Gail Omvedt said, "Public requires true representation, access, and membership, of all sections of the society. When this doesn't happen, it only becomes a means of masking private interest" (Mandal, "Upper Caste Domination"). According to the survey report of Oxfam-Newlaundary on digital media published in 2019,

1. Out of the 20 most followed on Twitter, 19 belong to the upper caste. No one belongs to the lower caste.
2. Out of the top 10 most popular new channels on YouTube, none belong to the Dalit.
3. 84% of the leadership positions in digital media are also occupied by the upper caste.
4. Of all the articles written on caste issues, 56% of the writers belong to the general category.
5. 72% of the bylined articles on news websites are written by general category writers.

2. Corporatisation

Before the digital revolution, running a media house was a mammoth exercise and involved big money. With the democratization of technology, it has become easier to start a media venture, especially in terms of finances. When the era of digital media started, there was all-around euphoria that the media matrix of the big four, namely huge capital, the veto power of the advertisers, dominant ideology, and government control could be challenged by the common folks of the country (Mandal, "India's oppressed").

But in the last five years, digital media space, too, has been hegemonized by the legacy media. The impression of social media and other digital platforms being a pluralistic democratic place where all voices will be heard and debated has taken a huge hit. According to the immigration data, 90% of technical immigrants to the USA belong to the upper caste.

There are no major tech giants or media houses in India headed by any Dalit. The majority of them are owned and run by the upper caste.

If we look upon the various governments in India since independence one thing we could easily conclude is that the power has mostly remained in the hands of the upper caste, irrespective of the political parties. There is a great possibility that they might lure tech companies to weaken encryption—the ultimate protection that journalists and others rely on to prevent third parties from snooping on their private messages. The arbitrary algorithm of the machine is biased and thus designed to suit the dominant discourse. Social media has created a hierarchy of discursive power by the arbitrary verification process and declaring it as the badge of authenticity.

3. Censorship

Looking at the history of ruling power anywhere in the world, the first thing they would try to achieve as rulers is the control over the mind of their subjects. Every regime attempts to feed the citizens with their own ideology and ensure the working of state institutes as ideological state apparatuses for them. And media as the most prominent tool of discourse making poses a great threat to the ruling ideology. In a democratic society, the ruling power are not entitled to use brute force to subdue the counter ideological apparatuses, so the best tool available for them to bring down the counter voices is to censor them through unreasonable and harsh regulations in the name of state peace and order. Post- independent, successive governments have tried to control the free voices of media through various legislative and executive means. The latest victim of the power politics is digital news and OTT platforms.

The digital media were supposed to work in favor of free speech which other mainstream media couldn't do due to the restrictions imposed on them under the guise of rules and regulations for public order and tranquility. They are supposed to serve as the platform of those who couldn't afford or access to the elite media of communication. Their features like easy accessibility, low-cost usability, free speech, unbiasedness, and non-political nature have ensured non-partial and just communication channels for all groups of people. It's only after the unnecessary and forced involvement of the high caste ruling ideology which has once jeopardized the progress of Indian political democracy towards achieving social democracy.

The various laws and rules regarding media have only extended the government's control over the media and the latest one regarding the digital media which has the provision of the removal of online content to news articles by the authority. This type of arbitrary power to any ruling class is quite a threat to the basic principle of any democracy i.e. freedom of speech. So, as a democratic country, irrespective of our ideological and political leanings, we must ensure that no government should be able to cut the freedom of speech of either individuals, institutions or any other organizations.

Conclusion

The existing matrix of structure and agency has resulted in a strong dominant group bias in media content. This is more visible whenever there is news involving subaltern groups. For example whenever there is a news involving the caste, like reservation, caste census, or SC/ST Act, majority of the narratives dominated by the hegemonic caste group start flooding the media outlets and the subaltern narratives get marginalized.

All politics of this era is driven by shareable content and virility. If you can control how content is created, published, and distributed, then you can shape politics.

Moreover, media houses are not yet ready for the diversity debate, which the US did 50 years ago. In the US, media houses embraced diversity with a conviction that it is good for the business. In India, that idea is yet to sink in.

Works Cited

Attri, Pradeep. "Transcript of Dr Ambedkar's 1953 Interview with BBC- When Dr Ambedkar Said Democracy Won't work in India." 2017.

Velivada. 12 July 2021. <www.velivada.com/2017/12/08/transcript-dr-ambedkar-1953-interview-with-bbc-dr-ambedkar-said-democracy-wont-work-india/>.

Cavalier, Robert J. "Introduction to Habermas's Discourse Ethics." CiteSeer. 11 July 2021. <www.citeserx.ist.psu.edu/viewdoc/download?doi=10.1.1.504.7531&rep=rep1&type=pdf>.

Mandal, Dilip. "Ambedkar knew about cartoons trolling him and he blamed 'Congress Press' for it." 9 June 2019. *The Print*. <www.theprint.in/opinion/ambedkar-knew-about-cartoons-trolling-him-and-he-blamed-congress-press-for-it/247623/>.

_____. "India's oppressed groups had high hopes from the Internet. But the Upper caste got into there too." 19 July 2020. *The Print*. www.theprint.in/opinion/indias-oppressed-groups-had-high-hopes-from-internet-but-upper-caste-got-into-there-too/463431.

_____. "Upper Caste Domination in India's Mainstream Media and Its Extension in Digital Media." 23 November 2020. *Economic and Political Weekly*. <www.epw.in/journal/2020/46/perspectives/upper-caste-domination-indias-mainstream-media-and.html>.

_____. "What Mooknayak was for Ambedkar, YouTube is for Dalits Today." 5 February 2020. The Print. 11 July 2021. <www.theprint.in/opinion/what-mooknayak-was-for-ambedkar-youtube-is-for-dalits-today/359196/?amp>.

Reading Hyperreality and Cultural Consumerism in the Songs 'Go West' and 'Californication'

LALTHANZAMI
Research Scholar
SMARIKA PAREEK
Chandigarh University

In a consumer society, not only the commodities are consumed, culture in the form of manufactured artifacts and signs is widely marketed and consumed by the masses through the mass media, serving as a cultural intermediary between cultural productions and consumption. The role of media in circulating the sign and images in the consumption of culture and how America being a hyperreal place, is discussed by Jean Baudrillard in his books *The Consumer Society* 1970, *America* 1989, and *Simulacra and Simulation* 1981. The selected songs in this paper, both their lyrics and music videos have a theme of consumerism and hyperreality and project the cultural hegemonic status of America satirically and critically. The song "Go West" by the disco band called 'Village People' was written in 1979. The title was taken from Horace Greeley's popular 1860s statement, "Go West, young man" during the Westward Expansion. The Village People took the theme into their terms, appropriating the 'Wild West' and the manifest destiny as a homosexual utopia. The rendition of the song "Go West" by Pet Shop Boys then projects the romanticization of the 'Wild West' through the eyes of the Eastern people and the song can also be read as the mocking of the Western simulated society. The second selected song "Californication" is a song by an American band called 'Red Hot Chili Peppers' in 1999, it conveys the process and impact of Californication in a cultural context. Both songs have shown the dream of California and the consumerism of its hyperrealism and cultural artifacts and beliefs.

Consumerism and California Dream

The California Dream has been featured in many literary works and pop songs. It started from the period of the Gold Rush, California the 'West' of America had been seen as a land of wealth, wild, and adventure. However, the Village People's "Go West" song depicts California as an LGBT destiny since the city of San Francisco in California had had the largest and prominent Queer Communities during the time. It was the epoch where myriads of queers were still in the closet but, it was also prevalent that even during the California Gold Rush, miner's ball (dance party) was held where only men attended and dance. It can be considered that the sexual liberation in the State is one of the things the 'Wild West' represented during the 1970s. Thus, the song states,

> (Together) We will go our way
> (Together) We will leave someday
> (Together) Your hand in my hand.
> (Together) We will make our plan. (People 0:14-29)

The counter culture of the 1960s was deemed to be largely influential as the movement preached love, peace, and liberation. It was made popular through songs, movies and, signs. The cassettes of American singers in many parts of the world, the adorning of denim which signifies freedom from constraints and the existence of hippie subculture, the queer culture, and feminist activists in many parts of the world is the evidence of how the counter culture was consumed by the people who resided outside America. The LGBT community in California and its Metropolitan Community Church, its project of the Stone Wall Nation was deemed to attract more queer people towards the State, thus, the song projects how people dreamt of California and the California dream in the song represents the LGBT utopia in the Wild West among many other things.

> (Go west) life is peaceful there
> (Go west) lots of open air
> (Go west) to begin new life
> (Go west) this is what we'll do. (People 0:46-58)

The original music video shows the singers danced excitingly, igniting the hopes and dreams of the sexual and gender minority. Their spirits can be considered as similar to the zeal spirit of young men during the Gold Rush who dreamed of wild adventure and wealth. Thus, re-enacting the historical Gold Rush period from their lyrics, costumes and performance spirit, the pursuit of the Wild West. It demonstrates how people felt the nostalgia that makes the consumption of the dream and its culture more powerful. Pastiche is one of the elements of Postmodernism and according to Fredric Jameson's *The Cultural Turn* (1998), it is not easy to have a new artistic creation in Postmodern time and that people imitate the styles and productions which existed in the past. Pastiche gave a nostalgic state of mind, which makes it easier for consumers to consume certain artefacts which have references to the past, as to how "Star Wars" (George Lukacs 1977) gave people the way to clutch the past generations' cultural experiences according to Fredric Jameson, the reason why the movie "Star Wars" has been enjoyed by many adults in the 1970s was because it employs Pastiche by giving the audience a sense of 1950s cultural experiences like watching Alien Movies in the Sunday afternoon. The song "Go West" also adopts the pastiche, and alludes to the spirit of Postmodern Western cultural consumption. Jean Baudrillard described cultural consumption in his book *The Consumer Society* 1970 and states, "Cultural consumption may thus be defined as the time and place of the caricatural resurrection, the parodic evocation of what already no longer exists" (99).

However, the rendition of the song by Pet Shop Boys in 1993 can be studied as having another representation of the Wild West. The song was remade in electronic music instead of disco. How the vocalist sings also differs greatly from the Village People, it lacks the enthusiasm and the hopeful spirit, the Pet Shop Boys' version was released after the disintegration of the Soviet Union, thus, projecting how the eastern European were looking at the West and how the former queer manifesto was not achieved. The member Chris Lowe in an interview said that one of the reasons they chose the song was because the way Neil Tennant would sing the song would ignite immense hopelessness about the California Dream ironically contrasting with the song lyrics. The version of the song represents how the world consumed the ideas of the culture of America even when the past's promised land did not flourish like how people imagined. As the song was remastered in 1993 when America's hegemony was on the spike, the song narrates the power of the Western media into constructing the idealization of America. The music video displays the image of a red star floating in the sky which signifies the Soviet Union, and the statue of liberty which signifies America, and, a group of men marching towards the West in uniformity. That represents how the eastern people identify the West as a land of individuality and freedom. "America always gives me a feeling of real asceticism. Culture, politics—and sexuality too—are seen exclusively in terms of the desert, which here assumes the status of a primal scene" (Baudrillard 27). The song "Californication" also conveys the idea of the consumption of America's cultural artefacts and mass media consumption by using California as a representation of the whole of America and, how America's media engaged in selling its culture. The lyrics of the song state,

> Psychic spies from China try to steal your mind's elation
> And little girls from Sweden dream of silver screen quotation
> And if you want this kind of dreams its Californication.
> It's the edge of the world and all of western civilization,

> The sun may rise in the east at least it's settled in the final location
> It's understood that Hollywood sells Californication.
>
> (Peppers 0:24-1:03)

The first line indicates how the products of California like its fictional characters, conspiracy theories and constructed figures in the media attracts and disturbs the mind from its spiritual and authentic reality. The second line suggests how the youth of the other parts of the world romanticize fame which is the product of California's Hollywood. The verse projects how people from the other parts of the world are affected by America's mass cultural imperialism and how media sells products from cultural artefacts and references. By encoding meanings in signs, the consumers are acquiring the signs and references through commodities along with the identities embedded in it. Hollywood produced Celebrities who act as an intermediary between culture and its consumption as television a medium of the message. Baudrillard described California as "ideally suited to the only truly profound pleasure" (52).

> Pay your surgeon very well to break the spell of aging,
> Celebrity skin, is this your chin, or is that war you're waging?
> Firstborn unicorn, hardcore soft porn
> Dream of Californication. (Peppers 1:16-1:31)

The verse depicts how beauty is being commodified and fetishized in Western society during the time and how people indulged in plastic surgery to preserve their youthful appearance and to meet the beauty standard of society. It alludes to how people battle with the scythe of time and nature. And celebrity being under the power of fame, engaged in plastic surgery that influences myriads of people across the world. "Firstborn unicorn, hardcore soft porn" suggests the fact that the great land which was dreamed of by many people as a mythical place, the place where people think of as 'Eldorado' in the past, is also a place where sexual liberation and consumption of erotic objects exists. "The body sells products. Beauty sells products. Eroticism sells products" (Baudrillard 135).

Where there is production, there is consumption, the line refers to the way movies, songs, and, videos sell out by injecting eroticism that entices the consumers. And as the Western cultural artefacts managed to be obtained by people in the other parts suggests the existence of cultural consumerism as the McDonald company managed to set up its business in many parts of the world. "Everybody's been there and I don't mean on vacation" (Peppers 2:45-49), the line hyperbolically suggests how California had been represented and popularized throughout history, literary works, and popular culture that sensitized people from different cultures and places about the productions and culture of California and how everybody grasps a glimpse of California in the products they used or what they dream.

Hyperreality

America is neither dream nor reality. It is a hyperreality because it is a utopia which has behaved from the very beginning as though it were already achieved. Everything here is real and pragmatic, and yet it is all the stuff of dreams too. It may be that the truth of America can only be seen by a European, since he alone will discover here the perfect simulacrum (Baudrillard 27).

To read the hyperreality, it is vital to observe the music videos of the two selected songs since they have connections with the lyrics and the message encoded. Taking the song 'Go West' by Pet Shop Boys, the music video depicts certain signs which are vital for semiotic studies of hyperreality.

According to the theory of hyperreality, there is no longer a pure reality, and sign is the meaning, and that consciousness between the real and the unreal erode. The video shows myriads of computer-generated images, showing the statue of liberty as a representation of the postmodern West (America), red star and red flag as well as grey buildings as a sign of representation of the Soviet Union (the east). The soldiers marching up a staircase towards the sky which leads to the West according to the video concept. It also projected men flying in the air with a surfboard. All these imageries highlight the integration between the real and unreal, blurring the line between them. The video concept depicts the technological development and the hyperreality of the West which was romancing by people in the east. The singer singing the song in a hopeless spirit rather than the enthusiasms exhibited by the Village People can be observed as the version of Pet Shop Boys as a mocking of the Western society, depicting how the reality of the West is hyperreality and that simulation is all that exists, although people keep having the dream of California, the dream of the West with its ideal manifesto acquired from the meanings and messages encoded in the mass media activities and productions. The Pet Shop Boys' version portrays the 'West' as a hyperreal place by manipulating and playing with cinematic images in the music video.

Red Hot Chili Peppers' music video for the song "Californication" is designed to be like an 'Unreal Engine' developed virtual three-dimensional game. The virtual reality game was developed in the 1980s but, it becomes popular in the late 90s. In America, Epic Games constructed the 'Unreal Engine' games which attracted a large amount of youth, they are the games that are made to produce perfect simulation. As technology developed, it produced the unreal simulated reality for the gamers which demonstrates how the consumers are thriving to buy anything to make them experience the world of simulation. But, in the postmodern western society, simulation and simulacrum is all that exists. Umberto Eco in *Travels in Hyperreality* remarks, "American imagination demands the real thing and, to attain it, must fabricate the absolute fake; where the boundaries between game and illusion are blurred" (Eco 8).

> Space may be the final frontier but it's made in a Hollywood basement.

> And Cobain can you hear the spheres singing songs off Station to
> station?
> And Alderaan's not far away, its Californication. (Peppers 2:16-30)

The above lyrics highlight the identification of California with its cinematic development. The verse is an allusion to the film 'Star Wars' 1977, as Alderaan is the fictional planet in the Star Wars universe. The verse depicts how Hollywood mastered the use of 'Green Screen' and computer-generated image to create cinematic pictures which are not real. "What you are presented with in the studios is the degeneration of the cinematographic illusion, its mockery, just as what is offered in Disneyland is a parody of the world of the imagination" (Baudrillard 54). 'Cobain' in the second line refers to Nirvana band's vocalist Kurt Cobain who passed away in the year 1994. The line tells how the images and the songs produced in Hollywood reach and captivate a large audience across the world, although being unreal, have the power to shape people's dreams and perception and that is the Californication which the song claims "tidal waves couldn't save the world from" (Peppers 4:19-21).

According to Baudrillard, the line between the cinema and reality fades, and that the whole city has the ability to make one feels the simulated experiences as cinema can. He states, "Where is the cinema? It's all around you outside, all over the city, that marvellous, continuous performance of films and scenarios" (54). "Pay your surgeon very well to break the spell of aging, Sicker than the rest, there is no test, but this is what you're craving?" (Peppers 4:34-43). The song has two separate verses for an allusion to plastic surgery, the former projects how celebrities wage a war with the power of time and nature to maintain beauty in the culture, the latter verse demonstrates that that is what people crave to consume, the plastic, the unreal, the ideal inauthentic versions although there is no forcing implemented. Thus, proves that the consumers' perception of attaining commodities is connected to their desired identities.

> Everything is destined to reappear as simulation. Landscapes as photography, women as the sexual scenario, thoughts as writing, terrorism as fashion and the media, events as television. Things seem only to exist by virtue of this strange destiny. You wonder whether the world itself isn't just here to serve as advertising copy in some other world. When the only physical beauty is created by plastic surgery, the only urban beauty by landscape surgery, the only opinion by opinion poll surgery. . . and now, with genetic engineering, along comes plastic surgery for the whole human species (Baudrillard 31).

The music video presents the scenes of California in a virtual game design, the characters running to escape from destructive forces evince the paranoia that governs the mind of various famous people in Hollywood. The video displays the city filled with signs, images, and architectural buildings, it also shows the destructive side of the dream by manipulating the actions in the game-video as a representation of the dark side of the Californication process and the hyperreality which people choose to embrace than the actual reality. "a 'message' city, entirely made up of signs, not a city like the others, which communicate to function, but a city that functions in order to communicate. But Las Vegas is still a 'real' city" (Eco 22). Fredric Jameson comments on the postmodern architectural buildings and calling them a "hyperspace" (23). He further states, "The newer architecture—like many of the other cultural products I have evoked in the preceding remarks—therefore stands as something like an imperative to grow new organs to expand our sensoria and our bodies to some new, as yet unimaginable, perhaps ultimately impossible, dimensions" (Jameson 23).

Conclusion

Both the selected song lyrics and their videos not only narrates the hyperreality of the West but also highlights the danger of its artificiality, the hyperreal truth that it feeds about freedom and individuality, thus, can have an impact on the questioning the concept and the line between the binary opposition of freedom and imprisonment. The cultural consumers consumed the idea of attaining freedom in the West but in the actual reality, it can be posited that in hyperreal society, people are consuming the simulacrum and are not free from materialism and simulation. And individuality breaks down in a society when people consume the trends set by influential figures. People entering the bandwagon towards individuality uniformly and searching for the promised land can be decoded and these are the critical irony that can be seen from the songs. Both of the songs have postmodern elements like intertextuality as the lyrics have multi references to other texts and, fragmentations, pastiche, and playfulness with signs, displaying characteristics of the postmodern society.

Works Cited

Baudrillard, Jean. America. Verso, 1989. Digital Libraries Monoskop, Monoskop.org/File: Baudrillard_Jean_America_1989.

_____. Simulacra and Simulation. University of Michigan Press., 1994.

_____. The Consumer Society: Myth and Structures. Sage, 1970. Digital Libraries Monoskop, monoskop.org/Jean_Baudrillard.

Boys, Pet Shop. "GoWest." Youtube, uploaded by Pet Shop Boys, 22 Apr. 2009, youtu.be/LNBjMRvOB5M.

Butler, Mark. "Taking It Seriously: Intertextuality and Authenticity in Two Covers by the Pet Shop Boys." Popular Music, vol. 22, no. 1, 2003, pp. 1-19. JSTOR, www.jstor.org/stable/853553.

"California Gold Rush." Encyclopedia Britannica. https://www.britannica.com/topic/California-Gold-Rush.

Eco, Umberto. Travels in Hyperreality. Harcourt Brace Jovanovich, 1986. www.columbia.edu/itc/architecture/ockman/pdfs/session_8/eco.

"Go West by the Village People." *Songfacts*, 1979, www.songfacts.com/facts/the-village-people/go-west.

Jadhav, Rukmini Bhimrao and R.B. Chougule. "A Conceptual Study of Postmodernism with Reference to Jean Baudrillard Michel Foucault

Jean Francois Lyotard and Jacques Derrida." *Shodhganga*, 2016. hdl.handle.net/10603/9746.

Jameson, Fredric. The Cultural Turn. Verso, 1998.

Little, Harriet Fitch. "Hoe the US Doctrine of Manifest Destiny Became the Gay Anthem Go West." *Financial Times*, 26 June 2017, www.ft.com/content/65131be4-5805-11e7-80b6-9bfa4c1f83d2.

Mohunta, Ratan Tilak, and B. Hariharan. "The Theory of the Postmodern." *Shodhganga*, 2012. hdl.handle.net/10603/36437.

Nayar, Pramod K. *An Introduction to Cultural Studies*. Viva Books, 2016.

People, Village. "Go West." Youtube, uploaded by Village People, 22 Sept. 2008, youtu.be/1wc-AQJ2Myo.

Peppers, Red Hot Chili. "Californication." Youtube, uploaded by Red Hot Chili Peppers, 27 Oct. 2009, youtube/YlUKcNNmywk.

"Go West (song)." Wikipedia, The Free Encyclopedia.

"Californication (song)." Wikipedia, The Free Encyclopedia.

"LGBT culture in San Francisco." Wikipedia, The Free Encyclopedia.

Politics of Terrorizing the Imperialists: A Postmodernist Reading of the Confessional Memoirs of Mark Rudd and Abdullah Anas

MAHIMA KASHYAP
Research Scholar, M.G. Central University, Motihari

Today, any prominent discourse on terrorism begins from 9/11. Can we, therefore, assume that terrorism began in 2001 with the terrorist attack in America? Probably not. The term terrorism is not new to the world. The origin of the very term dates back to the time of the French Revolution. Bruce Hoffman studies the change in the implication of the word terrorism. He argues that the meaning of the term changed with changing times. It was used for authoritarian and repressive regimes, for the ideologically motivated individuals or groups who resorted to violence to concretize their ideas and also for the freedom fighters who revolted against the imperialists. The meaning of the word 'terrorism' also changed to accommodate new instances which were not a part of the conventional vocabulary. Modern terrorism, however, seems to have conveniently let go of the secular counterpart with its concern and responses directed towards religious fanatics.

The terrorist attack on the World Trade Centre in the very heart of American pride challenged the secure boundaries of state and thus ensued, what is known as, the war on terror. The claims of safest boundaries and strongest democracy were threatened by the attack and in response, a new narrative emerged. In the name of providing safety to its citizens, the nations began curbing the fundamental democratic rights. Citizens' movement and their expressions are controlled for their safety. This also enables selective targeting of those who are assumed to be a threat to the authority. Any person or group who is seen as a possible threat to those in power, therefore, is indiscreetly and indiscriminately termed as 'terrorist.' The threat to power is automatically projected as a threat to the people or the state. This utmost control in the hands of the government of democratic states becomes a threat to democracy itself. Townshend maintains that "[the] 'terrorist' is a description that has almost never been voluntarily adopted by any individual or group. It is applied to them by others, first and foremost the governments of the states they attack" (3).

Jihad as a Concept

Abdullah Anas asserts that "there are those 'Jihadists' as they call themselves, namely al-Qaeda and its various factions, who commit unspeakable crimes and call it Jihad and completely abuse the concept" (3). This assertion is quite in contrast to the commonplace usage of the term Jihad which is frequently associated with the Islamist militants, terrorists, and Islamist radicals. The general connotation of the word has come to imply violence and terror. Several religious and mythical interpretations of the inspiration behind Jihad have been propagated. Anas maintains that the "western reformers and analysts who were to separate Jihad from its religious tradition will fail, but those Jihadist from within the Muslim world who sully that word are the greater danger" (33). Terrorism as a sign evokes mental images of a typical bearded terrorist and it seems like the assumed 'terrorising' religion Islam calls for the elimination of the *kafirs*. And though the scriptural sanctions are not completely undeniable, the postmodernist worldview would refuse to conform by its traditionally dictated meaning and would rather prefer to explore the possibilities and practicalities of the various truths in the light of postmodern circumstances. It also becomes imperative to investigate if such associations speak of a grander narrative that is propagated and endorsed by those who struggle to retain their hegemonic power, which is also mostly self-bestowed. Anas differentiates between the religious idea of 'Jihad' with 'Modern Jihadism' and calls the latter a misconstrued version of Jihad while reinforcing that Jihad is "as intrinsic to the faith as the Ramadan fast or the Hajj" (3). While Jihad has a religious sanction, Jihadism is an intersection point of religious propaganda and political power play.

This limitation imposed on people's expression is what Mark Rudd and his comrades oppose when they rise in protest against the Columbia university administration. The protest against the war in Vietnam soon veered into a resistance against the administrative authorities when the news that Marine recruiters will come "looking for prospective officers" in the campus reached them. This "direct provocation" led to a confrontation with the authorities and the SDS, known as Students for Democratic Society (Rudd 27). Mostly, it was the "poorer students" of the university who were lured into war. It is this initial resistance against the American imperialist policies and forced involvement of the public, and more often of the underprivileged, wherefrom the Weathermen organization emerged. Similarly, the Afghan war began with the idea of safeguarding Afghanistan's territory from the invasion of Soviet Russia, and Arabs joined the war to partake in Jihad which they considered a pious act "sanctioned by God" (Anas 3). Anas further explains the motivation behind the participation of people in what they considered 'moral' Jihad, "Sacrificing one's own being in God's service, to defend one's home, the weak and oppressed, was the ultimate testimony of one's faithfulness to God. One preferred God's pleasure over one's own comfort and love of life and this is why none of the men could refuse such an offer." (88-89)

This very war laid the foundation of al-Qaeda and the Taliban. The "Caravan" of Jihad was dominated by two influential groups:

Hekmatyar and Rabbani. The rivalry between the two factions later changed into enmity which is what Anas believes led to more radicalism and the formation of the infamous terrorist organization. While the latter group held onto Massoud's idea of defending one's territory, the former group with stronger political ambitions had associations in Pakistan and was mostly influenced by elements in Peshawar. Osama bin Laden who was once a close associate of Anas, the latter observes, gradually distanced himself and "was becoming his own man . . . caught up in the various political currents in Peshawar" (179). Anas attempts to reason the change and opines that "Bin Laden was not born out of social intellectual struggle; that is he, unlike the Egyptians or the Algerians, Tunisians, Sudanese and others, was not forged from the intellectual jousting of the left versus Islamists on university campuses" (182) and calls out his "political naivety" that "made him susceptible to the ideas of Islamic Jihad" (182). This intellectual struggle in the university campus is reminiscent of Mark Rudd and his friends' struggle in the Columbia Campus. Just the way, Afghan war was inspired by the thoughts of university-educated stalwarts, the struggle of SDS went beyond the university campus to form the Weathermen organization.

The support that SDS received, in the beginning, was overwhelming. In 1967, from a handful of SDS members, the count rose to "more than eight hundred students marching in a position to the marines" which Rudd notes, "was the largest antiwar demonstration yet at Columbia" (29). However, their actions were shunned as "unserious and terroristic" by the administration. (45) The atrocities of America in Vietnam were huge. It is hardly possible to estimate the losses and casualties in Vietnam. It is undeniably true that America too suffered a great loss for no reasonable cause. The ego-ridden state, in order to safeguard its interests, sacrificed many innocents on the impious altar of war. Rudd confesses that "this taught me never to underestimate the willingness of cynical old white men in Washington to sacrifice other people's children" (49). America was not only facing anti-war demonstrations but was also reeling under racial concerns. Afflicted by racial injustices and seeing no redemption from the present turmoil, the Blacks joined forces with SDS members. Their issues were different, but their enemy was the same.

Anti-West Stance

This anti-West stance is also apparent in Abdullah Anas's writing. He clearly states that the objective of his writing it to challenge the narratives promulgated by the West, and in particular America, "I write to counter those groups in the West who want to polarize the discourse and want to bring about this 'Clash of Civilizations' between the West and the Muslim world. Their declarations and statements attract various firebrands, demagogues and extremists who do not understand what impact their words have on the reputation of Islam and Muslims." (4)

In the wake of the 9/11 attack several narratives emerged whereof some were critical of America's stance and its imperialist policies. Townsend refers to American international policies as the crucial reason behind the attack: "American commentators, both official and unofficial, showed a marked reluctance to accept the fairly well-established view that Osama bin Laden's primary *casus belli* against the USA was the defilement of Saudi Arabia by the presence of US troops. Instead, they preferred more abstract explanations of the attacks rooted in envy or hostility towards American prosperity and democracy." (Townshend 9)

The exaggerated idea of the superiority was, thus, re-imposed to cover up the actions of the government and narratives developed to villainise the 'other.' However, in the postmodern world the binary of self/other or the dominant/dominated must be reassessed to understand the different standpoints especially in relation to terrorism. Terrorist is not a properly defined category and the definition of terrorism is wide and varied. Hoffman's assertion that terrorism is inherently political is as true as the fact that the very act of entitling someone as terrorist is political and thus, selective (2). For this very reason, state terrorism has been conveniently 'omitted' from the scope of terrorism in the United States' definition of terrorism. The act of emphasis and omissions are very crucial in understanding the biased narratives.

Media, in the present times, has become crucially instrumental in propagating such narratives. The media scrutiny, additions, selective omission, and misconstruction are how narratives emerge. Rudd accuses the media of exaggerations and selective representations of the veracity of the events during their protests. Media reports were mainly dictated by the administration and the voices of students were suppressed, even worse, sometimes, falsely construed. It is to counter such narratives that Weathermen began publishing their own pamphlets. Similar cynicism regarding media portrayal is seen in Afghan mujhhids too. Sheikh Abdullah, an esteemed figure for the Arab mujahids, gave in to such portrayals and suspiciously asks, "Is the situation really like how Western media has portrayed it?" (Anas 45)

However, Weathermen could not hold on to their initial characteristics and indulged itself in cult-making. Rudd's confession that "we had unwittingly reproduced conditions that all hermetically sealed cults use: isolation, sleep deprivation, demanding arbitrary acts of loyalty to the group, even sexual initiation as bonding" hint at the way the organization had begun fumbling (162-3). Their quest to appear radical and unconventional is reinforced in their claims that "monogamies had to be smashed" and they indulged in indiscriminate sex among the members as a result of which sexually transmitted disease spread among them like an "epidemic" (166).

Anti-women Proclivity

This sexual hysteria became the target of feminists who claimed that this was a tool for women's subjugation which they have been fighting against incessantly. Though the objective behind such experimentation was to liberate people of emotional and physical inhibitions, the result proved an utter failure. "Sex in Weatherman was manipulative. The anti-monogamy program created opportunity for women to be sexually exploited; it restricted women's control of their bodies. Sex, coerced or consented, solidified their obedience to male leadership and earned women leadership positions in their collective." (Wyker 73)

An inherent male chauvinism is also apparent when the women are expected to meet up the masculine standards in order to participate in the organization which further takes away their identity as women. Though they preferred to call themselves revolutionary seeking for equality and advocated women rights, the members of the Weather Underground Organization "were never truly able to reconcile their beliefs in women's equality with their beliefs that masculine traits were essential to revolution." (Silverman 94) The masculine strength and ideals were highly prized among them. Ironically, the idea that Rudd and his associates began with, didn't participate in their acts. The slogan, "WHAT DO YOU WANT? PEACE!!! WHEN DO YOU WANT IT? NOW!!!," was not their reality. The Weathermen often involved themselves in violent protests and bombing, so much so that Rudd lost his friends in one such bomb trial.

This masculinity or manhood is also celebrated by mujahids. Anas sees in Massoud a "Muslim manhood personified, that of a perfectly balanced sword, elegant, sharp, lithe, and strong with a handle made of ivory and verses of poetry and the Quran engraved in the finest calligraphy." (Anas 68) The description which has nothing feminine about it is conjoined by the absence of female characters, except a brief unnamed mention as someone's wife or someone's daughter, thus, establishing the nameless identities in relation to men. For Anas, Osama was a "shy man." Except occasionally, he refrains from using the term 'terrorism' and prefers other words like 'criminals.' The extent of criminality can vary but it becomes questionable if such a treatment is justifiable. The intention behind the memoir seems more than reclaiming the word 'Jihad' and the proclaimed aim to re-establish its traditional and religiously derived meaning of a "spiritually rewarding endeavour." Being a "proud" son-in-law of an infamously controversial figure of Afghan Jihad, Abdullah Anas' position is indeed contentious and his intentions vague.

The limitation with these memoirs is that their narrations are confined to the perspective of the authors. Naturally, they find their actions reasonable. They are actors, not receivers. The latter have their opinions. The author cannot distance himself completely with the character since s/he is writing about himself/herself. The author is the pivot in relation to whom the events occur and whose response to the event finds expression in the text. Several writers have attempted to delineate terrorists and terrorism in their fiction. "Literary depictions of terrorism often displace some other scene of violence. In the imagined act of terrorism, a writer may assess his or her own political commitments, actions, and failures. Thus the terrorist novel opens itself up to more general questions about the writer's ability to understand, respond to, and influence politics." (Scanlan 7)

Sometimes this fictionalization stands very close to romanticizing the terrorists and their predicament. Such portrayal as representing terrorists as a social victim who takes the weapon to avenge herself/himself is very common but far from reality. The 'melting of heart' is what follows and leads to their redemption. Such far from real treatment in fiction and emphasis on an individual's life and struggles is not how terrorism, with its widespread network, can be seen.

Conclusion

Modern terrorism began with the invention of dynamite in the late nineteenth century. The fluidity of knowledge poses a greater threat and thus, the possibility of proliferation of the knowledge of more dangerous chemical, nuclear, or biological weapons poses an unprecedented threat to mankind. The reason and goals behind the acts of terror have become more arbitrary in the recent times. In the postmodern times when human rights and democratic values have come to be cherished more than ever, the anti-imperialist war in Afghanistan indeed had many supporters from beyond the borders. It is for the same reason that Mark Rudd and his friends garnered support in various forms from European nations. Yet, the formation of al-Qaeda which is rooted in the same justifiable war is one the most criminal formations in the world. With time, most of such revolutionary groups too tend to astray from their major goals and begin striving for power. It can be, thus, noted that "the more vague the political goals, the more bound up with religious ones, the more postmodern today's terrorist groups have become" (O'Kane 188). But the narratives built by the dominant power pose an even greater threat in their attempts to overgrow other states and impose their worldview on others. Historicists and theorists like Walter Laqueur and others have familiarized that terrorism could not succeed. Those who have relied on violent strategies or terrorist activities could never successfully concretise their ideals. Townshend argues that "until they [the terrorists] and the state can speak at least a few halting phrases in the same language, the only response will be containment and coexistence rather than interaction. If terrorism cannot be eliminated, it must perforce at some level be tolerated—and it can be" (26). This negotiable ground, however, is difficult to arrive at because terrorism and narratives around it are, in Hoffman's opinion, "ineluctably about power: the pursuit of power, the acquisition of power and the use of power to achieve political change" and also, dominance (2).

Works Cited

Anas, Abdullah, Tam Hussein. *To the Mountains: My Jihad, from Algeria to Afghanistan*. Hurst, 2019.

Hoffman, Bruce. *Inside Terrorism*. Columbia University Press, 2006.

Laqueur, Walter. *A History of Terrorism*. Transaction Publishers, 2001.

O'Kane, Rosemary H. T. *Terrorism*. Pearson Education Limited, 2007.

Rudd, Mark. *Underground: My Days with SDS and the Weathermen*. HarperCollins, 2009.

Scanlan, Margaret. *Plotting Terror: Novelists and Terrorists in Contemporary Fiction*. University Press of Virginia, 2001.

Silverman, Liliana, "Masculinity and Violence in the Weather Underground." *Archive: An Underground Journal of History*. Vol. 19, May 2016.

Townshend, Charles. *Terrorism: A Very Short Introduction*. OUP, 2002.

Wyker, Cyrana B. "Women in Wargasm: The Politics of Women's Liberation in the Weather Underground Organization." *Graduate Theses and Dissertations,* 2009, www.scholarcommons.usf.edu/etd/93.

Death and Magic Realism in Murakami Haruki's "New York Mining Disaster"

NEELAM YADAV
Delhi College of Arts & Commerce, University of Delhi

We are living in a postmodernist world, where the Covid-19 pandemic has brought us face to face with death. Death is a gruesome reality. Hence, the depiction of death should be equally repulsive in whatsoever situation it is mentioned. But death meets a different treatment in the hands of Murakami Haruki, a renowned Japanese author, and a pioneer of postmodernist Japanese writing. Death is a recurrent theme in many of his bestselling novels like *Norwegian Wood*, *Kafka on the Shore*, *1Q84*, to name just a few. Although Murakami's novels have been vastly studied from numerous perspectives, there have only been a few sincere attempts to investigate the postmodern concepts and themes present in his short stories. This paper strives to study the theme of death and magic realism in accordance with Murakami Haruki's one of the famous short stories "New York Mining Disaster," the third story in his collection *Blind Willow, Sleeping Woman*, first published in English translation by Philip Gabriel in 2006.

Since childhood, Murakami has been profoundly influenced by Western culture, particularly Western music and literature. This is quite evident from many of his novels like *Hear The Wind Sing* (1979) and *A Wild Sheep Chase* (1982), or later work, *Kafka on the Shore* (2002), where, apparently, his protagonists are a connoisseur of western music, mainly Jazz. In the field of postmodernism, Murakami is influenced by American postmodern novelists such as Kurt Vonnegut, Richard Brautigan, and Thomas Pynchon and has often been criticized for Western influences in his works. Oe Kenzaburo, in his "The Novelist in Today's World," stated: "Murakami Haruki writes in Japanese, but his writing isn't really Japanese. If you translate it into American English, it can be read very naturally in New York" (Ishiguro & Kenzaburo 110). Murakami has won international stardom only after the publication of the translation of his two bestseller novels, *Wild Sheep Chase* and *Hard-Boiled Wonderland and the End of the World* in 1985 and 1989 respectively.

Postmodern Angle

Now, viewed from the postmodernist perspective, most of the stories in *Blind Willow, Sleeping Woman* represent contemporary Japan as they portray modern/post-modern issues like existentialism, search for identity, and death in all forms. Many stories also serve as a link connecting Murakami's traditional Japanese ideas and contemporary Western influences, like "The Folklore For My Generation: A Pre-History of Late-Stage Capitalism," "A Shinagawa Monkey" and etc.

"When I write a good story, I just keep writing. When you read a good story, you just keep reading," says Murakami in an interview. (Phelan). Stories of the collection, *Blind Willow, Sleeping Woman*, give its readers a similar sensation of readability. The collection has a total of 24 short stories of varying length and was written and published in Japan in various magazines and collections between 1980 and 2005. All the stories in *Blind Willow, Sleeping Woman* manifest Murakami's narrative skill and favorite themes, from the surreal to the monotonous, like talking to animals, mysterious cats, characters living with their imagination, and dreams that shape us and the things we might wish for, but could not attain. Though the stories in the collection deal with everyday life, most of these do not make any sense at first read. The titular story, "Blind Willow, Sleeping Woman" is about an unnamed adult narrator and his teenage cousin. Both of them are meeting each other after a long time. In present, they are waiting for a bus to the hospital so that the young cousin can have his ear problem examined, a disorder he has had since he was young. Later in the story, while waiting at the cafeteria of the hospital, the anonymous narrator had a flashback of this weird tree that was surrounded by flies and he had a surreal vision that when the flies entered anybody's ear they will eat up that person's body and he/she died sleeping. The story ends without any desirable conclusion.

Written in a similar fashion of post-modernist conclusion, the "New York Mining Disaster," the third story in the collection, takes the reader through the story of an unnamed twenty-eight-year-old narrator, accounting the tale of his unnamed friend who has a weird "habit of going to the zoo whenever there's a typhoon" (62) and an equally peculiar habit of changing his girlfriend exactly at every six months. He is the friend from whom the narrator borrowed a funeral suit, "My friend owns a nice used car, the collected works of Balzac, and a black suit, black tie, and black shoes that are perfect for attending funerals. Every time someone dies, I call him and ask if I can borrow them" (63), not once but five times as it is a 'Year of Funerals' for the narrator, "Friends and former friends died one after another, like ears of corn withering in a drought" (66). Later in the story, the unnamed narrator acquiesce that he is reluctant to buy a funeral suit of his own because of the superstitious belief that if buys his own suit, he will see more deaths, "if I buy funeral clothes, I'm saying that it's OK if somebody dies." (65)

Death as Motif

In "New York Mining Disaster," death is depicted both, explicitly and implicitly. At the beginning of the story, the unnamed narrator casually mentions death. He says that it is okay for a poet or a revolutionary or a Rockstar to die at the young age of twenty-one, but it is when you cross that age, "You've made it past Dead Man's Curve and you're out of the tunnel," (66) death is unacceptable. Death for the narrator is a divide between reality and unreality (or unreality and reality). During the course of a year, five of his friends straddle this dividing line between reality and unreality. First-person to die that year was a friend from college who teaches English at Junior high school and had been married for three years. This friend of the narrator had committed suicide by slitting his wrist with a German knife which he shopped two days before his suicide along with two packs of shaving cream. Murakami's portrayal, of the narrator's friend's death by suicide was meant to draw readers' attention to suicidal deaths in Japan which saw a sudden increase in the number in the last two decades. Though the reason for his suicide was unexplained, two packs of shaving cream which will never be used by his friend, create unease in the narrator's mind and he contemplates, what was his friend thinking before slitting his wrist?, "While he was waiting for the bath to fill, knocking back glass after glass of Haig on the rocks, he must have stared at those cans and thought something along the lines of I'll never have to shave again" (68)

Many scholars and academicians of Japanese culture and literature have shown that death psychology has a special status in Japanese society. As studied by a famous Japanese scholar, Nagamine Takahiko, 1988, "Attitudes toward death in rural areas of Japan," "Japanese people's perception of "death" is very different from that of other countries as reflected in media studies and literature as well. Japan has long been one of the countries with the highest suicide rate in the world. In 2018, more than 20,000 Japanese people ended their lives by suicide" (Takahiko 63). Murakami's works provide ample opportunities for analysis of suicide and the Japanese youth, as common themes of his novels include death, trauma, and coping among young adults. The best example could be Murakami's famous work, *Norwegian Wood.* All three major characters in the novel end their young lives by committing suicide.

Various scholars and critics like Yoshio Iwamoto and Matthew Carl Strecher have exercised numerous literary and psychological theories to analyze the impact of death (suicide/murder/natural) on various characters in Murakami's other works. This perception requires a different discourse and analysis for a different study altogether. After the death of this friend by suicide, four more friends of the narrator died in the course of one year. Out of these four, two died in road accidents, one of the heart attack and then another one at some oil field at "Saudi Arabia or Kuwait." None of these four, unlike the friend who died of suicide, says the narrator, "had the faintest idea their death" (68).

This story alludes to the death theme, which was represented in the beginning, by the deaths of five of the narrator's friends and at the end, by the scene of trapped miners awaiting rescue. Death is, here, informed with the nuances of magic realism, which is Murakami's one of the commonly used post-modernist techniques. Now, concerning magical realism, when trauma (which is an element of death) is represented in literature, it can include elements of the fantastic. As supported by Maggie Ann Bowers when she defines Magic Realism as, "referring to narrative art that presents extraordinary occurrences as an ordinary part of everyday reality" (Bowers 44).

Magic Realism

As the narrative proceeds, when does this element of fantastic becomes a reality is hard to distinguish. Magic realism is one of the famous narrative techniques in the post-colonial and postmodernism literature, used obsessively by Salman Rushdie and Gabriel Garcia Marquez, and post-1970's, more pertinently, by

Murakami Haruki. In "New York Mining Disaster" we comprehend that the narrative and plot are fragmented. Fragmentation, multiple narratives and, realism are significantly used by Murakami. The story does not narrate just one linear event or incident from the beginning till the end, instead, the story is a collation of three fragmented stories, separated in the narrative by the change in space and time. All three parts have a surreal dreamlike quality about them. The first part of the story takes place at the narrator's friend's house, where he went to return the borrowed 'funeral suit,' and ends with them having champagne and talking about the zoo in Paris and the animals that live there.

In the second part of the story, at an annual New Year's Eve party at a bar in Roppongi, the narrator was introduced to a mysterious woman who claims that she "killed" someone that looked like the narrator five years ago. They entered into a senseless conversation about this killing before they continued in their own ways. In the final section, a press release-style passage informs readers of the miners, trapped underground as the outside world tries to save them. The narrative in this final section of the story is explicitly uncanny and surreal.

Wendy Ferris in his 1995 published book, *Magic Realism: Theory, History, Community*, discussed five characteristics of magical realism. These characteristics are "the irreducible element, a phenomenal setting/world, unsettling doubts, the merging of different realms, and disturbances to time, space, and identity" (Ferris 17). Most of Murakami's works in general and "New York Mining Disaster" in particular meet Wendy Farris' five characteristics of magical realism.

"New York Mining Disaster" is set in a real but phenomenal world where people party on New Year's Eve, and drink chilled beer and champagne to celebrate. But, as the narrative proceeds, we see that there are irreducible elements in the story that alludes to fantastic. Why does the narrator's friend visit the zoo whenever there is a typhoon is inexplicable; the narrator says, "Typhoons aside, my friend's no different from anyone else" (63). The narrator was also amazed at his friend having a "new girlfriend every six months," "Why he insists on having a new one every six months (and it's always exactly six months) I'll never understand. "It is not just about a new girlfriend but also that "The girls all look the same, like perfect clones of one another" (63). All this information is passed on from the narrator to readers like casual remarks. Even though the above-mentioned incidences alluded to the theme of Magic Realism, the thin line dividing the fantastic and the reality vanishes with the casual narrative used by Murakami.

Then, in section two, the strange woman's declaration that she had killed the narrator's doppelganger, was equally mysterious and fantastic, but without any explanation. The two realms, the world of reality and the world of fantasy, that merge or overlap each other, are found at the end when there's a mention of trapped miners and alludes that there could be an alternate reality. Which is the real world?: the one where the narrator met the girl on New Year's Eve or the world presented at the end where there's a reportage of miners stuck in the dark mines, awaiting their rescue?— "They waited for hours. Reality began to melt away in the darkness. Everything began to feel as if it were happening a long time ago, in a world far away. Or was it happening in the future, in a different far-off world? Outside, people were digging a hole, trying to reach" (81).

Finally, the disturbances to time, space, and identity come about more on the surface with an inexplicable identity of the mysterious girl in the party, who meets the narrator, unfolds her secret murder mystery, and disappears, without any further explanation as to who she was and what prompted her to engage in that eerie conversation with the narrator. Disturbances with space were visible when people stuck in the mine, "blew out their lamps to save on air" and disturbances with time could be deduced from the narrative chronology. The story narrates the events that happened in the span of one year but lacks any chronology and can be read as events that could have occurred in one day: the death of the narrator's five friends, his 'peculiar' friend visiting the zoo, and changing his girlfriends, New Year Party at the bar, and finally, the miners fighting for their lives are the events which might have taken place in different dimensions and at different time period but conjoined by fragment narrative skills of Murakami. By fragmenting the narrative technique, Murakami creates a space between these moments of reality and fantasy, both for the characters who told the stories, and the readers who are spellbound to know what happens next. But by giving "New York Mining Disaster" a Magic Realist narration, it becomes convenient for the readers too to interpret the merging of the fantastic and the realistic worlds as per their proclivity.

"One of the unique features of magical realism is its reliance upon the reader to follow the example of the narrator in accepting both realistic and magical perspectives of reality on the same level" (Bowers, 44), says Maggie Ann Bowers. Magical realism is often invoked when a realistic world has magical elements that are taken as real. However, for Murakami, it is completely the opposite. His story looks at the magic in the real world. There is a very thin line between Magic realism and reality in his works. In most of his works, generally and this short story, particularly, reality and unreality are just naturally fused.

Murakami has often been questioned about the presence of an unreal world in his works. In an interview with *The Paris Review*, he remarked, "I can't always see the borderline between the unreal world and the real world. So, in many cases, they're mixed up. In Japan, I think that the other world is very close to our real life, and if we decide to go to the other side it's not so difficult. And you can't necessarily tell the difference between this side and the other side" (Wray)

Murakami also acknowledges in his *The New Yorker* interview that many of his works "often comment on the strangeness of the storyline, even call[s] the reader's attention to it" (Treisman). Like in this current story, the anonymous narrator draws readers' attention to the incidences which readers would have passed unnoticed, if not stressed with repetitive narratives like the oddness of clone girlfriends or the uncanny behavior of his friends drinking beer in the zoo, or never-to-be used-again-two-cans-of-shaving-gel his friend bought before committing suicide. First Person narration of the first two sections is taken over by an omniscient narrator in the final section of the story, when it was reported like a newspaper snippet, that miners (no definite number mentioned) are trapped underground, counting their final breath, waiting for some help from the outside world, "In the dark, the miners huddled together, straining to hear one sound. The sound of pickaxes. The sound of life. Outside, people were digging a hole, trying to reach them. It was like a scene from a movie" (81)

Hence, I would like to deduce from my study of this story in particular and other stories from collection in general that readers tend to experience a 'willing suspension of disbelief' when Murakami did not give any closure to the story. "New York Mining Disaster" is an open-ended story, which left its readers perplexed and bemused at the end.

Conclusion

Therfore I would like to submit my conclusion that it is the author's deliberate act to leave on readers to conclude the end accordingly, using their discretion, 'fancy and imagination.' But, end alone is not what matters to Murakami. His works often advised readers to look beyond the realistic detail and accept the dual ontological structure of the story in which the natural and the supernatural, and the explainable and the fantastic, coexist side by side in an ever-changing reality. This refusal of closure, I believe, is what gives Murakami's works magnetism, and with his intricate writing, he is able to leave readers longing for closure with ways to which one can interpret the work or try to find their own closure.

Murakami has used this characteristics of magical realism in order to explicate death and its trauma and by doing so, he managed to shed light on the connections between the magic realism genre and that of the trauma of death. Murakami in an interview with John Wary confirms that his "novels . . . often seem to resist a resolution of the kind that the reader is perhaps expecting." Murakami comments, "Conclusion means nothing at all." (Wray)

Though there's some fluidity in narration, not everything narrated in the story makes any logic. But, as Murakami calls his narrative, "very life-like" and since not everything in life makes sense, there are things and happenings which are hard to explain. Some events are like the dream, they do not make any sense always, yet they are sometimes so vivid as if real happenings of life. The end sometimes has no apparent relation to the beginning and many a times lacks resolution or the obvious resolution as they leave the reader thinking about what would happen next or what would have happened later.

So, if I could perceive an end to this story it would be this: The mining scene is the subconscious creation of the unnamed narrator. In his sub-conscious mind, the narrator sees himself one among the miners, who were stranded underground, and amidst the darkness, his sub-conscious mind entered the world where his friends die and he met a woman, who foreshadowed his death. Magic realist texts do not posit a qualitative difference between magical and rational world views. Hence, the eerie ending of the story gives it a perfect post-modernist end.

Works Cited

Bowers, Ann Maggie. *Magical Real(ism): The New Critical Idiom*, London, & New York, Routledge, 2005.

Ishiguro Kazuo and Oe Kenzaburo. "The Novelist in Today's World: A Conversation." *Japan in the World,* vol. 18, no. 3, 1991, pp. 109-22. https://doi.org/10.2307/303205.

Murakami, Haruki. "New York Mining Disaster," *Blind Willow, Sleeping Woman*, Apple Books, Vintage, 2007. Story 2.

Phelan, Stephan. "In The Basement." Interview by Stephan Phelan. *The Sunday Herald. January 2005,* https://www.stephenphelan.co.uk/articles/murakami/

Takahiko, Nagamine. "Attitudes Toward Death in Rural Areas of Japan." *Death Studies*, vol. 12, no. 1, 1988, pp. 61-68. https://doi.org/10.1080/07481188808252220

Treisman, Deborah. "The Underground Worlds of Haruki Murakami." Interview by Deborah Treisman. *The New Yorker*, 10 Feb. 2019, https://www.newyorker.com/culture/the-new-yorker-interview/the-underground-worlds-of-haruki-murakami

Wendy, Faris B. and Lois Parkinson Zamora. *Magic Realism: Theory, History, Community*. Durham, N.C, Duke University Press, 1995.

Wray, John. "The Art of Fiction." Interview by John Wray. *The Paris Review*, no. 182, issue 170, 2004, www.theparisreview.org/interviews/2/the-art-of-fiction-no-182-haruki-murakami.

Revisiting the *Ramayana* in Divakaruni's *The Forest of Enchantments*

PRATIBHA NEHRA
Ph.D. Scholar, Panjab University, Chandigarh

Adrienne Rich's *When We Dead Awaken: Writing as Re-Vision* considers re-vision as "the act of looking back, of seeing with fresh eyes, of entering an old text from a new critical direction." Rich further states, "We need to know the writing of the past, and know it differently than we have ever known it; not to pass on a tradition but to break its hold over us" (18-19). As opposed to the traditional interpretations of the *Ramayana*, the present paper posits a re-vision of the epic for feminist appropriation and a positive construction of femininity. Any discussion on the *Ramayana* hitherto has been dominated either by academic analysis or political debates on the figure of Rama; academic analysis thriving on Rama's portrayal as a patriarchal poet's fantasy while the political debates either assert Rama or reject Rama. In the din of these discourses on Rama, the discourse on Sita is pushed towards the margins.

The paper attempts to foreground Sita at the centre of the epic where she is able to negotiate a space for herself and other marginalized characters, since the epic sermonizes monovalently for the brahmanical patriarchs of ancient India, making little room available for discourses that run counter to the hegemonic and comprehensive regimes of patriarchal dominance. However the *Ramayana* is a multi-voiced entity as stated by Robert P. Goldman in *Many Ramayanas*, "encompassing tellings of the Rama story that vary according to historical period, regional literary tradition, religious affiliation, genre, intended audience, social location, gender, and political context" (Preface), the representational diversity of the *Ramayana* marks contradictory manifestations—as a hegemonic social text on the one hand and as a platform for resistance to that hegemony on the other. The paper also undertakes an assiduous revision of the debates and the silences present within the narrative framework of the epic, which will consequently illustrate its ideological underpinnings and its role in the production of the culture and society of India. Even the smallest of the loopholes of this monumental work become glaring due to its aspects of social normativity, its status as the family text par excellence, and as the ideal medium for the acculturation of children.

Feminist Interpretations

The avant-garde interpretations of the Indian mythology have fundamentally transformed the international literary climate. These writers have authored such works of literature that celebrate the Indian ethos and open avenues of cultural exchange with an international audience. *The Forest of Enchantments* is one such literary work that teleports the audience into the aesthetic retelling of the *Ramayana* with primary focus on Sita's narrative, or her side of the story in the form of Sita *yan* (Taskeen 39). Sita *yan* is Sita's project of storytelling where she addresses the issue of masculinized writing through male gendered language that does not accommodate the literary understanding of women's lives. Many feminist theorists have endeavoured to reclaim and redefine women through a re-structuring of language. In this novel, Divakaruni undertakes the task of re-vision and re-writing the narrative from a feminist lens as Sita embarks on an aesthetic venture, while she also tabulates the unrecorded historical accounts of women who had been deliberately silenced and coerced to the margins of literary expression.

The dark recesses, the silences, the pauses and the memories of Sita's journey fill the literary crevices of the *Ramayana*. Sita's character rehabilitates the journey of other female characters that had been silenced and forgotten in the din of masculinized writing. All these voices are tethered to Sita and they sincerely believe that as a woman of profound wisdom and with strength to empathize, Sita will not judge them on account of their misdemeanour or wrongdoings, rather she will give them a second chance to be aptly represented. The voices within Sita's mind plead, "Write our story, too. For always we've been pushed into corners, trivialized, misunderstood, blamed, forgotten—or maligned and used as cautionary tales" (Divakaruni 4). In *The Forest of Enchantments*, Sita takes an initiative to restore the lost dignity of these women by means of her re-writing.

Assimilation of the neglected and the marginalized into the mainstream is the central objective of 'Womanism' (Walker, 1994). The suppression of voices and the methodical marginalization is detrimental to the development of ethical representation. Therefore, Divakaruni—by employing the voice of Sita offers asylum to all the hitherto unheard voices. Alice Walker in her well-known work *In Search of Our Mothers' Gardens* states: "The writer—like the musician or painter—must be free to explore, otherwise she or he will never discover what is needed (by everyone) to be known" (264). Walker, famous as a devoted social activist and a candid writer, allocates sheer distinction to an author's intellectual freedom.

Sita's Image

Divakaruni's *Sitayan* is an example of Walker's spirit of intellectual freedom as it divulges the unsung acts of female valour. Divakaruni's storytelling in the voice of Sita is indiscriminatory in nature as she bleeds with her characters emotionally in order to be one with the humiliation and marginalization that they have undergone since ages. In the novel, at Valmiki's ashram, the pregnant Sita has a dream, where she finds Sunaina, Ahalya, Mandodari, Sarama, Kaikeyi, Tara, Shabari, even Surpanakha looking at her with wise and compassionate eyes and they appear to convey the message: "Endure as we do. Endure your challenges" (322). Meaningfully, afterwards, Sita ruminates over the word 'Endure,' "It didn't mean giving in. It didn't mean being weak or accepting injustice. It meant taking the challenges thrown at us and dealing with them as intelligently as we knew until we grew stronger than them" (322). Thus, the author imparts a new connotation to the term to empower women to fight against challenges and resist injustice.

Sita has always been construed as an epitome of endurance, which is often (mis)read as being submissive, obedient or meek, and is frequently cited as an example in the acculturation of girls in Indian society. Her wifely fidelity to her husband under any circumstances has been (mis)read as an embodiment of cultural conservatism. In fact, all the stories present in the novel are replete with instances of Sita questioning the injustices she witnessed in her journey. Sita's narration uncovers the muted stories hidden deep beneath the rigid and dominant discursive framework. In *The Madwoman in the Attic*, Gilbert and Gubar dub this mode of writing as 'palimpsest' and it is clearly subversive in its way of operating (45). Her writing seeks to explore the other female characters in the epic, namely Kaikeyi, Ahalya, Mandodari, and Urmila. Their roles have so far been analyzed by Valmiki, only from a masculine perspective, but she rewrites their journey from a unique feminine perspective. Narratives coming from diverse female characters merge into a unified whole in *Sitayan* and create a sense of interconnectedness. The margins are given an eloquent voice so as to initiate a dialogue with the mainstream.

The figure of Sita looms large in the collective unconscious of Indians; whether it promotes endurance, moral strength or rebellion. Sita becomes a point of reference; a model that one either accepts or rejects. There is almost an obsession, which contemporary writers have optimized in their art, to understand the complexities of the character of Sita. At present, Sita has become a site of contestations, where not one single meaning or message can be drawn out. She has become a site of rejections and emulations, where she is seen as the ideal woman, a title conferred by the upholders of patriarchal dominance. 'No More Sitas' was the headline of a letter published in a 1983 issue of *Manushi: A Journal about Women and Society*. The author is Saroj Visaria, a Banarasi woman, whose letter has been translated from Hindi:

> The ideals, ethics and morality heaped on women since time immemorial are suffocating and killing. The adjectives used to praise us have become oppressive. Calling us loving, they have locked us in the closed room of culture, calling us gentle, they have reflected us in a mirror of helplessness, calling us kind they have tied us in cowardice, they have handcuffed us with modesty and chained our feet with loyalty. . . . Now we must refuse to be Sitas. (qtd. Hess 16)

The above view also displays the contemporary attitude of Indian feminists, a position where they challenge and reject the ideal of *pativrata* (a woman who considers her husband lord's will dearer than her life) as it becomes synonymous with an oppressed woman. Just as the archetype of Rama has been exploited in the hands of a patriarchal Brahminical system to reproduce an ideal Hindu male, Sita too has been reproduced as an ideal Hindu female to help serve the status-quo. And although Sita's story cannot be called a happy one in its entirety, she nonetheless remains the ideal woman and becomes the medium through which the patriarchal values are loudly advocated. The tone of the *Ramayana* reeks of vehement orthodoxy normalizing the victimization of Sita and other women, where the *pativrata* Sita, who is utterly and unwaveringly devoted to her husband lord is worshipped, and the other women who slightly deviate from this ideal are meted out harsh punishments.

The iconic *Lakshmana* episode becomes symbolic of the restrictions imposed on women and the consequences meted out to them if they go against the patriarchal authority. The subsequent abduction becomes symbolic of the outcome when any woman asserts herself against her husband's will. In other words, when a woman goes against the moral directives laid out by the patriarch, she faces the wrath of fate, thereby reinstating the idea of Rama's word being supreme and that women must not aspire for any kind of independence or question the word of their husband. When Sita dares to cross the *Lakshmana Rekha*, which is an archetypal symbol of woman's accountability to the laws of man, she is condemned to confinement, exile and/or death in a masculinized text.

Interrogating an Icon

However, when women retell the *Ramayana*, this so-called transgression transforms into an act of assertion of one's free will. Another highly controversial instance, Sita's trial by fire or the *agnipariksha*, highlights the virtuous nature of Sita by glorifying her trial and tribulations, when viewed from the patriarchal lens. The male narration sung in patriarchal orthodoxy normalizes the silence revolving around this abuse instead of viewing Sita as a victim in the hands of not only Ravana but also Rama. In traditional versions of the *Ramayana*, this atrocious act is (mis)construed into the model of how an ideal woman must behave and sets precedent for the entire nation as it is internalized by a society that has a cult following of the *Ramayana*.

It is time to interrogate the trope of a troubled and brooding hero torn between his moral duty and his passions. While he may elicit sympathy from a selected section of society, this trope shifts the focus away from his unjust actions towards the victim, and redirects the attention to his own plight by self-victimization. The act of re-vision of the *Ramayana* assists to abolish the trope of a compassionate hero forced to be cruel and avoids the trappings of absolving the perpetrator's blame. As Lord Vishnu's avatar, the figure of *Rama* for many Indians literally embodies righteousness, duty, truth, and a commitment to *dharma* and is considered the ideal man, *satpurusha*. However, Sita's narrative is critical of Rama's attitude and intention—his obsession with imperial honour and obligations, disregard for the duties of a husband, and his decision to remain single being motivated by compassion, not by love for Sita. Divakaruni culls out the irony hidden in plain sight when she demands an answer to why the *sat-purusha* Rama threw an honest woman into fire? "If there is a problem about throwing a good woman into the fire, wouldn't the great exemplar of moral perfection want to communicate this? (10)" There is no visible difference in the treatment given by an ignorant common man and the enlightened avatar of Vishnu.

Lastly, in the final scene, Sita is asked to undergo the trial by fire a second time in front of her sons. Velcheru Narayana Rao in *When Does Sita Cease to be Sita* draws attention to the resistance inherent in the act where Sita chooses to return to the earth, and in doing so, she accomplishes two things: she has proven her chastity and demonstrated her independence, as well. It is both a declaration of her integrity and a powerful indictment against a culture that suspects and questions women at every step. It is difficult not to interpret this as Sita's protest against the way she was treated by her people and by her husband (Rao 226). In this episode, Divakaruni underlines the cruelty by Rama in the name of dharma and his disregard of not only a husband's duty towards his wife, but also a king's duty towards his subject. These episodes become all the more problematic when they are embedded in the cultural consciousness of Indian society where they are cited with such proverbial force that they become the gospel truth.

In order to challenge the dominant discourse, a counter-argument can only arise from revisiting and re-reading of the epic. Through these readings, one can identify various episodes in the epic that depict Sita's courage, strength and passion. In Bina Agarwal's 1985 poem on Sita, she labels her as "the victim twice" with reference to the *agni-pariksha* episode. Another contemporary response to the dominant discourse was Snehalata Reddy's 1973 one-act play Sita, where Sita bluntly declares "It is I who reject you!" (Reddy 40) when asked to undergo the trial by fire a second time. In these feminist writings, Sita questions Rama's verdict, his sense of justice and her right as a citizen and also points out Valmiki's limitations of his individual perspective, "What occurred when I was alone in the darkness, under the sorrow tree, you don't know. You don't know my despair. You don't even know my exhilaration" (Divakaruni 4).

In *The Forest of Enchantments*, Sita is depicted as feeling thoroughly uncomfortable with Valmiki's language since it is steeped in the discursive framework of masculine ideology and unable to address such issues which are clearly feminine in nature. The narration by a patriarchal or male author can push the woman subject into a position of passivity and this is the position that Sita seeks to encounter when she dips her quill in the ink. This is also the very essence of the true feminist criticism, through which the woman as a writer attempts to address the most intimate of details felt within the core of her being which are normally omitted or overlooked in the phallocentric writing. In fact, the color with which Sita wants to portray her narrative is "the colour of menstruation and childbirth, the colour of the marriage mark that changes women's lives, the colour of the flowers of the Ashoka tree under which I had spent my years of captivity in the palace of the demon king" (5).

Conclusion

Sita seeks to perturb the very foundation of patriarchal mode of narration through her writing. Sita, in fact, very emphatically states that the purpose of her writing is to challenge the foundational frameworks that contaminate the discourse with patriarchal ideology. Sita feels that the suppressed voices of all the 'other' women are speaking to her, urging her to write their raw tales of prolonged suffering and sustained suppression, "Write our story, too. For always we've been pushed into corners, trivialized, misunderstood, blamed, forgotten—or maligned and used as cautionary tales" (7). Sita, through her writing, thus reclaims an alternative space for femininity and deconstructs dominant male patterns of thought and social practices, and reconstructs female experience hitherto hidden or overlooked. *The Forest of Enchantments* accommodates the poignant *Sitayan* which addresses and inspires the contemporary and future women.

Works Cited

Divakaruni, Banerjee Chitra. *The Forest of Enchantments*. HarperCollins India, 2021.

Gilbert, Sandra M. and Susan Gubar, ed. "The Madwoman in the Attic." *Infection in the Sentence: The Woman Writer and the Anxiety of Authorship*, First Edition, Yale, 1979, p. 45.

Hess, Linda. "Rejecting Sita: Indian Responses to the Ideal Man's Cruel Treatment of His Ideal Wife." *Journal of the American Academy of Religion*, vol. 67, no. 1, 1999, pp. 1-32. *Crossref*, doi:10.1093/jaarel/67.1.1.

Rao, Velcheru Narayana. "When Does Sita Cease to Be Sita? Notes toward a Cultural Grammar of Indian Narrative." *The Ramayana Revisited*, ed. Mandakranta Bose, Oxford University Press, 2004, p. 224.

Reddy, Snehalata. *Sita*. Enact Magazine, 1974.

Rich, Adrienne. "When We Dead Awaken: Writing as Re-Vision." *College English*, vol. 34, no. 1, 1972, pp. 18-30. *Crossref*, doi:10.2307/375215.

Walker, Alice. *In Search of Our Mother's Gardens: Womanist Prose*. Women's Press, 1984.

_____. "The Complete Stories." *Coming Apart*, Women's Press, 1994, p. 170.

Predicament of Homosexuals: A Study of Selected Plays by Mahesh Dattani

PRERNA SRIVASTAVA & SANGEETHA NOVAL
Bhartiya Skill Development University, Jaipur

Postmodernism is a celebration of multiplicity in approach, multiculturalism, and denial of conventional ways of looking at things. The Postmodern Drama in English drew attention due to its sensitive demonstration of the arrangement, structure, variability, and presentation. Drama scripted and enacted during the post-modern time frame exhibits the nature of welcoming and desiring to deal with the captious yet solvable issues. Undoubtedly, such issues have been treated with better graciousness as compared to the other genres such as Poetry, fiction, etc. Holding the dominant spirit, drama of this period has projected the courage to reject the myths and mystic elements to a certain extent by embracing dauntless narrative as well as dramatic techniques. In a way, Postmodernism rejects pre-designed and pre-defined theories or concepts by allowing the intense concerns containing chaos, fluidity and multiplicity. Indeed, simultaneously, it pleads for conflicting multiple philosophical perspectives and ideologies in order to facilitate the unidentified solutions to the prevailing intense and unaddressed issues.

The contemporary playwrights have given a new orientation to Indian Drama by mirroring postmodern society in their plays. Dattani is one of them who carries innovative techniques and unique understanding to present the delicate emotions and plight of the deprived class of modern Indian society. Dattani portrays postmodernist tendencies through the themes of taboo relationships and homosexuality in his plays "On a Muggy Night in Mumbai," "Bravely Fought the Queen," and "Do the Needful" and thus ascends as a humanist bringing forth the trauma and distress experienced by these stigmatized sects of society. His plays are an amalgam of the traditional outlook and the contemporary culture. He revolutionized the genre by adapting various new techniques and has never projected a single sign of hesitation in defying harmful social and moral conventions for the sake of art. Dattani has dealt with the most sensitive and delicate issues of the country like India which has been led by orthodox traditions, and stringent conventions. Nevertheless, through the advocated social change in his plays, Dattani could break the chain of conventional norms by impressing the lawmakers to rethink and eventually the legal rights of homosexuals were revised on 6 September 2018 by the honorable Supreme Court of India. In the prestigious Newspaper of India, the head of the news was written as *Gay sex is not a crime,' says Supreme Court in historic judgment* and stated below were the key highlights of the news by the same newspaper:

- The Delhi HC in 2009 decriminalized sex between consenting adults of the same gender
- This 2009 judgement was overturned in 2013 by the SC which then also dismissed a review plea
- In 2017, the SC said privacy is a fundamental right, which opened the door for fresh pleas to familiarizing gay sex

Exposing Social and Cultural Rigidity

According to Aristotle, art is mimetic in nature as it replicates the society. The impact of culture on literature and its genres is unquestionable as it inevitably has a profound role in shaping the attitudes, actions and behavior of the people towards orthodox beliefs in particular societies. The reflection of the post modernistic tendencies is visible in the contemporary literature throughout the world. The behavioural patterns, interactions and mental constructs learned through the process of socialization forms the culture. The definition of culture which is acceptable by many sociologists given by Edward B. Tylor, the founding father of social anthropology is as follows: "Culture, or civilization, 'taken in its wide ethnographic sense, is that complex whole which includes knowledge, beliefs, art, morals, law, custom, and any other capabilities and habits acquired by man as a member of society" (Culture-def., Study.com).

Culture is the distinctive aspect that gives recognition and entity to any social group. It incorporates all acquired behaviours, etiquette, beliefs, knowledge, and norms and values including attitudes, dress and languages, etc. Culture means the aspects of social life that are ideal. It includes artistic, philosophical, the inherited arte-facts, ideas, habits and values, knowledge and belief, law, morals, customs, and all other capabilities and habits acquired by men as members of society. It also includes languages, ideas, customs, taboos, codes, institutions, rituals, ceremonies, symbols, and images. Thus, culture is a complex whole that dictates the cultivation of certain values in the social groups which society should abide by. In a way, without culture, any social group would face an identity crisis as culture promotes a sense of belongingness among the people of the same social group thereby developing a sense of affinity and social brotherhood.

Dattani's plays reveal the cultural diversity of modern India. The postmodern touch in his works sensitizes the readers or audience towards the hidden layers prevailing in the present society through the portrayal of his characters not only in a unique way but also as an actual representation of society. All the characters have their peculiar way of elegance in their echoes and reactions, they are with different mental conditions, sentiments and ideas, desires and objectives, strengths and weaknesses, basic morals and social questions as well as individual quandaries.

The voice of homosexuals was heard for the very first time in the history of Indian English theatre through Dattani's plays, especially the ones taken up here. The damaged psyche of those people is handled and exposed intensely in both plays. It is beyond our belief that these homosexuals would ever be accepted by the Indian society due to which they face trauma and also fear being exposed as homosexuals. These pathetic emotions have been captured realistically in these two plays. President and Founder of the Christian Apologetics and Research Ministry, Matt Slick feels his concern to write on the subject as: "Homosexuals want others in society to accept them as normal people with normal sexual behavior patterns. They are working hard to change moral, social, and political opinion to be more in line with what they want. They are not content to be by themselves. They want others to accept them as a philosophically, morally, and ideologically valid. They want to change the opinions of people. In short, they want to change society. Therefore, it is necessary to write about something that can so drastically affect the moral fabric of this country" (Matt Slick. CARM).

Although homosexuality is thought to be an aberration, it is rampant in every society. It is not immediately obvious because they live in a fear of revealing their sexual orientation. They know that when they come out with their true identities they face the dangers of isolation, physical and emotional violence. Their family members are forced to abandon their children or face ostracization themselves. The deviant sexual personalities in Dattani's "On a Muggy Night in Mumbai" lead a life of suppression, which affects their attitude in all spheres of life. The following lines from the play "On a Muggy Night in Mumbai" represent their mindset, their original relationships and the conflict that they face trying to adjust to in a society which is hostile to them.

Deepali. If you were a woman, we would be in love.

Kamlesh. If you were a man, we would be in love.

> Deepali. If we were heterosexual, we would be married.
> (*Collected Plays I:* 65)

Homosexuality is being normalized in Western countries but not without a bitter fight. In India homosexuals are marginalized and lead lives of quiet desperation. The following lines aptly depict the struggle by most of the Dattani's characters in the play to survive in the rigid, narrow minded social milieu of India. Hence, when Bunny tells Ranjit that he could leave the country because he was ashamed of being Indian. Ranjit responds that he is sometimes regretful being Indian and gay is not an option in India where traditional values are strictly adhered to.

> Bunny. Why don't you go back to England or wherever if you are ashamed to be here?
> Ranjit. Buggery do! I will be where I want to be, thank you.
> Bunny. You can leave the country, but you can never run away from being brown. You are ashamed of being Indian.
> Ranjit. That's really rich coming from a closet homosexual like you! Yes, I am sometimes regretful of being an Indian, because I can't seem to be both Indian and gay. But you are simply ashamed. All this sham is to cover up your shame. (*Collected Plays I:* 88)

The subject has been differently treated in "Bravely Fought the Queen" in which the character Nitin, a homosexual, is depicted in a very dominating style in contrast with the submissive homosexual characters in "On Muggy night in Mumbai." The Play deals with the modern Indian family and the plots revolve around the various emotional, financial and sexual complexities faced by the members of the family as it is about the battles being fought among the members of the same family at home. Jiten and Nitin the two brothers are the joint owners of an advertising agency who are married to two sisters Dolly and Alka, respectively. "Bravely fought the Queen" exposes the double standards prevailing in the society where women are projected to be esteemed but originally they are not only treated as a commodity by the males but also harassed by them.

As a consequence of homosexual relationships between Nitin (Alka's husband) and Praful (Alka's brother), Alka is doubly victimized. On the one hand, both her relationships i.e. married and brother-sister are staked and on the other hand, she experiences unbearable trauma as a result of such stigmatized indulgence. Both her brother and her husband ill-treat her for no evident reasons in order to camouflage their own guilt. Due to the cold marital relationship Alka resorts to drinking.

History is replete with similar cases like in the case of the famous Indian prince, Manvendra, who is the son and probable heir of the Maharaja of Rajpipla in Gujarat. He is the first openly gay prince in the world and he discusses the trauma faced by him in his own words about his marriage: "I thought that after marriage everything will be all right, that with a wife, I will have children and become "normal" and then I will be at peace. I was struggling and striving to be "normal." I never knew and nobody told me that I was gay and [that] this itself is normal and it will not change. That this is what is called homosexuality and it is not a disease. I tremendously regret for ruining (Chandrika's) life. I feel guilty, but I simply did not know better." ("Talk")

In Indian society, it is very difficult for society to accept such a homosexual psyche and different natural attributes. From the societal perspective, a person refusing to step into matrimony could be escapism from the liabilities of marriage but the actual reality behind this behavior could be homosexual tendencies that are beyond their comprehension or imagination. Hence, to fulfill the desires of the family members and society they have to indulge themselves in marital relationships and the inevitable result is the failure of such marriages which leads to lifelong trauma and pain for everyone involved. In one of the interviews with *Pink Pages*, India's most influential person Ashok Row Kavi when questioned about the most disappointed part of him being homosexual reacted thus: "What has left me most disappointed is the nastiness and malafide intentions of some of our own community members. If I find someone has purposefully hurt me, I usually pretend that the person doesn't exist but sometimes, one is forced to hit back because they do not allow you to live your life peacefully and then you have to stand up and fight. That's what hurts; human beings are cruel and callous to their own kind." (Interview on Pink Pages)

This is the strength of Mahesh Dattani that he places the same relation (Brother and sister) with two different angles in "Bravely Fought the Queen" and "On a Muggy Night in Mumbai." In "Bravely Fought the Queen" Alka is victimized by her own brother and on the other hand Kiran is getting all securities and pampering from her brother Kamlesh in "On a Muggy Night in Mumbai." This contrast is beautifully portrayed by Mahesh Dattani, a contemporary writer, who has showcased his imagination interestingly and captivatingly by crafting his subjects and characters according to the demands of the plot of the plays. It is not less than a surprise for both the reader and the audience that a single mind has defined the same relationship with two different viewpoints in almost similar conditions in the play. The words of Nitin (Alka's husband) reveal the true depiction of the relationship of Alka and Praful and how her brother betrayed her by keeping his homosexual relations with her husband behind her back:

> He tricked you too, didn't he? How can you still love your brother after what he did to you? . . . At other times I would lean forward to look at him. Close enough for my breath to fall gently on his face. And he would open his eyes. . . . I loved him too. He is . . . was attractive. And he responded. (*Collected Plays I*, 314)

On the other hand, the following lines gives the glimpse of the caring and affectionate bond of the brother and sister relationship in "On a Muggy Night in Mumbai."

> Kamlesh. I Just couldn't. You were so happy with him. I just could not take that away from you!

Kiran. And yet you did.

Deepali. He loves Ed, that is true. But he cared for you enough to let you marry Ed. Can't you see that? (*Collected Plays* 107)

It is quite evident that insecurity and uncertainty for the future lead a person's life towards violence and ferocity which we have observed through the characters of the above-discussed plays. Dattani's plays thrust for justice and equality in society for all the marginalized sections of society. He evokes the sensitivity of the readers towards all the tabooed topics by placing them for their attention and acceptance. "On a Muggy Night in Mumbai" talks about homosexuality in an open climate on the contrary to the camouflaged treatment of such a sensitive issue which society feels even hesitant to discuss openly. This play breaks the secrecy and unlocks this marginalized culture of homosexuals and their lifestyles. The deprived existence of homosexuals in the dominating presence of heterosexuals and the struggle to live with their real identity as homosexuals is the major theme of the play.

Narrative Strategies

Barbara Hardy defines it as a primary act of mind and she observes that we dream in narrative, remember, anticipate, hope, despair, believe, doubt, plan, revise, criticize, construct, gossip, learn, hate and love by narrative (31). Narratives encompass most of the activities of human beings and its simple meaning is anything that tells a story. According to D. C. Dennet: "Human selves are centers of narrative gravity since humans are programmed to extrude narratives as naturally as spider's spin webs or beavers build dams" (Nair 7).

A narrative technique is additionally known all the more intently for literary fictional narratives as an insightful technique, artistic device, or anecdotal device are some of the strategies, the author of a narrative uses to pass on what they intend to. Finally, a technique is utilized as a part of the making of a narrative to pass on information to the readers and audience. It is especially used to "build up" the narrative, typically keeping in mind the end goal to make the literary piece of art more outright, multifaceted, appealing and engaging as well. Literary techniques are distinguished from literary elements, which exist inherently in works of writing.

Postmodern narrative strategies include mainly non-adherence to any fixed technique. It takes up all types of registers besides the use of resources from different languages and cultures. Postmodern narratives, therefore, have no problem banking upon intertextuality in a big way. In fact, this is something that has always been there; only postmodern literature displays the confidence to own it. In this context, it would be fruitful to cite the intertextuality underlined by Jagdish Batra in his essay "The Shavian Sub-text in Mahesh Dattani's 'Dance Like a Man,'" wherein he juxtaposes Ratna, Dattani's heroine of the aforesaid play, with Raina, the heroine of the play *The Arms and the Man* by the renowned dramatist George Bernard Shaw: "What underlines true Shavianism is the mental make-up of Ratna, who can be classed as a typical Shavian heroine. Through this character, Dattani has also shattered the stereotyped image of woman" (Batra 217).

In stagecraft too, we find postmodern leanings. In the play "On a Muggy Night in Mumbai," Dattani uses postmodern techniques. Known for his inventions in the area of stagecraft, Dattani makes use of a multi-level stage to represent different spaces of Kamlesh's household and the different mental spaces of characters.

Another postmodern feature that marks Dattani's plays is the use of different linguistic registers. To lend a realistic touch to the play, he uses Hindi or other languages without any hesitation to couch dialogues in the character's native language: *Mere kuch dost ane wale hain. Tum unkoanadena. Tum to pehchante ho subko* (CPI 50). His preference and craving for the original and natural milieu for his plays makes him stand apart from the other contemporary writers. The usage of Hindi language or any other native language spoken by his characters are very lucid, articulate and striking. The most conspicuous element in Dattani's characters is that they use the English language which is neither stilled, nor antiquated, nor awkwardly coordinated but directed just towards a sophisticated group of people. Dattani has beautifully presented the regional utterance at the beginning of the play when Kamlesh talks to the guard and gives him money to buy some snacks and drinks for his friends. Dattani tries to show the emotions of Kamlesh in the language convenient for the guard to understand and complements the situation in the following conversation:

> Kamlesh. Tum, kya . . . yeh sab . . . paise ke liye karte ho?
> Guard. Hahn! Hahn, main paise ke liye hi to karta hoon sab kuch! . . . (a little nervously) Ab main jaon? . . . Duty chalu hai, saab. Secretary daantenga mujhe. (*Collected Plays I*: 51)

Dattani has done again justice by opting for regional language similarly, in "Do the Needful," when the servant boy Mali speaks in Tamil language in the play: "Akka! Latakka! (To Alpesh.) Why is she crying? Why did she run away? (*Collected Plays I:* 151)

Another brilliant narrative characteristic of Dattani's play is the use of cross dialogues to find the answer to the raised queries though the question asked between the two characters at different locations are answered by the conversation between two other characters in another part of the stage. In "Bravely Fought the Queen," Sridhar, Nitin and Jiten are together in the office and their questions are answered by the comments made by Baa, Dolly and Lalitha who are sighted in the house. Baa's refusal is brought out in the following dialogue when Jiten plans to sell the ancestral house:

> Nitin. That's where we grew up. BAA. Why should I not? It is my money!
> Nitin. Too many memories.
> Jiten. Sentimental fool. BAA. Mine! Every paisa is mine! Mine from my father!

> Nitin. It—it belongs to Daksha. Maybe we should do it up and all live there. BAA. This is my house! My house!
>
> (*Collected Plays I*: 277-78)

Through this very specific feature of coherently connecting the dialogues of various characters delivering their dialogues in different settings and different contexts promoting meaningful progress in the play, Dattani has portrayed his linguistic ability to justify this narrative strategy. The usage of utterances in various regional languages such as Hindi, Gujrati, Tamil, etc. exhibits his command over the multiple languages, effectively utilized to render an intense role in bringing the real image of the everyday language exchanges used by the characters as per their social status. For example, Kamlesh, the character in "On the Muggy Night in Mumbai" speaks in Hindi language with the guard who in reality is not expected to converse in English language. Similarly, Dattani has shown the conversation between the gardener and the character Lata in "Do the Needful" in Tamil language as English-speaking Mali would be a rare sight in the Indian society. Dattani has given a real portrayal of the linguistic usage in a country like India with diverse languages thereby removing the element of artificiality in the dialogues of the play. Dattani being a playwright surely not the initiator who encourages the elements of irony and humor in his writing but could be considered the pioneer of bringing out the toughest situation

As submitted before, postmodernism does not stick to any particular style. It also includes modernist techniques like symbolism as it does not lend itself directly to the portrayal of reality. Symbolism is used to explain thoughts, notions and emotions to readers through an object beyond its literal sense. It can be characterized as the specialty of communicating thoughts and feelings neither by portraying them straightforwardly nor by characterizing them through unmistakable correlations with solid pictures, yet by proposing what these thoughts and feelings are, by re-making them in the psyche of the readers using unexplained symbols. This aspect may be called the personal aspect.

Through the symbolic representation, he tries to represent the unrepresentable. The symbol of 'bonsai' has aptly been used by Dattani in "Bravely Fought the Queen" to demonstrate the stunted development of females in the male-centric society. The lives of the female characters namely Alka, Dolly and Lalitha in the play are quite the same as that of the bonsai. Aṣha Kuthari Chaudhuri appropriately comments: The stunted growth, the bizarre shape, the grotesque reality of the bonsai becomes resonant in the existence of all the characters that people the play (54). The emblematic introduction of bonsai uncovers the psyche of a power-ridden society towards women. Dattani through the dialogues of Lalitha has symbolically portrayed the confined space and opportunities for women which hinders their growth and progress in the following lines:

> You stunt their growth. You keep trimming the roots and bind their branches with wire and . . . Stunt them. . . . You've got to make sure the roots don't have enough space to spread. You still have to keep trimming them as they grow. . . . You can shape their branches into whatever shape you want—by pinching or wiring the shoots (*Collected Plays I*: 244-46).

The process of stunting a potential tree which can acquire full growth into a bonsai and confining women in gender roles and allotting them a position in family and society is not much different from it. Similarly, the way we follow to grow bonsais, women too are not exposed to enjoy a life free of all restrictions and compulsions. They are denied to flourish by gaining exposure from various means of learning and acquiring knowledge leading to emancipatory opportunities. Trimming the foundations of bonsais symbolize the curbing the potential intellectual growth by depriving them of their basic qualifications, intellectual independence and equality in society It also symbolizes the change of place the females encounter after marriage from their parents' home to their in-laws home and their exclusion from parental properties, are the striking features of Dattani's characters as well as the distinguishing characteristics of his sensational dramatic art. The changes and movements of the work are closely related to the stream of consciousness technique. This tool encourages the playwright to exhibit the twisted and fragmented pictures of life. In his plays, it is tactfully designed in the way thought process moves back and forth in time.

Conclusion

The analytical study of the three plays viz. "On a Muggy Night in Mumbai," "Bravely Fought the Queen" and "Do the Needful" by Dattani, endeavours to expose the sufferings and the hardships faced by homosexuals. They are boycotted and rejected by the heterosexual society for their variant sexual orientation against the social and cultural mandates. Dattani has realistically portrayed the struggle faced by the characters Kamlesh, Sharad and Prakash in the play "On a Muggy Night in Mumbai," Nitin in the play "Bravely Fought the Queen" and Alpesh in "Do the Needful" through their real-life situations. They are forced to live a life of alienation and seclusion which further fragments the society into different classes and categories thereby staking its harmony and togetherness.

In these three plays, Dattani handles the delicate issue of homosexuality in a sensitive manner by exposing the ill effects of the demeaning treatment towards them. It has been observed how the characters who follow a different sexual orientation suffer in modern Indian society. Dattani advocates for the fundamental rights to respect and dignity of homosexuals rather than mercy and sympathy shown towards them by an extremely judgmental society. Through the play "Bravely Fought the Queen" and "Do the Needful." Dattani throws light on the mandatory ritual of marriage between heterosexuals. The parents are forced by the cultural set of rules to settle their children in a heterosexual alliance without taking into consideration their sexual orientation. Depression, anxiety, violence and domestic scuffles are the obvious outcomes of these twisted and warped relationships which have been portrayed through the character Nitin in the play "Bravely Fought the Queen." Likewise, great pressure is created on the character Alpesh in "Do the Needful" for settling down into a marriage for the second time.

This brings out the additional stress borne by homosexuals. Dattani brings out the trauma encountered by homosexuals due to their vacillating identity as they are forced to pose as 'straight' in order to gain acceptance in society. Due to the fear of facing the stigma of being a homosexual they lack the courage to reveal their real identity. They unwillingly get into heterosexual marriages resulting in marital discord further complicating their lives. Dattani voices out for the acceptance of homosexuality in society without any stigma, so that homosexuals, who otherwise feel ashamed and tormented, can also become contributing members of society if they can lead a stress-free life. For the want of dignity and respect the homosexual character Ed/Prakash in "On a Muggy Night in Mumbai" crumbles down. Due to the fear of the revelation of the fact that he is a homosexual (who is posing to be a heterosexual) Prakash develops the unbearable feeling of guilt, shame and hatred towards himself to the extent that he attempts suicide.

Dattani could be described as a revolutionary playwright in that he treats the otherwise tabooed subjects in strikingly bold and uncanny idiom intending to alert society to the trauma and discrimination these so called non-normal humans experience in the society of normal humans. He analyses their problems from the social, cultural, and psychological point of view and pleads for their respectable place in society. His protagonists belong to no specific class, section, belief and philosophy, nevertheless, they own a strong and firm class and emerge as an inseparable section of society, possessing high values and beliefs. Dattani demands the revision in a conventional social and cultural milieu so as to secure them their due dignity. The bold treatment of such controversial issues has earned him the title of Social Activist advocating for lending dignity to the victims of discrimination on account of being 'different' as per the accepted socio-ethical parameters.

Works Cited

Batra, Jagdish. "The Shavian Heroine of Mahesh Dattani's Dance Like a Man." *The Critical Endeavour*, Vol. XVI, 2010, pp 216-225.

Dattani, Mahesh. *Collected Plays*. 2 vols. New Delhi: Penguin, 2000, 2005.

"Gay sex is not a crime,' says Supreme Court in historic judgment." *The Times of India*, 6 Sep. 2018. Web. < https://timesofindia.indiatimes.com/india/gay-sex-is-not-a-crime-says-supreme-court-in-historic-judgement/articleshow/65695172.cms >

Hardy, Barbara. "Towards Poetics of Fiction: An Approach Through Narrative." Towards A Poetics of Fiction. Ed. Mark Spilka. Bloomington: Indiana University Press, 1977.31.

Logan, Peter Melville. "On Culture: Edward B. Tylor's Primitive Culture, 1871." BRANCH: Britain, Representation and Nineteenth-Century History, ed. Dino Franco Felluga. Extension of Romanticism and Victorianism on the Net. Web. 18 Aug. 2021.

Nair, Rukmini B. *Narrative Gravity: Conversation, Cognition, Culture*. Routledge, 2003.7.

Pink Page. *Indias Most Influential Gays and Lesbians Ashok Row Kavi*. <https://pink-pages.co.in/features/indias-most-influential-gays-and-lesbians-ashok-row-kavi/>

Slick, Matt. "Why write about homosexuality?" *CARM*. N.d. n.p. <http://carm.org/write-about-homsexuality.>

"Talk- Manvendra Sigh Gohil." *Wikipedia*. 15 Jan. 2018. https://en.wikipedia.org/wiki/Manvendra_Singh_Gohil

Paranoia through Media in the Dystopian Societies of *Nineteen Eighty-Four* and *Oryx and Crake*

R. JAYA PRATHA
V.V. Vanniaperumal College for Women, Virudhunagar

Gerard Manley Hopkins in his poem "God's Grandeur" "Generations have trod, have trod, have trod." Together with the blemishes of colonization trauma and the warfare cues from the past, we have stepped into the postmodern era. In the matter of the 21st century, scientific and technological advances play a mighty role in shaping human evolution and in transforming human survival strategies. People are used to both the comfort and dismay sequenced by the surges and urges of science and technology. The changing modes of survival also contribute to the changing human behaviorism, psychology, wants, and needs. In this 21st century, every scientific innovation has become our everyday modus operandi. We, humans govern the media and media engage the population.

Media in Contemporary Culture

Throughout history, the human population has enjoyed the privileged varied forms of connectivity and communications. In the 20th and 21st centuries, the domination of media and technology became the everyday culture. It has expanded beyond what we might have guessed in the previous eras. Any guidance, instruction, information, communication, persuasion, suggestion, and even manipulation happens through the varied forms of media. Media has the power to break the boundaries and crack the limitations that prevail at reaching the global audience. On one hand, this media and technology make human survival so advanced, rational, and knowledgeable. On the other hand, it triggers a sense of insecurity and doubtfulness towards the concrete notion of survival. The major concern of today's media is its hypnotic tendencies, say, the manipulation of human consciousness and the imposed mutation on human survival strategies through the wide and overt scale of exposure.

Communication technology has evolved across the globe through telephone, radio, press, digital, and electronic gadgets, which are now taking a huge turn as 'media.' Though viewed as a part of entertainment and infotainment, media works as a pool for the circulation of ideologies, creating a survival space for propagation. The philosophies of the 1960s and 1970s relate the evolution of media with the revolutions caused by politics, capitalism, and social hierarchies. On the scale of cultural imperialism, the developed nations employed media as a tool to reach the developing. Soon media got its monstrous surge in the contemporary societal space, disconnecting humans from their traditional survival modes of the past. Providing every sort of supplementation and substitution, the media facilitates an interconnected global sphere, enlightened and entertained in multiple ways. One can ogle the disconnection from the traditional way of existence caused by the media and technology as both a boon and a bane.

Culture and history keep on switching and so are the innovations and existence mechanisms are. Media has created a culture of effective interaction, wider expression, mutual interdependency, and greater exposure. Apart from the media appealing to the mass audience, the power of media in influencing one's private sphere is also comparatively the strongest. With the world which is projected through media, an individual, as well as the society, gets a chance of perception. Through those entities, we embark on a survival mode to adapt. He creates his set of beliefs and explores his sense of reality through the choices provided by these driving forces. One comes to understand his sense of being in the present, the past, and the history only under the projection, either as restored documentation or as exposed perceptions. Media not only provides easy access to information, knowledge, and entertainment but also creates a survival space for propagation. With the varying assets such as e-learning applications, face detection features, surveillance mechanisms, gadget innovations, and artificial intelligence, we endure an entirely newer way of life and subsistence. As a whole, media functions as a "cultural socialization agent" with renewed survival stabilizing features.

Dystopian Science Fiction

When 'dystopia' hints at a place of suffering, dystopian fiction hints at fictional suffering setting empowered with totalitarianism, a dictatorship regime, surveillance threatening the basic human rights, abusive science and technology influences, and many more horrendous threads. The novel *Nineteen Eighty-Four,* written by George Orwell, features a dystopian society named Oceania, that works under a totalitarian regime and their continuous surveillance. Any persecution of the rules laid by the ruling party is condemned to brutal punishment. The violation of rules and the sequential punishments are the common actants of any civilization, but what constitutes the dystopia in the novel is the survival threat posed by the ruling power. The concepts such as 'thoughtcrime,' 'facecrime' and 'doublethink' deny the fundamental rights of humans for freedom, thought, and expression. Being a suppressed passive population, the people of Oceania adapt to the imposed way of life. What makes them so passive other than the punishment are the ideologies that propagate in Oceania through the doors of documentaries, media, and technology. Oceania is under the constant surveillance of the inner party, which as a whole, operates under Big Brother.

Under such surveillance, the thoughts, facial expressions, and actions are recorded and whenever they differ from the principles of Big Brother, the suspected are subjected to punishment and reformation. In addition to this, the media projects Big brother as their only hope and faith, symbolizing the figure of 'Big Brother' as the only supreme force with 'divine rights.' The documentaries and other materials about the history of Oceania are rewritten and altered to ensure only the strength and success of Oceania and Big Brother. It is a society where the population is conditioned in such a way to accept whatever the authority imposes and the authority imposed only an optimistic ideology that Big Brother and Inner Party are powerful of all. More than exercising their fundamental rights as human beings, all inhabitants of Oceania have offered their survival right to the party, combined with their dedication, sincerity, and due respect to Big Brother without interpretations or questions.

The novel *Oryx and Crake* offers a prognosis on the possibility of a future apocalypse, exploring the ecological destruction under a fictional dystopian setting. Before the apocalypse, the survival place is divided into three different regions based on the hierarchical status. Compounds are the location destined for people from higher status and Pheeblands are for people from lower status. In between are the Modules. The Compounds are provided with high security, complete surveillance, material benefits, and careful observation, whereas Pheeblands, lacking any security, remains a home for diseases and pathogens to reproduce, grow and propagate. All these pre-apocalyptic survival modes are recalled by the character named Snowman, who is the sole survivor of the apocalypse. As a result, the human population is wiped out, while a new population named 'Crakers' blooms. Snowman, whose real name is Jimmy in the pre-apocalyptic world, hints at the uncontrollable ecological demolition and the growth of destructive human materialistic desires of his time.

Dystopian fiction, being the genre that projects the possibility of a diabolic future, strikes hard at the contemporary flaws and faults, which we are passively enduring. Both the novels, *Nineteen*

Eighty-Four and *Oryx and Crake,* clearly illustrate the contemporary foibles and the existing fears of the masses. Primarily, postmodernism explores the tenets of anti-authoritarianism and science as 'hegemonic attempts' under the set conventions of socio-political constructs. These tenets form the frames in the dystopian genre, especially in the select novels, *Nineteen Eighty-Four* and *Oryx and Crake.* Acknowledging both knowledge and facts as futile elements of human existence, postmodernism highlights the paradox, chaos as well as shackles rooting from the scientific and political ideologies.

Postmodernism rejects objectivity and so the history as it can be viewed only at an objective tenet. Accordingly, an unstable historical matrix is projected in both novels. In *Nineteen Eighty-Four,* the totalitarian regime of Oceania alters the history and happenings as per the regime's needs and wants. The eradication of the historical past, the rejection of the existing bitter documentaries by throwing them in 'memoryholes,' and the cultivation of an admirable history for Oceania are all processed by the 'Ministry of Truth.' Those who are disliked by the party are turned into an 'unperson' by the authority, where the memory about the 'unperson' ceases to exist from the society. A similar stance occurs in *Oryx and Crake,* through the monstrous surge in consumerism. People before the apocalypse lived unconscious of their destructive scientific urges and usages which ultimately destroyed the entire civilization. Postmodernism views science as an entity that cannot claim any 'universal applicability.'

The stance is supported as the science in the pre-apocalyptic world in *Oryx and Crake,* turned nil in the post-apocalyptic world. The paradox and the fragmentation, which are emphasized in postmodernist literature, extend both to the communities and the individuals portrayed in the said novels. The novels project a fragmented world where the established morals, thoughts, beliefs, and values are rejected, and a new range of survival methodologies are revived as per the momentary needs. Moreover, the characters in the novel are seeking a perfect utopia and utopian happiness while all together they get avenged by the dystopian realities. The truth holds no values in the depicted societies, where what they have known, understood, and possessed as knowledge previously turned the contrast in the aftermath. In both the novels, technology, media, and science attempt to eliminate the concept of culture and history, thereby establishing a stronger sense of politics and control. Hyperreality has a major turn in dystopian societies as the protagonists suffer their consciousness while tracing the tracks of both reality and simulation. In both the novels, science and technology dominate the society, manipulates the population, separates them from history, and establishes new ideologies and strategies to cope up.

Paranoid Anxieties

The contemporary world is dominated by media and technology and similar are the stances in the dystopian novels. In the dystopian society called Oceania, media and technology rule the world. The prime authoritative figure, Big Brother could be seen only through the media and pictures. By sensing the omnipresence of Big Brother everywhere, set through the media and technology, the protagonist Winston Smith suffers paranoia. Winston Smith remains odd out of the entire population, being able to sense what the reality is and what the simulacrum is. He senses and survives the continuous fear and anxiety caused by paranoia, where it is a state of mind imparted consciously by the totalitarian regime. It is a strategy regulated by the party to keep the population in control of their activities and thoughts. When everyone in Oceania strived to keep their actions and thoughts as per the expectations of the party, Winston deviated from the 'statistics.' He committed all the actions that are restricted by the party including facecrime, thoughtcrime, and doublethink, knowing very well that some day or other he would be interrupted by the party. Orwell, who survived the horrors of world war and its aftermath, creates a parallel tension of fear and anxiety in his dystopian fiction under the political context.

The surveillance technology, which got its acceleration during the 20th century, was initially used for the supervision and spying of weapons. George Orwell's depiction of the usage of mass surveillance technologies is not strange to contemporary society. More than just surveillance, all these mechanisms take a chance in regulating the collective mentality of humans, conditioning them for political benefit. In the context of war and aftermath, the media and influence had a major effect on the population during the early 20th century, which in turn is reflected by George Orwell with a futuristic imagination towards the year 1984.

In the novel *Oryx and Crake,* the paranoid fear through media is paralleled with science and technological advancements. Jimmy experiences paranoia as a result of his survival in compounds. Jimmy is the one grown-up in modules who got a chance to move into compounds, where the enormous materialistic pursuits are provided under surveillance and scrutiny. He encounters paranoid anxieties whenever the surveillance agencies, 'the corpsecorps,' approached him in the name of inquiry, as everything they said threatened Jimmy beyond the factual entity. Jimmy's mother, Sharon escaped the Compound as she too suffered paranoia amid the horrors, materialism, and espionage. Media access in the pre-apocalyptic society exerted an authority on its population, familiarizing and easing them with what are considered bizarre in the contemporary context.

The brutality done to animals in the name of scientific experiments, the tight security across privacy in the name of safety measures, and the unrealistic reality which Jimmy's mother mentioned as 'vile,' made her experience a worse paranoia, making her run away from the reality. It haunts the Compounds more than Pheeblands, as people are driven into a state of paranoia together with the scientific cold wars and industrial baffles. Anyone who is opposing the notions of the corporate authorities is eventually 'eliminated' from society. Jimmy sees the world only through the eyes of media and technology, about how manipulated the people are and how untrustworthy the things are. The exposure to violent media, pornography, gaming, and addiction without restrictions cultivated a sense of social paranoia but equally exerted passion and trust on science and technological advancements. The repeated exposure to the subjective survival and the lingering addiction towards technology and materialistic pursuits, attempt the best to rid off the existential anxieties among the population, except for the few who could realize the dystopian nature of their residing societies.

Conclusion

"The paranoid is never entirely mistaken," says Sigmund Freud. Paranoia is a state of mind probably associated with the unhealthy psychology of people. But studying paranoia in the backdrop of the societal frameworks provides a wider insight into the drive of human survival and consciousness. Literature explores paranoia through an epistemological understanding of social constructs and survival context. The novels offer a dystopian climate but they are not so far from the contemporary stances. We can analyze our sense of paranoia in the frames of cultural groups and the collective society. There exists a reiteration effect about the limited choices of survival, conditioned passivity, and trained dependency among the societies of *Oryx and Crake* and *Nineteen Eighty-Four,* making it a mere dystopia. It occurs in the midst of an individual's attempt to fit somewhere in the advanced global spaces. More than a psychological condition, paranoia is an alert to sense through the falsities and vile deviations of our existence. The delusion and distrust embarked today's survival is rooted in the active entities of technology and materialism, and when it outdates nature's limitations, the 'vile' soars.

Works Cited

Atwood, Margaret. *Oryx and Crake*. Virago Press, London. 2003.

Orwell, George. *Nineteen Eighty-Four*. Penguin, London. 1949.

Baker C., Crawford P., Brown B.J., Lipsedge M., Carter R. *Madness in Post-1945 British and American Fiction.* Palgrave Macmillan, London. 2010. https://doi.org/10.1057/ 9780230290440_6

Best, Steven, Douglas Kellner. *Postmodern Theory: Critical Interrogations*. Macmillan, 1991.

Butler, Christopher. *Post Modernism: A Very Short Introduction*. Oxford University Press, 2002.

Bywater, William. "The Paranoia of Postmodernism." *Philosophy and Literature*, 14: 1, 1990, pp. 79-84. Project MUSE, doi: 10.1353/phl.1990.0063.

Jameson, Frederick. *Post Modernism or The Cultural Logic of Late Capitalism.* Durham: Duke University Press. 1991.

Matos, C. "Globalization and the mass media." *Encyclopedia of Globalization*. Oxford: Wiley-Blackwell, 2012.

Trauma of Diasporic Double Displacement in M.G. Vassanji's *No New Land*

RAVITA
Ph.D. Scholar, SRM University, Sonipat, Haryana

The term "Diaspora" refers to the dispersal of people from an original homeland, often traumatically. It also presents movement from the homeland in search of work or trade or forced migration due to compelling factors . It presents a strong ethnic group consciousness sustained over a long period of time and often a troubled relationship with host society. It also shows a sense of solidarity with co-ethnic members in other countries and the possibility of a distinctive creative, enriching life in tolerant host country. Generally, diasporic literature deals with alienation, displacement, nostalgia and quest for identity. It also addresses issues like amalgamation or disintegration of cultures. It reflects the immigrant experience that comes out of the immigrant settlement. Mostly, the migrants seem to suffer from the pain of being far away from their homeland, the memories of their homeland, and the anguish of leaving behind everything familiar agonizes their minds. William Safran observed that, "They continue to relate personally or vicariously, to the homeland in a way or another, and their ethnic communal consciousness and solidarity are importantly defined by the existence of such a relationship" (Safran 84). The feeling of rootlessness, alienation, confusion, nostalgia, dislocation and suffering due to discrimination on the basis of race, culture, religion and language concludes into conflicts, fight for identity and leads to the birth of feeling of marginality in the minority diasporic group which results in the creation of a fractured identity. They maintain a memory about their homeland and also believe that they are not and perhaps cannot be fully accepted by the host society.

Moyez G. Vassanji raises some of these issues through the portrayal of events and characters in his acclaimed novel *No New Land.* He is a Canadian novelist and editor, and a keen observer of lives caught between one world and the another. He has received considerable literary awards which include Commonwealth Writers Prize in 1990, Harbourfront Festival Prize (1994), Giller Prize (1994), The Governor General's Prize in 2009. Vassanji is described as the "most promising novelist" in South Asian Community. (Birbalsingh 102). He writes about the migration and displacement that took place in the African nations like Kenya and Tanzania. He was born in Kenya, brought up in Tanzania and studied in the United States before coming to Canada to settle there. So the sentiments of marginality and alienation are well infused by him in his characters as he himself is a victim of migration.

Diaspora Turns Immigrant

The novel *No New Land* presents how Indian immigrants struggle to find place in host countries such as Africa and Canada. It describes the agony of double migration of Shamsi community, "an Indian Muslim sect, the Shamsis, somewhat unorthodox, hence insecure." (13). Vassanji shows how the immigrants have no option except to keep on living on the alien land and discovering: "We are but creatures neither of our origins, and however stalwarts we march forward, paving new roads, seeking new worlds , the ghosts from our past stand not behind and are not easily shaken off." (9).

The members of this community made their first voyage to East Africa in the 19th century taken in by the British empire through their exploitative agreements with semi-skilled labour, small traders, and junior colonial functionaries. Since slavery had been abolished in Europe in 1833, the British colonizers thought of this alternative to hoodwink the ignorant Indians living in the Bihar, Bengal, western U.P. and other parts of the country. Some decades later, the girmitiyas, as these bonded labourers were known, were followed by small traders, mostly from Gujarat, who were enterprising people and established themselves in different parts of Africa. Mahatma Gandhi went to South Africa towards the close of the 19 century. He saw the rampant discrimination of black and brown-skinned people by the British rulers there, who also sowed the seeds of distrust among Africans towards Indians and made them believe that the Indian traders were exploiting them—a well-known strategy that they also adopted in India and brought about the Partition.

The result of this distrust was the second voyage of the Indian diaspora that began in the 1960s from the postcolonial Africa towards Europe and North America. So, this second wave of migration was caused because the South Asian community felt threatened with the rise of African nationalism. With the Black coming to the power, the era of the White domination came to an end. As Indian migrants didn't belong to either of the groups, neither White nor Black, they faced discrimination and were expelled out of the country.

The novel describes the hardships that the characters had to suffer while living in an alien city. When Lalani family was thrown out of Tanzania, they moved to Canada which was thought to be a land of hope with promising prospects. Roshan, the sister of Nurdin's wife, urges them to come to Canada. But when Nurdin, with his wife Zara, and their two children Hanif and Fatima, take a flight to London to reach Canada, the situation of Nurdin in the plane predicts the predicaments he has to face in Canada: "Goodness, was Canada going to be like this: every step a mystery and trap, fraught with belittling embarrassments, and people waiting to show you up." (32)

At London airport, the immigration officers shatter their dream to see London. At Toronto airport in Canada, Roshan and her husband receive the Lalanis. Roshan gives them a pack of chewing gum saying: "You'll want more. And you'll get it. This is Canada." (37). In fact, the chewing gum is symbolic of the problems that never come to an end. If you want to get rid of the chewing gum, you can't throw it out of your mouth. The Lalanis' abode in Toronto presents a microscopic view of Indian macrocosm in Canada. The very first experience of the overwhelming winter can be seen as the representation of cold and aloof behaviour of the host country. The snow that Nurdin and his family encounter on entering Canada becomes metonymic of otherness. The hostility of the weather anticipates that the place is going to cause alienation and isolation for Nurdin and his family. The dawning of pleasant feelings and exhilaration when one sets his foot in Canada installs an illusion that all the monetary differences might be shelved, but when people from developing countries like Africa and India enter here, they are welcomed by a series of negative experiences: "These are the first days and you hate yourself for arriving in winter. Braving the punishing cold, you beat the footpaths, searching for vacancies." (44).

In African city Dar-es-Salam, Nurdin had to face discrimination. He was neglected there for his fair complexion and realized that even the peons rose above him merely because of their black skin: "Peon, it seemed to Nurdin, rose above him merely because of their black skins. The Europeans had always been masters; their higher positions he had taken as a matter of course." (28)

Racism in Canada

In Canada too, he has to suffer due to racial discrimination. He hunts for the job and in spite of being qualified as a seller of shoes, he remains unemployed for a long time just because of having a different identity: "I am a salesman, I was a salesman. Just give me a chance. Why don't they understand we can do the job?" (44) The employers, however, have one simple way to reject him; they want "Canadian experience" which is the "trump they always call, against which you have no answer." (44). The discrimination is at its climax in the following observation:

> "I know I don't have Canadian experience," he breathed hotly and with emotion on the phone, "but how can I get Canadian experience if you don't give me a chance? I've sold shoes for eight years! Eight years-"
>
> "Perhaps you were overqualified, sir."
>
> "That was a new one. Overqualified. Good for laughs, and it got many." (48).

The horrible face of discrimination is visible in an incident that takes place in the subway tunnel in Canada. It shows that the discrimination rules the roost here too. At the tunnel three white youths attack Esmail, an Asian immigrant from Dar es Salaam. They joyfully abuse him and shout, "What do you have there, Paki? Hey, hey? Paki-paki-paki" (95-96). They push him in the stomach. The onlookers can't do anything among whom Nanji is also included. These three youths force their dominion over others. They think themselves superior because they are born white. This incident provokes the immigrants for agitation who later assemble at Esmail's residence. This incident forces them to think of their existence in Canada: "What now? Was this a sign of things to come danger to self and property, to wife and kids? Have we come to the right place after all?" (102). Once more They are bound to think of their existence: "The blacks kicked us out, now the whites will do the same. . . . Where do we go from here? (103).

Canada is a land of opportunities but at the same time becomes the place of cultural confusion and disconnection. People give much priority to the colour of the skin rather than the person. Nanji, a young immigrant professor, also suffers from racial discrimination. Often returning from the university by bus, Nanji sits alone on the seat. Many passengers remain standing but do not sit near him and all the way Nanji thinks about racism: "Racism, the word kept intruding into his mind and he kept pushing it back. On what basis racism? It could be my face, dark, brooding, scowling, cratered. Perhaps I look like a bum. Professor Nanji?" (93).

Nurdin's daughter Fatima gets admission in art and science instead of pharmacy, the prestigious one, and Nurdin is accused of raping a white girl. Fatima accepts her plight and decides that art and science was not so bad after all. But Nurdin has to face many problems in and out of the family. After this incident everyone was looking on him as a rapist without investigating him. The white lady Mrs. Broadbent refuses to serve him lunch and further adds: "Where he comes from, both his hands would be chopped off. (180).

Every one believed the girl just because she was white. Nurdin is suspended from work, booked, and finally his own family and community started looking at him suspiciously. This made Nurdin excessively enraged on the society where people give importance to race and colour. Only Romesh believed him who said: "I thought in this country a man was innocent until proved guilty."

Fellow Feeling Helps

But all is not as it seems. In the entire novel the reader can find that there is a thin layer between the reality and the appearance. Only two things bring happiness in Nurdin Lalani's life and other immigrants that are past memories and their own community people in host country. Their past memories are not only memories to them, but immigrants live and create their identities in these memories and changed their life. In the novel they narrate stories of their home to white Canadian friends hoping to counterbalance the negative portrayal of Indians to which they are exposed. Agnew writes: "There is not one imagined India but many and it is the differences in these imagined worlds that alienate and make immigrants feel that they do not belong here in Canada. Such feelings heighten their nostalgia for their cultures and lost "homes" in India." (Jayaram 17).

As a member of minority community, the life of immigrants depends on the fellow immigrants. The readers notice many such incidents when people survived only because of their fellow immigrants' support. When Esmail is attacked by three white Canadian boys, people took the incident seriously and protested. They also conducted protest march in streets. The following speech expresses their suffering very well:

> "The blacks kicked us out, now the whites will do the same. . . . Where do we go from here?"
>
> "Look like Pakistan for us."
>
> "There are worse goons there. Did you hear of two murders?"
>
> A woman cut in impatiently. "Why doesn't someone tell these Canadians we are not Pakis." (103).

Once the immigrant lives in his ethnic community, he gets a chance to keep his identity and to practice his culture. Community life may give the immigrant an economic independence.

Conclusion

The novel illustrates the similarities between other tales of marginalization as a racial minority. The characters move back and forth between Indian practice and Canadian reality in order to pursue a better livelihood. They are prepared to bear hardships, cultural shocks of unfamiliar policies, contrariness of climate and live far away from their family, relatives, and friends for the desire of attaining economic security, but the result is finally dictated by political climate, whether in Africa or Canada, as a critic observes with regard to the cultural equation that evolves over time between the immigrants and the host community: "It is seen that the [multicultural] interface progresses along the trajectory of initial prejudices, culture shock, economic hardships, nostalgia and sense of loss, creation of imaginary homelands, adjustment with host culture to the extent possible, shaped finally by the politics which decides if the adjustment will be favourable to the native or the migrant." (Batra 223).

Works Cited

Vassanji, M.G. *No New Land.* New York: McClelland & Stewart, 1991.

Batra, Jagdish. "The Triad of Economics, Politics and Culture and the Fate of the Immigrant." *Multiculturalism and the Need for Recognition & The Border: World Reconfigurations of the 21st Century.* Eds. Anamaria Falaus & Ligia Tomoiaga. Bucharest: Eikon Publishing, 2019, pp. 223-237.

Safran, William. "Diasporas in the Modern Societies: Myth of Homeland and Return." *Diaspora: A Journal of Transnational Studies*, Vol. 1 No. 1 Spring 1991, pp 83-99.

Jayaram, N, Ed. *Diversities in the Indian Diaspora: Nature, Implications, Responses*. New Delhi: Oxford Indian Paperbacks, 2012.

Birbalsingh, Frank. *Writers of the Indian Diaspora: Neil Bissoondath, Indo-Caribbean-Canadian Diaspora.* New Delhi: Rawat, 2005.

Dwindling Divisions of Hierarchy: A Postmodern Examination of Bama's *Sangati*

S. Smruthi, PG Student, Stella Maris College, Chennai

Dalit literature from Tamil Nadu has significantly contributed to the narrative of discrimination faced by people owing to their caste, in accordance with the age-old hierarchy of caste, which people adhere to, till this day and age. The hierarchy, initially intended to allocate professions among the *Brahmins, Kshatriyas, Vaishyas* and the *Shudras,* to facilitate the smooth functioning of a society as a holistic unit, later came to be known notoriously for its discriminatory and oppressive practices, wherein the members of the upper-class resorted to inhuman treatment of the lower classes and took advantage of their supposed superiority.

This shift from the intended purpose of formation of the system of *varna* to the ruthless exploitation meted to the members of the caste, lower in this hierarchy with the passage of time, was influenced by manipulatory practices at the personal level. This later got established as the "norm," sanctioned by the upper-caste benefiters through propagation of institutionalized discriminatory practices. Hence, the personal became the political and these individual acts of extracting the maximum advantage out of their access to privileges, by virtue of belonging to a position of power according to the hierarchy, eventually snowballed into a highly inequitable and lopsided society.

The Dalits were oppressed even more, owing to their position in the lowest rungs of the hierarchy of caste and were subsequently subject to abuse and ill-treatment by the upper-caste populace.

Apart from denial to basic amenities and education, they were also made to pursue tasks that compromised on their dignity, which included manual scavenging. The Tamil Dalits too shared a similar experience of subservience and systematized marginalization. The Dalit women, were doubly marginalized, owing to their "disadvantageous" position in terms of both caste as well as gender, as they were subjugated to maltreatment both by members of the upper-caste outside the house, and the man, inside the house. It is essential to notice this juncture of suppression of Dalit women from all sides and the fact that it unfortunately is not known by many. As a result, all Dalits are categorized under a homogenous compartment and are studied as victims of the caste system, without really penetrating deep and unraveling the various factors that cause their misery, the various degrees in which the members experience abuse, how the Dalit women suffer differently from the Dalit men and more than often, more than them, and also their spirit of endurance and resilience, to name a few.

Narrative of Victimization

A single, homogenized narrative of the victimization of Dalits, can do no justice to this nexus of layered and complex nature of repression. It is necessary to refrain from participating in this incomplete narrative, as it leads to marginalizing once again, the suffering of the Dalit women, by not discussing about it. Hence, it becomes important that we do not negate or disregard these experiences of Dalit women or just include their voices for the namesake. Mere inclusion might not be sufficient for recording a comprehensive perspective of the Dalit women, as it would be platonic in nature, and more so, because the very term "inclusion" brings about a hierarchy in the narrative, as what is included, is automatically acknowledged as the margin, to the central and dominant narrative that exists. A narrative, that is sensitive to the heterogenous experiences of the Dalit community, and one that captures not just their suffering but also the dynamism of their lives, is crucial to alter and remodel the deficient narrative.

Bama Faustina Soosairaj is a writer known for bringing about a revolution in the sphere of Tamil literature with her radical and matter-of-fact style of writing and chronicling. She is most popularly known for *Karukku* and *Sangati*, which are excellent mirrors of the lifestyle of the Dalit community. Coming from a Dalit family, where her grandfather switched to Christianity from Hinduism, Bama records the authentic and plural stories of Dalits, especially that of women, in *Sangati*: *Events*. In doing so, she produces a fresh narrative concerning the psyche of Dalit women, the trauma they undergo on an everyday basis, on account of their doubly marginalized status in the society among other issues. The many events that Bama covers in this novel, prove to bring about a discourse that challenges the single and unidimensional narrative that only depicts them as victims, without discussing their other experiences. This attempt of Bama's to produce an alternate narrative of Dalit people as opposed to the Absolute Truth, can be studied as a postmodern trope.

Not only in providing an alternate narrative is Bama's *Sangati* postmodern in nature, but also with respect to its content, as she engages in a style of writing that protests against conforming to what may be understood as "elitist" literature. Her writing contains the local Tamil Dalit flavour, which adds to the text's authenticity, and also stands as a stark contrast to the conventional approach to "good" and "refined" literature, which usually refrains from containing slangs and derogatory remarks. In subverting this notion, Bama brings in a very realistic picture of everyday speech that one is bound to encounter in a typical street in the Dalit settlement mentioned in the novel. This blurring of hierarchy of "refined" and "unrefined" literature again resonates with the postmodern tent of the lack of adherence to following strict divisions. This paper attempts to trace these postmodern tropes in Bama's

Sangati, that defies any form hierarchies, be it in terms of caste or literature.

Tropes of Postmodernism

Bama, in the very beginning claims to offer an unsung narrative of Dalit women, under the section of Acknowledgements in *Sangati*, as she writes: "My mind is crowded with many anecdotes: stories not only about the sorrows and tears of Dalit women, but also about their lively and rebellious culture, their eagerness not to let life crush or shatter them, but to swim vigorously against the tide; about the self-confidence and self-respect that enables them to leap over threatening adversities by laughing at and ridiculing them; about their passion to live life with vitality, truth, and enjoyment; about their hard labour. I wanted to shout out these stories. I was eager that through them, everyone should know about us and our lives." (ix)

Lakshmi Holmstrom, the translator of Sangati, in the Introduction to this novel opines; "*Sangati* flouts received notions of what a novel should be, just as *Karukku* flouts conventions of autobiography. It has no plot in the normal sense, only powerful stories of a series of memorable protagonists. 'Sangati' means news, events, happenings, and the book is one of interconnected anecdotes." (xvi)

The novel undermines the typical structure of a novel, as Bama acts as the chronicler and also goes on to provide her reflections on the particular incident discussed, towards the end of an event. Her commentary not just remains a mere observation, but also includes questions that she asks the reader, which emphasizes the self-reflexive nature of the text, again highlighting its postmodernist nature. Though these questions and comments, the readers grow increasingly aware of the act of reading this text, which also demands action on their part, to rethink the unfortunately normalized subjugation of Dalit women.

Treatment of Language

Sangati is also rich in Tamil proverbs and sayings, as the translator efficiently retains the linguistic essence of the original saying. In one of the events, to mention the biased treatment of the boys and girls in their community, Bama uses a Tamil proverb to convey the partial treatment: "It's you folk who put butter in one eye and quicklime in the other" (29). Similarly, the tradition of ululating and singing songs spontaneously for each situation is another brilliant talent that the Dalit women possess in this novel and is beautifully mentioned in several events, as Velliamma Kizhavi says, 'Even if there's no kanji to eat, the women can never be stopped from singing loudly and ululating' (17), after which she starts singing extemporaneously on the occasion of a girl who came of age.

The novel pays close attention to the disorientations common in natural speech, as Bama has to constantly remind Velliamma Kizhavi, about the topic they started discussing about, each time she digresses. The characters are referred to by the area where they dwelled, such as, "South Street Sesamma," "West Street Bhakkiyam," "East Street Mariapossupam" and so on, who gather at or stop by Velliamma Kizhavi's residence for a short span of period, as they come to grind their millets at her house, borrowing the pounder and stone grinder, during which they strike a conversation. Their speech is loaded with imprecations and abuses hurled at one another, such as "you stinking munde" (38). In one of the events, we see Maikuuzh Kizhavi, who "shook out the four or so strands which spread out from her head, tied them into a knot, spat out to one side, and went off leaning against her stick and shouting abuses in her turn, "Go away you whores . . . Thuu!" (38)

Bama, in consciously choosing to preserve and weave in the raw and natural fashion of language and vocabulary central and integral to the lifestyle of the Dalit characters in the novel, does complete justice in transforming the narrative not just any chronicle, but an authentic one. Holmstrom in her Introduction throws light on how Bama's lack of adherence the conventions of grammar is a conscious and intentional attempt at subverting the tradition of gatekeeping in literature: "Raj Gauthaman sees it (Dalit writing) as essentially subversive in character, bringing both content and forms which challenge received literary norms. . . . 'Dalit literature describes the world differently, from a Dalit perspective. Therefore, it should outrage and even repel the guardians of caste and class. It should provoke them into asking if this is indeed literature.' . . . He claims that it is the stated design of Dalit writing to disrupt received modern (upper-caste) language proprieties and to 'expose and discredit the existing language, its grammar, its refinements, and its falsifying order of as symbols of dominance . . . for it is according to these measures that language of Dalits is marginalized as a vulgar and obscene language, the language of slums' (xii-xiii).

Bama, by writing in the everyday Dalit style of speech, dismantles the hierarchies of sen Tamil (refined language, used in literary texts) and kodun Tamil (the colloquial, non-literary language), which reiterates the postmodern trait of effacing hierarchy in literature. The events relating to the women being possessed by *peys* (ghosts) is yet another idea that Bama brings to limelight in this novel. The idea of being possessed, which is usually shunned with ridicule, for its associations with the supernatural and therefore automatically being against reason and rationality is skilfully discussed here, as Bama decodes the reasons behind women uttering such obscene language and acting possessed. In one of the events, Bama describes the torture that a woman undergoes, as "she was heavily pregnant, her whole stomach dragged on the earth as he pulled her along" (62). In one of her commentaries towards the end of an event, Bama, the chronicler opines:

> why must she submit to being beaten and stamped upon for no rhyme or reason? That's why she quarrels with him. If he shows his

> strength of muscle, she reveals the sharpness of her tongue. Because she can't hit him back, she curses him roundly. What else can she do? . . . When you examine the words they use in their quarrels, you will notice they are full of obscenities, very direct and ugly, often dealing with sexual relations. . . . I sometimes think that they have neither pleasure nor fulfilment in their own sexual lives, they derive a sort of bitter comfort by using these terms of abuse which are usually names of their body parts . . . by shouting and fighting first thing at dawn and last thing at night, if need be, our women survive without going crazy . . . we find ways of coping in the best way we can. (67-68).

Bama also carefully locates the position of Dalit men, in the power structure: "there was nowhere else for them to exert their male pride or to show off their authority. All that suppressed anger was vented when they came home and beat their wives to a pulp. Even though they are male, because they are Dalits, they have to be like dogs with their tails rolled up when they are in the fields and, dealing with their landlords." (65)

Conclusion

It is through deviating the established standards of novel writing tradition, that Bama has been able to achieve the raw and real presentation of the Dalit lives, especially that of the women, as she transports the readers to the streets in the novel. The very title, which translates to "events" has postmodern tropes to it, as it brings about plurality and a "multiverse," as opposed to a straight-jacket narrative, which may be seen as "universe." Moreover, the novel is heavily dependent on the tradition of orature, as almost all characters engage in impromptu singing and tales and myths of the *peys* and local beliefs.

Each event in this novel disrupts the homogenized narrative of suffering of the Dalits, as Bama introduces the reader to multiples voices through many characters, who have different stories, of not just suffering but also their small acts of rebellion, such as the incident, where Sanmuga Kizhavi encounters caste-based discrimination through mischief, and Maikanni who is very innocent but also has the immense will to survive against all odds, even at such a tender age, as, "The day Maikanni learnt to walk, she started working as well" (70). This novel therefore, proves to be a mosaic of several narratives, through several events of not just their struggles and challenges, but of their endurance and varied experiences.

The postmodernist features found in the style of writing can also be seen as "experimental" according to Thiara, at its core, given that the technique employed to tell the stories of the Dalit characters, disrupts the "etiquettes" and "customs" of what may be considered to be literature of "good quality." The texture of the writing is hence characterized by resistance to abide by any convention that restricts the natural flow of the narrative. By rewriting the skewed narrative of Dalits and offering an insight into the intricate female experiences in *Sangati,* Bama presents the commonplace as truly as possible, even if it requires defying the standards of language and content that are of "literary merit." *Sangati* is therefore a sincere representation of the ordinary, possessing the spirit of postmodernism and shattering cultural, linguistic as well as literary hierarchies at the same time.

Works Cited

Bama, and Lakshmi Holmstrom. *Sangati*. Oxford UP, 2012.

"Explaining the Destabilization of Identity: Postmodernization, Commodification, and the Leveling of Cultural Hierarchy." *Identity Crises: A Social Critique of Postmodernity*, Robert G. Dunn, ed., University of Minnesota Press, Minneapolis; London, 1998, pp. 107-42. www.jstor.org/stable/10.5749/j.ctttt1s1.8.

Gopal Guru. "Dalit Women Talk Differently." *Economic and Political Weekly*, vol. 30, no. 41/42, 1995, pp. 2548-2550. www.jstor.org/stable/4403327.

Singh, Manjari, and Bama Faustina Susairaj. "Dalit Text As Testimony: A Conversation with Bama." *Indian Literature*, vol. 60, no. 3 (293), 2016, pp. 23-44. www.jstor.org/stable/44478990.

Thiara, Nicole. "Subaltern Experimental Writing: Dalit Literature in Dialogue with the World." *Ariel: A Review of International English Literature* 47.1-2 (2016): 253-80.

Tambe, Shruti. *Sociological Bulletin*, vol. 66, no. 2, 2017, pp. 243-44. www.jstor.org/stable/26625754.

Dystopian Writings in Postmodern Literature

SERIR LINA
M.A. Student, University of Tlemcen, Algeria

Art and literature are intertwined with movements that constantly spin, rotate, and progress to reach a revolution which responds to the tart philosophical ruminations, and prepare humanity to adapt to the vicissitudes of life. Art and literature have always been of a vital and protean nature as history restores those vivid stages, resulting from its fertile ground, including Miltonian and Shakespearean Renaissance, Rousseau's Enlightenment, Romanticism with Austen and Delacroix, and the observant life of Realism; along with Cubism, Impressionism, Psychoanalysis and surrealism which continue in the Modern era. The pervasive aftermath of Modernism was so heavy and complex to be absorbed that the expressed art in the half of the twentieth century "merely means moderner modern" (345), to use the words of Christine Brooke-Rose, because it spans the tendencies of Modernism, yet, "at the heart of modernist culture is a distrust of the very idea of culture itself" (Declan 1992). Indicatively, we refer here to an "awkward and faintly epigonic, suggestive less of a vigorous or even interesting new direction in the old art of storytelling than of something anti-climactic, feebly following a very hard act to follow" (McHale 18) that is named 'Postmodernism'.

Obsolescence of the Modern

Chronologically, the interval between Modernism and Postmodernism is nigh for they both occupied a great share from the Caveman's century[1]. The prefix "Post" literally means after, later, behind, subsequent to, or posterior to." Thus far, Postmodernism is purported to be the posterity of Modernism because as McHale argued in his book *Postmodernist Fiction (1987)* that "every literary historical moment is *post* some other moment, just as it is *pre* some other moment, though of course we are not in the position to say exactly what it is *pre* - what it precedes and prepares the way for except retrospectively, while we are always able to say, in principle, what it is *post* what is it the posterity of" (20). However, McHale observed that the prefix 'post' is merely a sham that mostly bothered people, whenever subjects of postmodernism are debated. From another philosophical point of view, the prefix 'post' intends to indicate that whatever is after is 'contrary to' or 'anti' as stated by Noel Carroll (1997), or in other words, whatever comes 'after' is 'incompatible with.'

Hence, modernism and postmodernism coexist at the same time, in the same world. Still, postmodernism dethroned a myriad of modernist trends and practices for "whatever counts as postmodern is not simply after whatever is modern; the former is also somehow contrary, in certain core respects, to whatever is said to be modern" (89) argued Noel Carroll. Is it typically the prefix '*post*' annexed to 'modernism' to mean what follows modernism? or should we have a glance at the verb 'to post' to merely 'announce' 'modernism' publicly and officially?

The term 'postmodernism' is hard to fathom. Perhaps, this is due to its birth from the ashes of wars, or it is due to the severe jolt of the raised ideologies that smothered individuality and inured human to alienation: the loot of the Second World War. Be it as it may, postmodernism indeed came after modernism but it seemed to be unfaithful to its predecessors. Modernism introduced discernible changes in art and literature and endeavoured to experiment new forms of expression that respond to the conditions of the modern world, while politics stands at bay. By way of contrast, postmodernism has rather a complex system that is based on the heavy rejection of any sort of traditional notions.

It is thus necessary to gauge the dissimilarity between Modernism and Postmodernism since the latter has never been content of the responses the former strived to formulate. According to Oxford Learner's Dictionaries, postmodernism is "a style and movement in art, architecture, literature, etc. in the late twentieth century that reacts against modern styles, for example by mixing features from traditional and modern style." In other words, postmodernism has an unsettled state that is divided between following modernist ideas besides tolerating high and low forms of art. However, while modernists tried to represent fragmentation and alienation, postmodernists preferred to celebrate that fragmented view with an unwatchful roving eye.

The artistic style of the period that touched many spheres including cinema, literature, and philosophy has, in fact, produced a strong sense of hybridity; based on the concept of unifying different genres and cultural forms from different time periods and diverse sources of high and low art; as well as converting past styles into a unique postmodern design. In this vein, Hans Bertens in his introductory essay *The Debate on Postmodernism* declared that every postmodernist was primarily "insisting on difference and declaring war on sameness in the same intellectual, moral, and political freedom, and seeing never-ending process where other worldview saw (and see) stability" (3).

Literary Theory in Postmodern Era

Postmodernism pushed its way through the throng of literary criticism to become one of the widely ranged theories used in many books and novels to lament modern aesthetic styles and ideas. In fact, postmodernism, as any concept, stems from curiosity and human thirst for change. When an inquiry into the implications of modernism was requested, the line between approving these implications and refusing them has been blurred. The American essayist Clement Greenberg claimed that "the post in postmodernism can be taken in a temporal chronological sense" he continued that "anything that comes after something else is "post" that something else." He finds that postmodernism followed modernism only in a temporal sense, because the latter witnessed a cessation mainly when the art that demands high standards began to face new rationalization and lower standards. However, as man ceaselessly engages in evolutionary progress, postmodernism as a movement, a theory, a style, a philosophy, or a new literary form imposed its weight to describe man's status of delirium, and re-evaluate Western culture.

Critics agree that in the years that followed the end of the Second World War, postmodernism strived to claim its superiority over modernism and mainly in 1950; a year that coincided with the manifestation of "les nouveaux Romanciers" in France. Along with Michel Butor, Nathalie Sarraute, and Claude Simon, Alain Robbe- Grillet overtly expressed his fatigue from historical novels and introduced "le Nouveau Roman" or "the New Novel" that holds new techniques and features where omniscient point of view is rejected and writing becomes an adventure rather than a merely traditional narrative with plot and characters. As a matter of fact, these practices have been already exhibited by Joyce in *Ulysses* (1922) or Woolf in *To The Lighthouse* (1927) with accelerated plots, and by Proust, who lingers on details to create a deceleration in his novel *In Search of Lost Time* (1922).

Thus, postmodernism is also a controversial concept that suspects reason and marginalizes universal truth and traditions. Its theories have been implied in literature; the often-open gate of change to renew the zest for creative ideas. Writers like John Barth, Kurt Vonnegut, Thomas Pynchon, Umberto Eco, and Angela Carter introduced postmodern techniques in their novels. Eco's tour de force in the late twentieth century *Foucault's Pendulum* (1988) claims the origins of fascism. Whilst Pynchon's *Gravity's Rainbow* (1973) combines black humor and fantasy to point out fragmentation and alienation through his unreliable narrator who is no longer able to make distinction between reality and fiction. These narratives symbolize the acutely disturbed state of mind that is caused by the traumas of the post world war II, i.e., incoherence of thoughts, chronological disorder, and loss of faith.

Literary theories emerged fiercely to put literary texts under scrutiny, and tried to decipher the truest meaning behind them. Plato in *The Republic* (360 B.C.E) examined justice on the scale of the state and explained that "we shall be satisfied; or, if there be a difference in the individual, we will come back to the State and have another trial of the theory" (166). Indeed, progress or regress stems from theory. The latter holds interesting meaning to indicate "a formal set of ideas that is intended to explain why something happens or exists" (oxford learner's dictionaries), "a plausible or scientifically acceptable general principle or body of principles offered to explain phenomena" (Merriam Webster dictionary), or as Jonathan Culler simply put it "*theory* signals 'speculation'(2). In fact, what is quite interesting about the word 'theory' is its fickle foundation that constantly evolved, mainly with poststructuralist thinkers who made great endeavors to overcome traditional structures and create a powerful engine to analyze and interpret any sort of literary text.

The juggernauts of literary theory for whom we remain indebted are the editors and collaborators of the Tel Quel literary magazine that was founded in 1960 in France. The pioneers of this magazine revisited crucial issues of sexuality, ethnicity, power, and politics. Michel Foucault investigated power and knowledge in the social context, Jacques Derrida focused on language and introduced a unique way to read the text through his deconstructive theory, Julia Kristeva discovered other layers of the literary text using intertextual relations, Louis Althusser discussed the supremacy of ideology, while Jacques Lacan attempted "to 'rewrite' Freudianism" (Eagleton 142). Post-structuralism is another legacy of postmodernism and its theories are one of the greatest devices of literature. Notoriously, the fanciful life of virtue and values was condemned to oblivion. In fact, the fissure in the traditional form of literature, be it poetry or prose, appeared manifestly in the works of T.S. Eliot, Ezra Pound, William Faulkner, James Joyce, Virginia Woolf, and so forth. Their writings, in fact, addressed the turmoil of the First World War that alienated humanity and sentenced individuality to the abyss. However, the readership wanted something more powerful that depicts the destiny of their societies and gauges the extent of regression they may reach if they keep transgressing the limits. The literature in turbulent times gave birth to a special genre that proliferated rapidly after the Russian writer Yevgeny Zamyatin published his masterpiece *We* (1924) that is dystopia.

Dystopia in Postmodernism

Just like any literary genre, dystopia came as a reaction against its rival utopia. 'Happily forever after' was forbidden in the twentieth century for utopia failed to occupy a strong place among the literature of the period. Instead, dystopia, as perplexing as postmodernism, aimed at presenting the utopian failure ascribed to the spread regimes and ideologies practised on societies. Communism struggled to manifest a Marxist utopia based on Karl Marx and Friedrich Engel's *Communist Manifesto* (1848), but this was not the utopia Marx once sought, for the "hellish state brought about by attempts to construct unrealizable ideal systems" (Rosefielde 246) gained a new term which is failed utopia or dystopia. According to Gregory Claeys "the 1960s produced the first extensive literature on dystopia" while Arthur O. Lewis in *The Anti Utopian Novel* (1956) states that anti-utopia, regressive utopia, negative utopia or as commonly known dystopia aims at "depicting a society which is officially "perfect" but which is demonstrated to have flaws making it unacceptable to the author's—and presumably the reader's- point of view" (qtd. Claeys 275).

To illustrate the twentieth century, the atrocity of the period is resulting from the new-born ideologies, the deplorable systems of governance, or more properly, from the widespread of totalitarian regimes, the dreadful biological influx and the grievous technological development. Part of the allure, these events could alienate people out of their imaginative comfort zone provided by utopia to diverge in the tragic part of history. Writers of the era engaged in a dystopian fiction to both treat and to add insult to injury, "whereas utopias describe an escape from history, these anti-utopias describe an escape, or attempted escape, to history, which is to say, to the world of contingency, conflicts, and uncertainty" (qtd. Booker 4).

Many writers opted for dystopia in their literary works; however, few have guided the convoy of the genre. Yevgeny Zamyatin, Aldous Huxley, Ray Bradbury, Margaret Atwood, and George Orwell are worthy to be mentioned in order to adduce the last claim. Henceforth, dystopia seems to be another version of postmodernism exhibited profusely in contemporary literature. George Orwell's *Nineteen Eighty-Four* (1949) is written in postmodern fashion, by means that the language of the text "is written by culture and not authors" (171) as argued by Aaron S. Rosenfeld in *Character and Dystopia* (2021). Again, totalitarianism, communism, late capitalism, and ideological power, are notable elements in postmodern writings.

George Orwell's *Nineteen Eighty-four* (1949) is set in a futuristic state named Oceania. The novel holds a political prophecy and a warning to prevent a dystopian future led by totalitarian ideals. Oceania is allegedly believed to be a utopian place due to the growth of science and technology with an attempt to create modern civilization. As discourse remained under scrutiny by structuralists and post-structuralists, language became of paramount importance to transcribe political satire and persuade readers to rethink about the certainty of totalitarianism and communism. The past and memory threaten the governing system, the reason why these systems keep deteriorating the individual, the self, the I when he/she is unable to recall the restored information in their minds. Patrick Parrinder argues that "it was in *Nineteen Eighty-*

four that he [Orwell] noted how the falsification of reality is seamlessly welded into the obliteration of memory" (266). Winston, the novel's protagonist, tried to remember London street (which become Oceania in 1984) "squeeze out some childhood memory that should tell him whether London had always been quite like this" the author carries "but it was no use, he could not remember: nothing remained of his childhood" (chapter1). Orwell, in fact, attempts to visualize the difficulty of remembering past things using the verb "squeeze out" to display the amount of pressure and eagerness of Oceania's citizens to take a trip down memory lane but the trial goes in vain.

Postmodernist texts also celebrate the usage of black humour, irony, parody, satire, inter-textuality, fragmentation, and playfulness. In this vein, we should recall the first dystopian novel that inaugurated the anti-utopian genre in the twentieth century written by the devil of Russian literature Yevgeny Zamyatin named *We* (1924). In the narrative, Zamyatin mastered playfulness perfectly when he accurately and intentionally selected a special jargon for a futuristic dystopian society. In the dystopia of *We*, citizens are regimented by a ruling power that is the omniscience of their "Now Jehovah," the Benefactor, or the Well-Doer. Zamyatin tried to shape irony in using such a name for the head of his authoritative state. How does it come that the ruler of a community based on dictatorship is associated with philanthropy while his policy is a misanthropic fallacy?

As the case presents, there is a strong link between Zamyatin's *We* and any dystopia written in modern or postmodern time. Worthy to mention is that Zamyatin's OneState is founded on the basis of tyranny and control. Soon, this society has become a paradigm for many dystopian writers including Aldous Huxley's *Brave New World*, Orwell's *Nineteen Eighty-four* and the sixth novel of the Canadian writer Atwood; *The Handmaid's Tale*. As a fact, dystopia is based on totalitarian regimes which practise oppression and coercion upon its citizens. From submission and tyranny, the ruling class derives its power to manage, command, and control. After four decades, Orwell used the same technique of irony and playfulness in his narrative *Nineteen Eighty-four* (1949) by dividing his government into four ministries that are: Ministry of Truth in which Orwell presented his popular parody "WAR IS PEACE FREEDOM IS SLAVERY IGNORANCE IS STRENGTH" (Chapter1), Ministry of Peace whose aims are far from being peaceful, Ministry of Love that is the most 'frightening one' as Orwell put it, and the Ministry of Plenty that deals with economy. However "their names, In Newspeak: Minitrue, Minipax, Miniluv, and Miniplenty" (Chapter 1). Notoriously, every ministry's aspect is being reduced and minimized in Oceania to show how small and minor love, peace, truth, and playfulness are.

Again, communism, late capitalism, ideological power, and faction are key concepts of postmodern texts. These narratives are, according to Jean-François Lyotard, 'meta-narratives' or 'grand narratives' and argued that "the narrative function is losing its functors, its great hero, its great danger, its great voyage, its great goals" (xxiv). According to the French literary theorist "the decline of narrative can be seen as an effect to the blossoming of techniques and technologies since the Second World War" (37). Dystopias as well go beyond narration to set the alarm of warning from an absurd future.

Reading *Brave New World (1932), Nineteen Eighty-four (1949), Walden Two (1948), Anthem (1938)*, or *Kallocain (1940)*, is absolutely leading us to dystopian fiction, because they settle the traits of dystopian tradition in form and content. Actually, what all of these narratives share strongly is the notion of power and surveillance over individuals. According to James K.A Smith, Michel Foucault believes that "the root of our most cherished and central institutions—hospitals, schools, business, and, yes, prisons- is a network of power relations." (p). Surveillance is a form of control that Orwell overtly announced it in the beginning of his novel “BIG BROTHER IS WATCHING YOU.” Nevertheless, citizens are supervised by patrol police and Thought Police.

Foucault in his book *Discipline and Punish* (1975) explained that justice and surveillance are mechanisms that work side by side in order to prevent man from committing crime and if it is committed, then police and justice must punish, while “legal procedures should not remain secret, that the reasons why a defendant is condemned or acquitted should be known to all, and each individual must be able to recognize the reasons for a penalty” (Foucault 108). As dystopian societies must be settled in isolation, what is beyond the boundaries of society is irrational and savage. They are, often, isolated by barriers or walls. Atwood interprets what Foucault aimed to present, by means that legal procedures are exposed in the Gilead through the wall: a reminder to the Gileadeans to restrict themselves according to the norms of the state or else they die. On Atwood’s Wall, persecuted prisoners are hanged; a means to horrify citizens in order to avoid resistance or rebellion. Offred, the narrative’s heroine, powerlessly, prayed: “I don’t want to be a doll hung up on the Wall, I don’t want to be a wingless angel. I want to keep on living, in any form, I resign my body freely, to the uses of others. They can do what they like with me. I am abject” (256). Indeed, the idea of the wall and what it symbolizes succeeds in making the populace resigned and acquiesced to any order the system dictates. In a perfect state, dystopian citizens are prisoners whose sins are not venial but cardinal.

In a similar vein, Foucault referred to this kind of public manifestation of truth to the eighteenth century and writes “It was the task of the guilty man to bear openly his condemnation and the truth of the crime that he had committed. His body, displayed, exhibited in procession, tortured, served as the public support of a procedure that had hitherto remained in the shade; in him, on him, the sentence had to be legible for all” (43).

In the *Meditationes Sacrae* (1597), Sir Francis Bacon mentioned his maxim “knowledge is power” to indicate that it is only through knowledge that man reaches prosperity and improvement. However, four centuries later, Foucault diffused a mirror reflection on Bacon's maxim to read it backwards: "power is knowledge."

In the first part of his book *Discipline and Punish* (1975), he claims that "we should abandon a whole tradition that allows us to imagine that knowledge can exist only where the power relations are suspended" he added "we should admit rather that power produces knowledge" and "that power and knowledge directly imply one another; that there is no power relation without the correlative constitution of a field of knowledge, nor any knowledge that does not presuppose and constitute at the same time power relations." (27). The concept of power is one of the contemporary debated conundrums, because it has been repeatedly used and abused. All terror of the twentieth century arises from the intense desire for power. Dystopias try to address that political, economic, and social greed which ended the life of millions.

Back to Orwell's dystopian masterpiece *Nineteen Eighty-four*, knowledge is controlled, inspected, and eyed at the utmost interest. In Oceania, the government put Thought police as guardians who would even intrude on the minds of citizens. Neither freedom of thought nor freedom of speech is tolerated; thus, any sort of knowledge is associated with dictatorial power. In Ray Bradbury's dystopia *Fahrenheit 451* (1950), totalitarianism and technological revolution (the state's strength) determine what knowledge individuals should acquire by banning books and eliminating literature using mass media. In the novel, Beatty, the chief of book burners and the state's faithful believer, declaimed to Montag, the novel's protagonist, that "the important thing for you to remember, Montag, is we're the Happiness Boys, the Dixie Duo, you and I and the others. We stand against the small tide of those who want to make everyone unhappy with conflicting theory and thought. We have our fingers in the dyke. Hold steady. Don't let the torrent of melancholy and drear philosophy drown our world" (49). Again, "knowledge is power" when "Power becomes unbreachable if textual information is monolithic" (Bloom 33) the reason why in Fahrenheit 45, books are dangerous because as Beatty stated "None of those books agree with each other" (Bradbury 29). While "power is knowledge" because the source of any right or truth is power per se as mentioned Michael Kelly "power cannot be exercised except through the production of truth and with the aid of right, but that power is to some extent constitutive of (the discourse of) truth and right, and knowledge as a whole" (378).

Conclusion

As addressed in my analysis, the reaction against modern styles has bewildered has both and enlightened many to live in better terms. The celebration of the modern character was marred by the factual interpretations that have been presented, more than elsewhere, in the postmodern era in which universal truths had been rejected and distrusted. Another main point addressed in the postmodern period is the rise of dystopian genre as a warning of things to come and a cautionary advice to cease the occurrence of different fatalities. This sort of study aims also at fathoming the ideological topics of fragmentation, submission, power and control. The latter was manifested distinctively Foucault's ideas of tyranny and prison. This research would help to learn effectively about various dystopian narratives that overtly refute the theory of oppression, and proved that man is born free and would break the chains.

Works Cited

Althusser, Louis. "Ideology and Ideological State Apparatuses." *Mapping Ideology*, ed. SlavojŽižek. London: Cromwell Press, 1994.

Atwood, Margaret. *The Handmaid's Tale.* Houghton Mifflin

Bertens, Hans. *The Debate on Postmodernism International Postmodernism Theory and Literary Theory*, ed. Hans Bertens, Douwe Fokkema. Amsterdam/ Philadelphia, John Benjamins, 1997, 3-14.

Booker, M. Keith. *The Dystopian Impulse in Modern Literature: Fiction as Social Criticism*, London: Greenwood Press, 1994.

Bradbury, Ray, ed. *Harold Bloom*. Chelsea, 2008.

_____. *Fahrenheit 451*, Project Gutenberg Ebook, 2008.

Brooke-Rose, Christine. *A Rhetoric of the Unreal: Studies in Narrative and Structure, Especially of the Fantastic*, Cambridge, Cambridge University Press, 1981.

Carroll, Noel. *The Concept of Postmodernism from a Philosophical Point of View. International Postmodernism Theory and Literary Theory*, ed. Hans Bertens, Douwe Fokkema, Amesterdam/ Philadelphia, John Benjamins 1997, pp. 89-102.

Claeys, Gregory. *Dystopia a natural history*, United Kingdom: Oxford University Press, 2017.

Culler, Jonathan. *Literary Theory : A Very Short Introduction*, Oxford University Press, New York, 1997.

Eagleton, Terry. *Literary Theory: An Introduction*, Blackwell, 1996.

Foucault, Michel. *Discipline and Punish: The Birth of the Prison*, Trans. Alan Sheridan, Vintage Books, 1991

Greenberg, Clement. *Modernism and Postmodernism*, William Dobell Memorial Lecture, Australia, 1979. http://www.sharecom.ca/greenberg/postmodernism.html. Harcourt, 1986

Kelly, Michael. *Critique and Power: Recasting the Foucault/ Habermas Debate*, the MIT Press, 1994

Kiberd, Decan. Introduction. *Ulysses*. London, Penguin, 1992

Lyotard, Jean-François. *The Postmodern Condition: A Report on Knowledge*, Translated by Geoff Bennington and Brian Massumi, Manchester University Press, 1984.

McHale, Brian. *Postmodernist Fiction,* London and New York, Routledge, 1987.

Orwell, George. *Nineteen Eighty-four*. Buccaneer Books, 1982

Plato. *The Republic,* Translated by Benjamin Jowett, Project Gutenberg Ebook, 2008

Rosefielde, Steven. *Red Holocaust*, Routledge, 2010.

Rosenfeld, Aaron, S. *Character and Dystopia; The Last Men*. Routledge, 2021.

Smith, James, K.A. *Who's Afraid of Postmodernism ? Taking Derrida, Lyotard, and Foucault to Church*, Baker Academic, 2006.

Zamiatin, Eugene. *We*, trans. Gregory Zilboorg, E.P Dutton, New York, 1924.

Why Publish or Perish? Re-reading the Report on Knowledge

UMESH PATRA
Mahatma Gandhi Central University, Motihari

Looking at the history of English literature, one finds several literary and allied intellectual movements that were regarded as modern in comparison with their immediate predecessors, yet none of these movements were daubed as "modernism" per se. After the medieval stupor, Europe, at large, underwent a religious and cultural revival. This period is called the 'Renaissance.' The Renaissance artists and scholars questioned beliefs hitherto held sacred and considered themselves to be modern. Yet, their modernity was deemed as a reawakening, not as an altogether new phenomenon. The age of enlightenment carried the tradition of anthropocentrism that had set in a century ago. The Victorian period, with unprecedented changes brought in through industrialism looked back nostalgically at a bucolic and wholesome past and looked ahead sceptically towards an uncertain future. Yet, its relation to history was reverential. It was only during the twentieth century that the artists and intellectuals had the gumption to call themselves modern in the sense no other age had called itself. The advent of modernism in the first half of the twentieth century in Europe was a rupture in the Western intellectual tradition. The flipside of calling a movement "modernism" is that it arrests the continuous flow towards an unknown goal and brings history to a grinding halt. It was no wonder that the subsequent age had to both continue the tradition and oppose their predecessors by calling themselves "postmodern."

The cultural and intellectual phenomenon called "postmodernism" could be understood as a paradox. On one hand, the postmodern artists rebelled against traditional aesthetics, attempt to destabilize any fixed notion of art, while on the other, their praxis became the foundation of a new aesthetic or an anti-aesthetic. The onslaught of non-representational art, that denounced individuality and venerated chance findings, drew bouquets and brickbats from various quarters. One of the fiercest critics of "postmodernism," Jurgen Habermas considered this trend to be a derailing of the project of enlightenment that had been initiated since the seventeenth century. According to Habermas, postmodernism was not a successor (to enlightenment), but a rebellious counter-culture movement that sought to challenge the glorious intellectual and cultural tradition of the West. At this juncture, Jean Francois Lyotard came to the defence of "postmodernism" and rightly regarded this as a "condition," not a unified movement of sorts. Moreover, this condition was caused by a severe critique and questioning of what passed as knowledge. His essay "The Postmodern Condition: A Report on Knowledge" analyses the changing attitude towards knowledge during the second half of the twentieth century. In the essay, Lyotard celebrates the lack of hankering after any universal definition of truth and celebrates what he calls "dissensus."

In this paper, I look at Lyotard's predictions regarding epistemology in the context of contemporary publication market in academic journals in the field of literary studies. I claim that multiple publication platforms of dubious origin have led to a chaotic condition and given assent to the culture of "anything goes." Reluctant teachers are often dragged into the vortex of mandatory publishing and their half-hearted attempts to write research papers, primarily for career goals, have created an abundant wasteland of dispensable output, often termed "trash." Various legitimizing agencies have come forward to clear the trash from the academic corridors, and their efforts have led to a new but somewhat skewed hierarchy.

Spectre of 'Publish or Perish'

A strange spectre is haunting the corridors of university departments, conference venues, PhD viva voces, and other academic events in India. The spectre, in its hectoring voice, charges at the academic tyro, with a simple exclamation, "Publish or Perish." The poetic beauty of this phrase cannot be ignored. It appears like a haiku. Like many ancient proverbs, this too crystallizes the opulence of thought in the economy of words. Further, its utterance highlights its alliterative effect. Like "Do or Die," "Get Busy Living or Get Busy Dying," this phrase too has a sing-song pattern. The sound complements the sense. Like any good poem, it could mean a lot of things. Who is the speaker here? It could be a seasoned academician with grey hair and a ten-page long curriculum vitae. Who is the addressee of this imperative sentence? It could be any ambitious academic neophyte. What is the message? It states that one must publish, or else . . . ! But publish what? The answer will be different for each addressee. An academician in the field of English literature in India could publish research papers, articles, book reviews, interviews with prominent authors, case studies, and the like. And publish where? At 'reputed publication platforms' such as blind/double-blind peer-reviewed journals, conference proceedings, edited books and the like. But most importantly, publish why? The ominous 'or' in the dictum "Publish or Perish," coldly connotes that those with no publications at all, or publications not in genres mentioned above, or publications not in the platforms mentioned above, are doomed in their career. Their academic credibility is brought to question.

The dictum "Publish or Perish" glorifies publication of articles of a certain type on platforms of a certain type. It deliberately shifts the focus from the act of writing to that of publishing. If writing is considered an intimate act, publishing by its very nature is an act undertaken in the public sphere. The ceremonies organized for publication such as book-launch events are the rites of passage for an idea. The publication of an article announces the end of writing. It signals that no more editing can be done on a given piece of work, unless there is a revised publication, of course. It declares the fruition, and therefore the end of the growth of an idea that might have been conceived by the author in an unceremonious manner. It might have been affected by the tides and ebbs of enthusiasm. It would have encountered several problems on its way to the printing press, its credibility being denied on one or more occasions. It might have been sceptically renounced as a fruitless germ by none other than its own author. But once published, the piece of writing would be evaluated, appreciated, criticized, or misunderstood by the readers. The work now enters the public domain, leaving for good the nurturing abode of its author. What the author had in mind during the composition of the article does not affect it anymore. What appears on the page are nothing but "words, words, and words."

Roland Barthes cogently takes this idea to its logical conclusion in his essay "The Death of the Author." He announced that once the task of writing is complete, the authority of the author ceases. He no longer remains a lurking presence whose personal life is brought to bear on the writing. The words will be interpreted by the individual reader based on their own socio-cultural positions, their experiences of life. His essay ends with a bold assertion that "the birth of the reader must be at the cost of the death of the Author" (Barthes 148). The new academic publishing seems to signify the dawn of a new era: the birth of the publisher.

Today publishing houses act not only as platforms which collate scholarly writing, but more as legitimating agencies that certify scholarship of the papers published therein. Thus, the publication in a reputed journal guarantees the authenticity of research. In the field of humanities, it has led to a unique problem. A research paper in the field of English studies attempts to present an idea following a scientific method. Imagine a research paper on "Waiting for Godot": a rational study of a play that resists any rational interpretation. It is difficult to determine how much of a research paper is objective and how much is subjective? For instance, take Caroline Spurgeon's *Shakespeare's Imagery and What it Tells Us.* Spurgeon counts the number of recurrent words in a Shakespearean play to conclude that a particular play of Shakespeare is dominated by a particular mood. The question is: does this study enhance our enjoyment of Shakespeare? The horde of masses who watched *Hamlet* didn't watch it with a calculator in hand adding each time the word 'rotten' was used. Nor can we imagine Shakespeare composing *Romeo and Juliet* in a tavern careful to use the word 'star' only for a specific number of occurrences, neither more nor less. Without denying the meticulous perseverance of Spurgeon that too at a time when Shakespeare was not available in digital form (or any literary work for that matter), one may venture of ask, what is the effort worth? The answer could be offered by another Shakespearean scholar Harold Bloom. According to Bloom, each reading is a misreading of a text. What matters is whether one misreading is more interesting than another misreading. Therefore, Spurgeon's reading of Shakespeare could be read not as the only, not the final, but an interesting reading of Shakespeare as valid as Thomas De Quincey's reading of Shakespeare in his essay "On Knocking at the Gate in Macbeth." The existence of multiple versions of reading or misreading could be the domain of literary research. Lyotard's observation on the postmodern condition becomes an important contribution to epistemological discussions in this context.

Lyotard on Scientific Truth

Lyotard titled his treatise as "The Postmodern Condition: A Report on Knowledge." Lyotard claims that science, which deals with verifiable or falsifiable denotative statements, also takes recourse to a grand narrative of the growth of Life or the Spirit of the mind. He traces the beginning of scientific thinking in Socratic dialogues by Plato. Take for example the allegory of the cave. Socrates explains the existence of three worlds:

a) the world of ideas which is the sole domain of the philosopher (the lover of wisdom);
b) the material world—a poor replica of the world of ideas, thus once-removed from reality; this is the world perceived by the prisoners
c) The imaginary world—a poor replica of the material world which is twice removed from reality. This world is created by poets who unwittingly copy the imperfect world of sensory perceptions. (Plato)

To denounce the knowledge derived from sensory perceptions in the material world as well as the imaginary world created by artists in their narratives, Plato too took recourse to a form of narrative. He built a simple plot consisting of a dialogue between two characters: one being Socrates and the other Glaucon. His advocacy of scientific thinking was based on a concocted fable concerning underground prisoners facing a wall of shadows. If science too takes recourse to narratives for denoting its findings, and each narrative is as valid as another, then science cannot claim the ultimate possession of knowledge or truth.

According to Lyotard, the post-modern art claims no possession of truth. If modern art bemoaned the loss of truth (in the works of Yeats and Proust for example), post-modern art becomes free from the irritable hankering after truth, revels at the surface level, and claims that there is no truth to depict. Take W. H. Auden's poem "The Shield of Achilles" for example. In this poem, Auden contrasts the scenes of modern warfare fought in barren lands with the scenes of the epic battle of Troy. The craftsmanship on Achilles' shield is nowhere to be found in the weaponry of the twentieth century. The tone of the poem is elegiac, not heroic, not even mock-heroic. The atmosphere is that of mourning. The entire opus of "War Poetry" composed by soldier poets and veterans of the first world war attests to this claim by Auden.

The same atmosphere can be found in several literary works created during the early half of the twentieth century. "The Wasteland" by T.S. Eliot, "The Second Coming" by W.B. Yeats could be read as elegies that bemoan the death of a civilization that was once prosperous, but now on the verge of ruin. One reads the lines "London Bridge is falling down" (Eliot) and "The best lack all conviction while the worst are full of passionate intensity" (Yeats) with the melancholic memory of a bridge that was once intact and a time when the best had all conviction. The poem "The Church Going" by Philip Larkin attempts to make sense of a religion that, according to him, was bound to lose its believers, yet is of immense mysterious value. The theme of disillusionment and a sense of failure was rampant in modern art and criticism. Scholars like Arthur Koestler, Andre Gide, Stephen Spender, and others who were initially influenced by Marxism but denounced it eventually, titled their collection of essays as "The God That Failed." It is significant that they chose the word 'God' to signify a system of political philosophy that considered religion to be an opium of the masses. There was a theological basis under threat. The belief in the dictum "God is in the heaven and all's right in the world" had been shaken. The attempt to replace that theological order with a Marxist order had also failed.

This disenchantment is nowhere to be found in Postmodernism. Take for example the poem "Karawane" by Hugo Ball. This poem is a random assemblage of meaningless sounds. There is no meaning behind the words, no rhyme, no rhythm. The poem does not adhere to any rule governing generic classifications. It is neither a sonnet, nor an ode, nor an elegy. It is neither descriptive nor narrative. I quote here an excerpt from the poem:

> jolifanto bambla o falli bambla
> großiga m'pfa habla horem
> egiga goramen

higo bloiko russula huju
hollaka hollala
anlogo bung
blago bung blago bung
bosso fataka
ü üü ü (Ball)

To recite this poem, one neither needs practice, nor some knowledge in English phonetics. One cannot go wrong in its recitation as there is no right way to pronounce these sounds. Painting, collage, and montage proliferated during this period. Jean Arp created a collage titled "Squares Arranged According to the Laws of Chance" in which he did exactly what he promised in the title. The artist simply cut colourful sheets of paper into squares and dropped them on the canvas. He attached the fallen pieces wherever they fell. Such a collage does not require artistic intuition or genius. Similar is the case with Marcel Duchamp's famous artwork *Fountain,* which was nothing, but a mass-produced urinal arranged upside down bearing the signature of the artist. When it was lost from the museum, Duchamp brought another such urinal and made it a work of art. According to Peter Burger, "the signature whose very purpose is to mark what is individual in the work, that it owes its existence to the particular artist, is inscribed on an arbitrarily chosen mass product because all claims to individual creativity are to be mocked" (51-52). The Dadaists too had created "noise concerts," which assailed all preconceived notions concerning Western art. They brought art closer to chaos, stripped it of all the quasi-divine romantic glory concerning the creator and represented disorder and disharmony. Marcel Juno represents this agony thus: "We had lost confidence in our culture. Everything had to be demolished. We would begin again after the tabula rasa. At the Cabaret Voltaire we began by shocking the bourgeois, demolishing his idea of art, attacking common sense, public opinion, education, institutions, museums, good taste, in short, the whole prevailing order." (qtd. Hoffmann)

It is apparent here how the postmodern artists and scholars differed in their relation to the past. While the priests of "modernism" like Yeats, Eliot and Auden bemoaned the loss of a theological guiding force, the postmodern artists sought to annihilate whatever little remained of the past with "a passionate intensity." They wished to create a democratic environment in which appreciation of art did not require a certain training and erudition, but a sensibility to find what is beautiful in an upside-down urinal, for instance.

It comes as no surprise that Habermas, like many others, found this environment to be anarchic and stripped of any inherent values. Habermas advocated the use of consensus between discursive actors to arrive at a judgement as to which version of truth can be amenable to both. Habermas wished to reconstruct the bridge that was rapidly crumbling, to arrive at any minimal agreement concerning what is beautiful, what is logical, what is rational. In opposition to Habermas, Lyotard invents and propagates dissensus. According to Lyotard, each consensus will lead to a crystallization of a view conceded by most members of a rational conversation, mostly the occident. Any opposition to that will not be tolerated. Here, he invokes the idea of terror: "By terror I mean the efficiency gained by eliminating, or threatening to eliminate, a player from the language game one shares with him. He is silenced or consents, not because he has been refuted, but because his inability to participate has been threatened (there are many ways to prevent someone from playing). The decision makers' arrogance, which in principle has no equivalent in the sciences, consists in the exercise of terror. It says: 'Adapt your aspirations to our ends—or else.'" (Lyotard, 64)

By exercising terror, one can silence the other and obviate any resistance to the agreed version of the truth. The post-modern mind, Lyotard argues, does not claim the finality of the conclusion arrived by consensus. According to him, "Postmodern knowledge is not simply a tool of the authorities, it refines our sensitivity to differences and reinforces our ability to tolerate the incommensurable. Its principle is not the expert's homology, but the inventor's paralogy" (Lyotard 23). Instead of a dialogue, he champions the cause of 'paralogy' which may be understood as varying, overlapping, or contradictory views which do not allow a unifying judgement.

Paralogy and Multiple Publication Platforms

The current situation of research in higher education in India provides an interesting ground for this discussion. The presence of multiple platforms for the publication of research papers comes to terms with the idea of 'paralogy.' In the absence of a sole truth, a transcendental signified, the proliferation of these numerous research papers could also be seen as language games between tricksters. For a small fee, one can publish whatever one wishes. As each research paper, germinating from a unique worldview, is at par with any other research paper, there remains no question of quality. Publication of research papers is deemed essential in academia and provides the author the opportunity of career progression. Publication could be the product of joy. "Great joy is had in the endless invention of turns of phrase, of words and meanings, the process behind the evolution of language on the level of *parole*" (Lyotard 10). For Lyotard, speech is necessary for joy. One must speak or write to exist in a paralogical world. However, the contrary is also true. There is also great joy in silence, in standing aloof from the invention of new turns of phrases and new meanings. The compulsion of publishing forces those, who would have retained a dignified silence, also to take up the battle of words. Without the tools, the competence, or perhaps the mere will to write, they produce articles and papers that are not little narratives in opposition to the grand narratives but are no narratives at all. There is no communication taking place. There are neither senders, nor receivers, let alone the referent or the message. What matters most or what only matters in the mere fact that the paper has been published and the ritual performed. The proof of this ceremony will be used for future gains. It will neither add to the conversation nor lead to a new conversation. This brings to light the prediction that Lyotard had made concerning knowledge: 'The question (overt or implied) now asked by the professional student of higher education is no longer "Is it true?" but "What use is it?" In the context of the mercantilization of knowledge, more often than not this question is equivalent to: "Is it saleable?" And in the context of power-growth: "Is it efficient?"' (51).

In today's context, the knowledge is not even saleable. It is merely a confirmation that a transaction has been made. There is an abundance of material masquerading as research output, often referred to as 'trash.' This trash is littered on websites that claim speedy publication with a nominal sum. The publisher becomes the controller and sole indulger of the published texts. Most of these papers may not have been written at all. They may be a computerized re-working of some older work that is sent to a journal and later published purely for a mercantile purpose. As there is no steadfast criterion to distinguish what constitutes credible knowledge, this has led to a culture of "anything goes." Those who are not willing to actively take part in the conversation or initiate a conversation, take recourse to plagiarism: that is turning other thoughts as their own, salami slicing: repeating a single idea over and over again, or relying upon ghost or gift authorship.

This situation stands at the opposite end of paralogy. For Lyotard, "terror" consisted in silencing opposing voices, desiring a consensus through a discourse among parties. The dictum "Publish or Perish" also uses terror. It asks reluctant parties to produce knowledge adhering to the rules of the language game involved in academic writing. It forces non-seekers of knowledge to seek knowledge. Such people take the easy way out by exploiting the very lacuna of this doctrine. If anything can pass as knowledge in the absence of any totalizing, norm-assigning grand narrative, then they can publish anything. It brings us back to the mythological tower of babel where no one can understand the other. Further, it brings us to a situation where neither the sender nor the receiver is willing to communicate, yet they produce noise, because being silent is either seen as assent or ineptitude.

In the cacophony of deafening unintended conversations, there was still a requirement of at least some communication to be made. This very abundance of trash led to the re-emergence of certain agencies that now legitimize knowledge through peer approval. These agencies are the reputed publishing houses, not surprising that most of them are the occidental. Institutions across the globe realized the value of legitimation. The University Grants Commission (UGC), "a statutory Organization of the Government of India by an Act of Parliament in 1956, for the coordination, determination and maintenance of standards of teaching, examination and research in university education," attempted to legitimize the sources of knowledge for academicians in India (UGC). In its first attempt to curb the menace of predatory publishing in 2017, it brought up a gargantuan list of journals, publications in which will be approved as credible research output. This list itself was so huge that it comprised all such journals which it had sought to keep outside the pale of authentic knowledge platforms. Professor Bhushan Patwardhan, Vice Chairman of UGC says: "To deal with the problem of predatory journals, UGC created a white list of quality journals as a proactive step. However, due to some flaws during the list's creation and implementation, it was polluted with poor-quality journals and faced severe criticism. A large number of poor-quality journals were included in the UGC approved list, which opened the floodgates for desperate authors." (Tao)

Therefore, in a landmark decision in 2018, the UGC delegitimized its previously approved list. It published a document with the list of all such journals that it had earlier approved with "Cancelled" written in red letters in watermark ("UGC Approved (old) List of Journals"). UGC delisted 3000 titles from its category of approved journals. Supposing that each of these journals had at least 10 issues with 10 articles in each issue, then 3,00,000 (pseudo?) research papers were considered invalid. Imagine a pile of three hundred thousand research papers delegitimized at one stroke. The actual size could be 10 times more than that. The decision did not create any existential threat to epistemology, nor a stir among intellectuals to roll back the move. Rather, it merited a grudging approval among all stakeholders.

UGC did not stop there. It also led a scrutiny of the 10 years of Ph.D. dissertations in Indian universities (Jain). In 2019, It created a platform called "Consortium for Academic Research and Ethics" (CARE), a body which will approve the list of journals, publications in which will now be considered for publication. Along with the list, UGC also approved the international journals that are listed in SCOPUS and Web of Science. There is an inherent hierarchy among these journals. They are listed on various platforms which assign them a score mostly based on the number of citations merited by these journals. For example, a journal that publishes 10 articles and each article gets 10 citations, that journal is supposed to be of a higher standard than a journal with 9 citations per article. The most valuable article is the one that is the most popular. The value of an article now is not determined by the content of the article but based on the platform where it is published.

Conclusion

Even though the platforms for predatory publishing were delegitimized, the dictum "publish or perish" still holds sway. Now the slogan could be read as "Publish (in such and such journals) or Perish." While in the earlier model, good writing also got discredited because of the platform. So, now the platform becomes more important than the content. One is more likely to write in one's bio-data that the author has been published by these reputed journals, than mention the ideas discussed therein or even the title of the paper. Now con-versation could continue on platforms that were at least hitherto held sacred or new platforms will be created to lure a clientele that's still reluctant to take part in conversation. This compulsion to produce knowledge and its consequences will persist as long as the slogan "publish or perish" does not itself perish!

Works Cited

Ball, Hugo. "Karawane." *Poets.org,* https://poets.org/poem/karawane. Accessed 10 Nov 2021. Web.

Barthes, Roland. "The Death of the Author." *Image, Music, Text*, Translated by S Heath, London: Fontana, 1977, pp. 142-148.

Bloom, Harold. *A Map of Misreading*. Oxford: Oxford University Press, 1980.

Burger, Peter. Theory of the Avant-Garde. Minneapolis: Manchester University Press, 1984.

De Quincey, Thomas. "On the Knocking at the Gate, In Macbeth." *Miscellaneous Essays. Project Gutenberg,* 2004, https://www.gutenberg.org/cache/epub/10708/pg10708.html.

Eliot, T.S. "The Waste Land." *Poetry Foundation*, https://www.poetryfoundation.org/poems/47311/the-waste-land.

Habermas, Jürgen. "Modernity: An Unfinished Project." *Habermas and the Unfinished Project of Modernity*. Edited by Maurizio Passerin D'entreves and Seyla Benhabib. Massachusetts: The MIT Press, 1997, pp 38-58.

Hoffman, Irene E. "Documents of Dada and Surrealism: Dada and Surrealist Journals in the Mary Reynolds Collection." *Bulletin Dada*. Ed. Tristen Tzara. The Art Institution of Chicago-Reyson & Bunham Libraries.

Jain, Rajnish. "Quality of PhD Thesis in Indian Universities." *UGC*. 21 May 2019.

Koestler, Arthur, et al. *The God That Failed*. New York: Harper & Row. 1949.

Larkin, Philip. "Church Going." *Blue Ridge Journal*, www.blueridge journal.com/poems/pl-church.htm.

Lyotard, Jean-François. *The Post-modern Condition: A Report on Knowledge.* Translated by Geoff Bennington, Manchester: Manchester University Press, 1984.

Plato. *The Republic*. Translated by B Jowett. *Project Gutenberg*, 1998, https://www.gutenberg.org/cache/epub/1497/pg1497-images.html. Web.

Spurgeon, Caroline. *Shakespeare's Imagery and What it Tells Us*. Cambridge: Cambridge University Press. 2005.

Tao, Tao. "India's Fight Against Predatory Journals: An Interview with Professor Bhushan Patwardhan." *The Scholarly Kitchen*. 5 Feb 2020, https://scholarlykitchen.sspnet.org/2020/02/05/indias-fight-against-predatory-journals-an-interview-with-professor-bhushan-patwardhan

UGC Approved (old) List of Journals. *UGC*, www.ugc.ac.in/pdfnews/5283580_UGC-Cancelled-List.pdf.

UGC. "About University Grants Commission." www.ugc.ac.in.

Yeats, W.B. "The Second Coming." *Poetry Foundation*, www.poetryfoundation.org/poems/43290/the-second-coming

Postmodernist Nature of the New Wave of Interactive Fiction on Television

VINITA NAIR
Research Scholar
MEKHALA VENKATESH
Jain University, Bengaluru

Imagine getting to make choices for the characters in a story, instead of the narrator informing you of the direction the story takes and how it ends. That would be a common feature in the world of Interactive Fiction. Interactive Fiction (IF) has been explored across various mediums including books, gaming, educational software, and various other visual mediums. This genre of fiction is also something that matches with what appeals to a modern audience, a fiction that allows what Bakhtin calls 'truthpravda' or truth for itself which means that there are many truths unlike 'truthistina' of truth in itself, a universal truth or in post-modernist terms a meta narrative.(Jamali 645). With each version of the storyline comes the individual's version , a truth based on his or her set of experiences and perspectives.

Interactive Fiction

Interactive fiction, as the name suggests, is the kind of literature in which the user of the fiction plays an important role in creating the narrative. Montfort explains Interactive Fiction as a system that produces a unique storyline when interacted with. There is also a necessity of action from the user's end which leads the direction of the narrative.

Such kind of fiction was seen in Choose Your Adventure Books in the 1980's where stories were written in second person and the reader assumed the role of the protagonist determining the course of action. Readers would be asked to move to particular page numbers based on their choices. A more recent version of such fiction can be seen in creations like Ryan North's Romeo And / Or Juliet , where one can either be Romeo or Juliet and decide which way the story should move. It's further refined versions are now seen in gaming, educational software and even OTTs.

In a computer mediated narrative which is seen in gaming, the story resembles a fine grained 'Choose your Adventure' experience depending on a demand-based feedback loop for the whole story to take shape. There have been some attempts in to bringing interactive fiction into television medium. There are movies like Possibilia, a story about a couple which is undergoing a breakup. It is designed in such a way that there are up to 16 possibilities one can end up with based on the audience choices. Another such example is 'A Week in the Life of Milly' where the protagonist Milly is a child prodigy facing many dilemmas and the audience helps with those choices she faces (Keeley). The narratives for these types of fiction seem like a deviation from the regular or acceptable and are rather abnormal in their form and structure. Another attribute of such fiction is that it allows multiple narratives. All these features create a platform to further gauge whether this fiction is post-modernist in nature.

Postmodernism represents a shift in perspective in various disciplines like art, literature, architecture, fashion, social sciences and many more. Power shifts in the post second world war era and various other phenomena like consumer capitalism led to this theory being a mouthpiece of the fragmentation, disorientation and insecurities stemming from it. Post Modernism expressed a disbelief in coherence, cynically suggesting that there is disorder everywhere.

Gibson says that Postmodernism as a culture negates systemization and structuralist thinking. Staying away from a metanarrative (Lyotard et al. 54) or grand narratives that are created by power wielders and are incomplete truths is an important part of this school of thought. Metanarrative is an all-encompassing narrative in which covers historical meaning, knowledge, social and cultural phenomena and experience along with adhering to the universal beliefs or truths. These narratives basically work to legitimize power. Instead, the focus is on 'mini narratives' which then creates a chance for many such narratives to emerge. Post modernism pushes the theory of constructivism and strongly advocates that everything is ideologically constructed which further means that there is scope for multiple realities.

Postmodern Proclivities

Bandersnatch on the OTT platform Netflix gave viewers a taste of how this type of fiction can manifest in a television series and on a much more participative level. Unlike a regular series on the platform, the story stops at strategic points asking the user to click on one of the choices given on the screen using the remote controller. Thus, the story has multiple paths through which the audience can travel, and each path would be unique to the user. Also, the story becomes the user's unique story because the choices are made by the users themselves.

Postmodernism saw the rise of new artistic practices, rejecting Modernism's reliance on linearity, coherence, realism, and internal consciousness as frameworks for creating plots and characters. Hutcheon(180) talks about 'absence of centre' in a postmodernist narrative. She calls it an opportunity to open-up ideology to appreciating differences. Unlike a regular narrative interactive fiction allows multiple interpretations, thus there is not one interpretation but many of the story idea. A new version of storytelling, the narrative actually adjusts the timing according to the choices made, some versions take more time and some take less depending on the choices made. The absence of centre here, in this kind of narration is the fact that it is not standardized with an author directed perspective, thus open to the differences in perspectives.

Aristotle is considered to be the first to apply logical reasoning into investigation of narratives. The Aristotelian theory of narratives was re-presented by Laurel where she points out two different types of relations between the components of the structure of a narrative (41). She calls it two opposite causal chains. One which goes from enactment to action, by an authorial view of the narrative represented by the plot, called the formal cause and the other in the opposite direction, from action to enactment, by the audience view of the narrative represented by its understanding of the plot, called the material cause.

For interactive fiction, Mateas put forward a neo-Aristotelian theory where user becomes a character (143). The user's intention plays the role of the formal cause, from language to enactment, also giving an authorial perspective on the narrative. The material cause is represented by the limitations on the user represented by material resources constraints from below and plot constraints from the plot authorial level. What is interesting in this model is that the user action level is situated at the character level in Aristotle's narrative structure. This reworking of narratives aligns to what Laurel talks about post-modernism opining that it advocates the process of re-historize and not de-historize art and literature.

Textuality in interactive fiction represents a flagrant divergence from the long-established conventions of narratives. These narratives resist discipline, not adhering to most narratological methods. Narrative theorists such as Gibson term the narratives of Interactive fiction as textual monstrosity in the context of postmodernism: texts that defy structuralist thinking, systematization, and classification (212).

Another attribute of interactive fiction is fictional mediation (Thabet 105) The user gets to co-narrate, trigger events thus projecting a narrative voice into the text. This voice depends on the user's perceptions and also the options provided by the system. Agency is a key factor and has huge narratological implications. With some dimensions under the user's control it gives the narrative a personal version, which is also subjective to a large extent. This means that there are multiple narratives based on user's perceptions. This adheres to the notion of resistance of meta or grand narratives which is a post modernism feature introduced by Lyotard (xxiv), where he talks instead on focussing on the fragmented and the marginalized. This meta narrative can be defined as an overarching interpretation of circumstances that provides a pattern for people's beliefs.

Postmodernism disrupts this narrative schema and its formulaic codes to give way to little narratives or 'petit recits' as Lyotard preferred to call it. Every user in Interactive fiction creates a little narrative and the grand narrative in these versions of the story, that is going the way the author's perceptions work, stands nullified. Traditional relationships between dominant and subordinate, in this case an author and reader became less formal and less predictable. The erosion of traditional identities also shook fixed ideas and took into consideration the effect of discourses that construct and enforce preferred narratives for understanding the self, other, and world.

Postmodernism describes knowledge and claims as socially constructed stemming from political, historical and cultural discourses. Postmodernism rejects any singular and constant reality. This is basically because of its constructivist background and it's rejection of any kind of parallelism or similarity (Farmahini 124). Again this aligns to the attribute of interactive fiction where there is no singular path or a set end to the story and new versions are created based on users' choices. Each version would also be based on the prior experiences gathered by the user. Postmodernism rejects universal values and accepts the relativity of all values in all areas, which means no specific value preference exists. Everyone should order their own values, value preferences, and approaches

(Rahnama 25), thus fundamentalism is replaced by activism. The school of constructivism advocates that the main component of morality is the concept of "experience." Rejection of absolute values, emphasis on experience, relativity of moralities, and their fluid nature connects the ideas of constructivism and post modernism.

While perusing a piece of interactive fiction like Bandersnatch, a person's experience will decide his or her choices thus denying the piece an absolute structure. Each piece of the story is constructed by the user thus different from another version of the same story. The story can be entirely different or parts of it can be. This will lead to one out of the five endings for the series yet the structure of the story would be different, the incidences, decisions of the protagonist would differ. This is much like constructivism where John Dewey refused the tabula rasa theory and advocated that each learner comes with a set of prior knowledge based on experiences, which allows the learner to consolidate knowledge in his or her own way (Duschinsky 509).

Conclusion

Postmodernism works towards heightening our awareness of ambiguity, uncertainty, emergence, and difference(Taylor 113). It works almost like a virus disrupting the tendencies of modernist thinking of turning process into structure (Chia 579). It reminds us that our knowledge and identities which we may have viewed as total, transcendent, or even permanent, are suddenly vulnerable (Mumby 6).

As compared to gaming, Interactive Fiction maybe a less explored area as far as television goes but it's certainly something that is creating excitement in the field of television entertainment. The success of the series led to Netflix bring out the interactive version of 'You vs Wild' where survival expert Bear Grylls is directed by the audience on his actions. India too got its first interactive trailer with Guneet Monga's Monsoon Shootout offering the audience to make choices for the protagonist. Its postmodern nature of uncertainty is what appeals to the audience along with the power it renders to create one's own unique narratives.

Works Cited

Chia, Robert. "From Modern to Postmodern Organizational Analysis." *Organization Studies*, vol. 16, no. 4, 1995, pp. 579-604. *Crossref*, doi:10.1177/017084069501600406.

Duschinsky, Robert. "'Tabula Rasa' and Human Nature." *Philosophy*, vol. 87, no. 342, Cambridge University Press, 2012, pp. 509-29, www.jstor.org/stable/41682980.

Farmani, M. *Postmodernism and Education*. Tehran, Avizh, 2010.

Gibson, Andrew. *Towards a Postmodern Theory of Narrative*. 1st ed., Edinburgh University Press, 1996.

Hutcheon, Linda. *The Politics of Postmodernism*. Routledge, 2002.

Keeley, J. "10 Interactive Movies You Can Watch and Control Online." *MUO*, 24 Feb. 2020, www.makeuseof.com/tag/3-free-interactive-movies-web-control.

Laurel, B. *Towards a Postmodern Theory of Narrative*. Edinburgh, 2003.

Lyotard, Jean-Francois, et al. *The Postmodern Condition: A Report on Knowledge*. University of Minnesota Press, 1984.

Mateas, M. *A Preliminary Poetics for Interactive Drama and Games*. Edinburgh University Press, 2020, edinburghuniversitypress.com/book-towards-a-postmodern-theory-of-narrative.html.

Montfort, Nick. "Toward a Theory of Interactive Fiction." *Toward a Theory of Interactive Fiction*, 2003, nickm.com/if/toward.html

Mumby, Dennis K. "Modernism, Postmodernism, and Communication Studies: A Rereading of an Ongoing Debate." *Communication Theory*, vol. 7, no. 1, 1997, pp. 1-28. *Crossref*, doi:10.1111/j.1468-2885.1997.tb00140.x.

North, Ryan. *Romeo and/or Juliet: A Chooseable-Path Adventure*. Illustrated, Riverhead Books, 2016.

Nesari, Ali Jamali. "Dialogism versus Monologism: A Bakhtinian Approach to Teaching." *Procedia - Social and Behavioral Sciences*, vol. 205, 2015, pp. 642-47. *Crossref*, doi:10.1016/j.sbspro.2015.09.101.

Rahnama, A. *An Introduction on Moral Education (Philosophical-Psychological Fundamentals and Moral Teaching Methods)*. Tehran, Ayizh, 2009.

Taylor, B. et al. "Engaging Organizational Communication Theory & Research: Multiple Perspectives Engaging Organizational Communication Theory & Research: Multiple Perspectives." *Postmodern Theory*, 2005. *Crossref*, doi:10.4135/9781452204536.

Thabet, T. "Monstrous Textuality: Game Fiction Between Postmodernism and Structuralism." *Loading*, vol. 5, no. 8, 2018, journals.sfu.ca.

Fluidity of Fiction and Non-Fiction: A Postmodernist Reading of *The Diary of Cotton Mather*

VIOLETTA TROFIMOVA
Independent Scholar, St. Petersburg, Russia

Postmodernism is usually associated with the second half of the twentieth century. Nevertheless, some thinkers, above all, Jean-Francois Lyotard, taking a cyclical view of cultural history, considered postmodernism an essential part of it. In his concept postmodernism and modernism succeeded each other in the past and will go one after another in the future.

Postmodernism can tell us a lot about literature and its history. Among the important predecessors of postmodernist novelists we can mention Miguel de Cervantes with his *Don Quixote* (1605; 1615), Laurence Sterne with his *Life and Opinions of Tristram Shandy* (1759-1767), and Denis Diderot with his *Rameau's Nephew*. While *Don Quixote* and *Tristram Shandy* are good examples of metafiction and metafictional parody. *Rameau's Nephew* presents a nihilistic and ironic character that questions the norms of morality and declares himself totally amoral. Lyotard also called Rabelais a postmodern because he, as well as Sterne, emphasized paradoxes ("Rules" 218).

Apart from Lyotard, a literary critic Stephen Greenblatt was also interested in historical texts including non-literary texts. He claimed "non-literary texts are not simply neutral transcriptions of reality; instead, historical fact and experience are available to us only in 'textual traces,' with all the concomitant rhetorical strategies which characterize textuality" (Sim 263). As history can be presented only in the form of narrative, Greenblatt easily connects non-literary historical texts with the literary artifact (Sim 264). That is how he reads Shakespearean plays. Before turning to the relationships between fiction and non-fiction, or, as Umberto Eco called them, natural and artificial narrative, I will give a number of important postmodernist notions that work not only for twentieth- and twenty-first-century texts, but also for much earlier narratives.

Lyotard made a distinction between grand narratives, or metanarratives—theories that claim to provide universal explanations, and little narratives. He defined postmodernism as incredulity towards metanarratives (Lyotard, "Postmodern" xxiv). Among grand narratives we can mention Hegelian, Marxist and other philosophical systems. An event is "an occurrence that dramatically alters the way we view the world, and calls all our ideological assumptions into question in the process" (Sim 10). Such events cannot be predicted, and to acknowledge them means to acknowledge both the limitations of grand narrative and "the essential openness of the future" (Sim 10).

Svelteness is a concept proposed by Lyotard which "attempts to capture the flexibility and lack of dogmatic belief" (Sim 369). To be svelte means to be open to events and to respond to them without the prejudices springing out of a belief in grand narratives. Literary scholars make distinction between a "readerly" and "writerly" text. A "readerly" text "reads itself for us," and a reader is a consumer in relation to it (Nicol 44). A 'readerly' text is finite. A "writerly" text treats the reader as a "co-writer"; it is the reader who activates its meaning. A "writerly" text "exists nowhere" (Nicol 44). Postmodern texts serve as examples of "writerly" texts. Finally, natural narrative "describes events that actually occurred (or which the speaker claims actually occurred)," while artificial narrative "is represented by fiction which only pretends to tell the truth about the actual universe, or which claims to tell the truth about a fictional universe" (Eco 119-20).

In this paper, I am going to analyze a piece of non-fiction—*The Diary* of an American Puritan thinker, historian and natural philosopher Cotton Mather (1663-1728)—as a text which often transgresses the boundaries between non-fiction and fiction, natural and artificial narrative. This text is considered to be one of the major historical sources for the period, but it has not attracted much attention of literary scholars. It remained unpublished for almost 200 years, although some fragments appeared in print almost immediately after author's death. As I am going to show, this text is much more complex than just a traditional account of the life of a Puritan with its self-analysis, prayers and other religious practices.

Genre Peculiarities of Mather's Times

Cotton Mather (1663-1728), a New England Puritan priest and intellectual, spent his entire life in Boston, where he became the most prolific writer of his times with more than 400 publications on history, religious matters, natural philosophy and medicine. He apparently did not leave any works of fiction. He is infamous for his involvement in Salem witch trials, as he published a book on witchcraft and an account of this event entitled *The Wonders of the Invisible World* in 1693. He has published the history of New England, books on education and ethics, as well as *The Christian Philosopher*—the first systematic book of science in America. He made experiments on plant hybridization in 1716 and was instrumental in introducing smallpox inoculation in America together with a doctor Zabdiel Boylston in 1721-1722. His *Biblia Americana* and his medical treatise *Angel of Bethesda* did not appear in print until recent years.

Mather can be considered a creator of a grand narrative in early American literature. Around 1697 he completed his history of New England in the seventeenth century—*Magnalia Christi*

Americana, which was published in 1702 and made him a name in the history of literature. It told about the great deeds of the founders of the colonies, and the most important historical events of the period. Because of this work Mather got a reputation of a pedant with a heavy style, an author whose writings are very difficult to read. His *Diary* can be read as a little narrative which unfolds his secret aspirations, tells about seemingly ordinary and unimportant domestic events and everyday life. Moreover, Mather's *Diary* poses a problem of whether it is a fictional or non-fictional text.

One of the great figures of postmodern literature Umberto Eco in his *Six Walks in the Fictional Woods* showed the fluidity of the boundaries between fictional and non-fictional texts, natural and artificial narratives. He claimed that "an incontrovertible signal of fictionality does not exist," and "any attempt to determine the structural differences between natural and artificial narrative can usually be falsified by a series of counterexamples" (Eco 125, 121). Eco emphasized the idea that "we are continually tempted to give shape to life through narrative schemes," and it may be profitable to "read life as if it were fiction, to read fiction as if it were life" (Eco 99, 118). Actually, the most visible mark that shows that the text is artificial can be found in the "para-text," which is defined by Eco as "the external messages that surround a text" (Eco 120). The most typical paratextual signal for fiction is "the designation 'A Novel' on the book's cover" (Eco 120).

Postmodern literature followed Eco's advice to read life as fiction and bent towards representing "fictional" quality of contemporary life. Such US authors as John Barth and Thomas Pynchon widely used the elements of autobiography and diary in their novels and short stories. For example, John Barth's collection of short stories *Lost in the Funhouse* (1968) included such works as "Life-Story" and "Autobiography," and Thomas Pynchon's novel *V.* had an entry in the character's late father's diary as a starting point for the quest. The same tendency can be seen in British post-modern fiction. A fine example of British historical fiction, A.S. Byatt's Booker Prize winner *Possession* included several extracts from characters' diaries.

David Levin in his biography of Cotton Mather entitled *Cotton Mather: the young life of the Lord's Remembrancer, (1663-1703)* pointed out that the entries for the decade starting with 1681 "are not a diary at all" (63). Mather called them his "Reserved Memorials." The narrative "had been copied and revised retrospectively from originals which Mather destroyed" (Levin 63). Despite the fact the entries are dated precisely, "these papers do not record his daily experience, secular or devotional" (Levin 63). Actually, it poses a big question over a genre of Mather's *Diary* and whether it is correct to call it a piece of non-fiction. It obviously loses its documentary quality in the process of rewriting, and transforms into a piece of advisory literature—a set of examples from author's religious life that can be imitated by his children.

The "Event" in Mather's *Diary*

The "event" in Lyotard's sense happened to Mather in the year 1702. Levin attributed it to his failure in "particular faith," that is, the voice of Heaven the author of the *Diary* seemed to hear in answer to his prayers. Levin exposed the double nature of this "event"—the failure of God's promise about Mather's father's important and profitable mission to England and, above all, the failure of his belief in his wife's recovery from consumption (Levin). His wife Abigail's illness and final death became a period of heavy trial for Cotton Mather. It lasted for more than half a year. He persuaded himself that God promised him her recovery and despite her obviously hopeless condition, he waited for a miracle which did not happen. His wife, tired of long suffering, expected death and lamented the fact she had become a burden for her family: "I shall make you all weary" (1: 452). The only person her words did not apply to was her husband: "I don't mean you, Mr. Mather" Abigail told him (1: 452). She even came to believe in her own miraculous recovery and dreamt of a medicine which was to help her. Besides Abigail's illness, Mather was faced with his children being sick with smallpox. Contrary to his wife, they all fortunately recover.

Mather makes a most detailed account of the "event"—his sufferings in the second half of the year 1702. The diary entries from this period are full of distress and mark author's doubts in his faith. As early as on May 1 he writes: "And now, I see once again, that Faith is no Fancy" (1: 427). On June 3 he admits: "An Uncomfortable Dullness accompanied the Devotions of the Day. I could not but fear, lest the Death of my Consort and all the Unhappy Effects of it upon a broken Family must overtake me" (1: 430). On the same day he founds "the evil spirit buffeting of my mind, with impure Thoughts, which exceedingly abased me before the Lord" (1: 430). "But Lord!—exclaims he on June 25,—how aggravated a Calamity must be her Death, if such a Sting, as the Disappointment of my Particular Faith, must be added unto it" (1: 434). Mather still tries to find support in religion: "I resigned her unto the Lord and submitted unto all the sorrowful Consequences, of a rejected Prayer, and a defeated Faith, and a desolate broken Family, if He should order them for me" (1: 435). But religion gives little support in his situation, as the diary entries from July, August and October show: "My Faith, and my poor Consort's Patience, is mightily tried by her continuing in a dubious, dangerous, deplorable Condition of Illness" (July 21); "I am kept up all Night, that I may see her die, and therewith see the terrible Death of my Prayer and Faith" (August 1), "And being in extreme Distress about my poor, feeble, wasted Consort, who after more than twenty Week's Languishment, is, for my further Trial, fallen into the Symptoms of an hopeless Consumption" (October 22) (1: 436-37, 443).

Mather feels his condition is in concordance with the sad condition of the town and even the entire colony, that is, his private life is inseparable from his public life of a priest: "I kept this Day . . . in my Study. Both with respect unto the Condition of my Consort, and with respect unto the condition of the Town, where the Small-pox begins to spread; and the Land, where a War is now proclaimed, and other sad Circumstances we have in our Government" (July 4); "More than fourscore people were in this black Month of December carried from this Town to their long Home" (1: 435, 451). Mather's prose is rhythmic and musical, reflecting his own and his people's tragic situation.

Cotton Mather gives the exact date that marked a change in his life and calls it "the black Day": "At last the black Day arrives: Tuesday, the first of December. I had never yet seen such a black Day, in all the Time of my Pilgrimage. The Desire of my Eyes is this Day to be taken from me. Her Death is lingering, and painful" (1: 448). No other diary entry by this date had had such an intense tragic quality.

The same as with the entries from the 1680's, the part related to "the event" from 1702 was obviously written much later and cannot be called a genuine diary. It looks more like memoirs. We find here elements of retrospection that add lyrical quality to the narrative full of drama and pain: "I cannot remember the Discourses that passed between us. . . . This I remember, that a little before she died, I asked her to tell me faithfully, what Fault she had seen in my Conversation, that she would advise me to rectify. She replied . . . that she knew of none" (1: 448).

After the "event" the *Diary* changes its narrative structure. Mather puts aside purely religious explanations of what happened to him and his wife and proposes secular reflections on the situation. We cannot say he has become svelte, as he still believes in the dogmas of his religion, but he is more open to other, non-dogmatic interpretations of his painful experience.

Mather admits his wife's staying in this world would have brought nothing but unhappiness to her family: "Had she lived, it would probably have been, in continual weakness, and Languor, and Sorrow, that would have been at last uneasy to us all" (1: 451). He is sure he would have been infected from her "if she had recovered a little more, and so far that I should have run the venture of sleeping with her. My feeble Constitution would undoubtedly have run into a consumption" (1: 452). Mather also points out her "melancholy temper" aggravated by family problems—remarriage of her widowed father and deplorable condition of her brothers: "The Sight of these Things, would without a Miracle, have brought such a Disorder of Mind upon her, as would have rendered my Condition insupportable" (1: 452).

Despite these reasonable thoughts, grief overcomes Mather. He would have done everything to make his wife stay with him in this world, and now he hardly bears being without her: "Before the late weeks of my Life, I had rarely known any Tears, except those that were for the Joy of the Salvation of God. But now scarce a Day passes me, without a Flood of Tears, and my Eyes even decay with weeping" (1: 457). The account of the "event" in Mather's Diary is moving and full of human sentiments.

Narrative after the "Event"

A couple of months pass, and the narrative structure of the *Diary* changes again and starts resembling a romantic novella in a nutshell. The heroine of this story remains unnamed, and the narrative bears the quality of a fictional text—the reader wants to know what happens next and what the end of the story is. Mather calls the girl "a young Gentlewoman of incomparable Accomplishments" with "polite Education" (1: 457). He says she is "of rare Wit and Sense"—the characteristic strongly resembling a quotation from the play *Silent Woman* by Ben Jonson: "It has something in it like rare wit and sense" (1: 457; Johnson 152). She is "extremely winning in her conversation" (1: 457).

He is forty years old, a widower with several children, and she "is not much more than twenty years old" (1: 458). The girl is active and full of initiative. At first she sends him letters, and then pays him a visit. She is not shy to press him to marry her veiling her request under religious issues: her marriage to him seems to have a wholesome effect on her soul. Mather knows she is an "airy person" with not very good reputation (1: 458).

The girl manages to raise strong feelings in Mather. He tells of "a mighty tenderness for a person so very amiable," using an expression which resembles even the words of one of Aphra Behn's characters in a play *Feigned Courtesans*: "as long as my Person is so amiable" (1: 467; Behn 152). He also admits that "breeding" requires him "to treat her with honour and respect" (1: 467). Nevertheless, his feelings have little to do with his religion and his ministry. Moreover, he starts to consider this affair as an obstacle to his work and mission.

Mather does not go into details what was wrong with the girl's reputation and why his family was so much against his marriage to her. But he was obviously afraid of breaking family connections because of this affair: "that I may be left utterly destitute of all humane support, my relatives, through their extreme distaste at the talk of my respects for the person above mentioned; and fear lest I should over-value her; do treat me with unsupportable strangeness and harshness" (1: 469). Finally, Mather decides to break with the girl: "I struck the knife, into the Heart of my sacrifice, by a Letter to her mother" (1: 474).

Despite his resolution not to marry a girl so much disliked by his family, Mather still has strong doubts in his faith. His *Diary* entries from 1703 give lengthy account of his spiritual crisis. The failure of his "particular faith" may mean that the God does not hear him: "[Satan] fills me with fears, that I am a man rejected and abhorred of God; and given up to the worst of Delusions; and that the Lord will make no more use of me to glorify Him. I am scarce able to live under these doleful Disconsolations" (1: 468-69). Another explanation may be the God does not exist at all: "Sometimes, Temptations, to impurities; and sometimes to Blasphemy, and Atheism, and the Abandonment of all Religion, as a mere Delusion; and sometimes, to self-Destruction itself" (1: 475). He even talks about himself in the third person: "These, even these, O miserable Mather, do follow thee, with an astonishing Fury" (1: 475). Mather admits his "spirit is excessively broken" (1: 471). Besides spiritual crisis his human sentiments are hurt, as his friends tell him about matches for him. His father also presses him not to continue in widowed state and to remarry.

This romantic episode from Mather's *Diary* has a happy ending. He finds a good woman living not far from him, a widow with a little son, proposes to her and marries her. Despite such a conventional denouement, this part of his *Diary* is still a "writerly" text, a narrative demanding deciphering on the side of a reader. This text is open for interpretation, as it has a number of blank spaces and a very limited point of view. Although it is a non-fictional narrative, it can also be read as fiction, as Umberto Eco proposed to do, as it has a plot, main characters, conflict, and insight into the principal character's psychology.

In the pieces of fiction, diaries are often incomplete, partly lost or destroyed. The same thing happened, as Cotton Mather claimed, to his own *Diary*. It misses some years because, as the author said, these parts were destroyed or hidden by his third wife Lydia: "She not only detains them from me, but either she has destroyed them, or she does protest, that I shall never see them any more" (2: 584). Lydia seems to have notions of privacy very similar to those of our own time. The entire story of their courtship and wedding remains untold, opening a wide space for speculations.

Conclusion

Cotton Mather's *Diary* is not a diary in full sense of this word, as it has been edited and rewritten, and considerable parts of it read as memoirs. Moreover, it can be called a postmodern text in the same way as those by Rabelais, Sterne and Diderot, with one important difference—it is still a piece of non-fiction. It is an example of little narrative, a "writerly" text which changes a lot after the "event"—the untimely death of Mather's first wife. The romantic episode from the year 1703 show that the boundaries between fiction and non-fiction are sometimes difficult to define, and only extratextual signs—para-text—can establish them.

Works Cited

Behn, Aphra. *The Rover and Other Plays*. Ed. Jane Spencer. Oxford: Oxford University Press, 1998.

Johnson, Ben. *Epicene, or The Silent Woman*. Manchester: Manchester University Press, 2003.

Levin, David. *Cotton Mather: The Young Life of the Lord's Remembrancer, 1663-1703*. Cambridge, Massachusetts: Harvard University Press, 1978.

Lyotard, Jean-François, and Brian Massumi. "Rules and Paradoxes and Svelte Appendix." *Cultural Critique* 5 (1986), pp. 209-19.

Lyotard, Jean-François. *The Postmodern Condition: A Report on Knowledge*. Manchester: Manchester University Press, 1984.

Mather, Cotton. *Diary of Cotton Mather*. 2 vols. Boston: Massachusetts Historical Society, 1911-1912.

Nicol, Brian. *The Cambridge Introduction to Postmodern Fiction*. Cambridge: Cambridge University Press, 2009.

Sim, Stuart, ed. *The Routledge Companion to Postmodernism*. London and New York: Routledge, 2002.

Resisting Authority in *The Merchant of Venice*: A View of Shylock

PRIYANKA LAMBA
Dronacharya Government College, Gurugram

The Merchant of Venice is one of the most reputational comedies of William Shakespeare. It has a relatively simple main plot about the romance between a young gentleman Bassanio and a pretty lady Portia and the complex subplot about the traditional revenge story of Elizabethan times. In the story of "a pound of flesh," Antonio's counterpart, Shylock is the most noteworthy figure. The characterization of Shylock has been a controversial topic for four hundred years. The character of Shylock has continuously fueled debate over Shakespeare's questionable endowment of "humanity" upon the Jew. Interpretations of Shylock have changed over the years. Over the year's theatre and film productions have also portrayed Shylock in various ways. Literary critic Anne Barton asserts that Shylock has at times been characterized as the devil incarnate, a comic villain. He has also been described as a "wronged and suffering father nobler by far than the people who triumph over him." In the recent studies and productions, he is presented as a justifiably angry man struggling to resist the constructions of his alterity imposed upon him by the dominant culture.

Racial and Religious Biases

In Shakespeare's time, Jews were despised for their religion, culture and occupation. Anti-Semitism ethos were rampant in the Christian dominant England, ranging from that of the court to the common people. Recent historians and critics have agreed that there was a considerable number of Jews in England in Elizabethan period. They were generally teachers, merchant and physicians who had arrived from Portugal and Spain after their expulsion from there and "their presence complicated the anti-Semitic ideologies that had percolated down from earlier times." Although England at that time was expanding its own frontiers, reached for new market and colonies abroad yet it displayed a great hostility and anxiety about the presence of outsiders like Jews, Turks and Africans in its own society. Ania Loomba reveals that in 16th and 17th centuries, there was a substantial increase in nationalist feelings and hostility towards outsiders. In England Jews were not given equal opportunities, they lived in ghettos, paid higher taxes and wore caps and dresses that distinguished them from others. In order to limit the economic as well as legal rights of outsiders, various laws were proposed. They were thought to be demonic, scheming and cruel. So, Jews can very well be labeled as "others" as they were considered different from the main values of the society and therefore deserved discrimination and persecution. They were labeled "others" in every aspect of life, from career to social life, from religion to culture. During the period of Shakespeare's plays, the issue of hysteria relating to Jews was being voiced due to the allegation against Roy Lopez who was Queen Elizabeth's physician being Jewish, for trying to murder her. Public opinion about outsiders was instrumental in influencing their stage representations. By 1600, over twenty thousand Londoner's were going to the theatre each weak. Marlowe in The Jew Of Malta presents a colossal caricature of a Jew Barabas who says, "I walk abroad at nights and kill sick people groaning under walls, sometimes I go about and poison wells." As a result of this wickedness, he is boiled alive to the universal delight of the Christian audience.

Apart from *The Merchant of Venice*, anti-Semitic passages appear in briefly in Shakespeare's other two plays also i.e. *The Two*

Gentlemen of Verona and *Macbeth*. In *The Two Gentlemen of Verona*, Launce, is the clownish servant of Proteus, who describes his dog as being so unsympathetic that it would not shed a tear even when "a Jew would have wept to have seen our parting" In *Macbeth,* the witches include "liver of blaspheming Jew" in their hellish recipe. The play *The Merchant of Venice* is about the consequences of being a Jew in medieval England. Shylock, the Jew, a demonized "other" is depicted as a devil in the shape of human, who is a greedy usurer, a merciless murderer, a patriarchal father and a mean master. The villainy image of Shylock is the concentrated embodiment of anti-Semitic ethos of Shakespeare's times. From the very first line he is devising a plan to entrap Antonio, and most importantly we learn that his fortune is made by withholding money in a sense by the practice of usury. He is greedy, legalistic, clever schemer, lacking in compassion in short a "devil" (1.3.96; 22.19) or 'the very devil incarnation" (2.2.25) who secretly loathes the Christians he lends money to—"I hate him for he is a Christian" (1.3.24) Shylock the Jew introduced the "pound of flesh" penalty in the loan agreement with Antonio, the Christian merchant. The condition laid by him points to some evil trick as he declares, "If it will feed nothing else it will feed my revenge." (3.1.36) In the trial scene he rejects the New Testament notion of forgiveness and condemns himself by rejecting God's mercy. Juxtaposed to him are the Christians-Antonio, Bassanio and Portia who are presented as paragons of virtue, examples and personification of the ideals of their religion.

The vengefulness of Shylock who lacks the religious grace to comprehend mercy is contrasted with the generosity of Antonio and the Duke. The Duke grants him pardon without being asked, Antonio gives up his share of Shylock's wealth and to redeem himself he is asked to convert to Christianity. H.B. Charlton asserts that going according to the current sensibilities of his time Shakespeare "planned a Merchant of Venice to let the Jew dog have it." Thus, in the Elizabethan times, *The Merchant of Venice* celebrated the superiority of the civilized races and reinforced the cultural and racial hierarchies of his times. As Ania Loomba says, "Shakespeare was made to perform such ideological work both by interpreting his plays in highly conservative ways (so that they are seen as endorsing existing social, gender and other hierarchies, never as questioning or destabilizing them) and by constructing him as one of the best if not 'the best' writer in the whole world. He became, "during the colonial period, the quintessence of Englishness and a measure of humanity itself."

Though it is difficult to perceive Shylock as being exempted of the stereotypical aspects of his negative character, but Shakespeare succeeds in establishing the first seed of humanity within his character. Shylock questions and resists the dominant culture of the English which constructs him as "other" and denies him a fully human status. Shakespeare reveals a great sympathy for Shylock making him the victim of "Otherness." In Act 1 Scene 3 Shylock makes an aside where he justifies his hatred for Antonio because "he hates our sacred nation, and he rails, Even there where merchants most do congregate, On me, my bargains, and my well-worn thrift." Here Shylock reminds us that his own religion is as sacred to him as Christianity is to Antonio and his friends. Shylock in another major speech "cite scripture" about the biblical story of Jacob and Laban as the justification for the practice of charging interests on loan. He actually negates his image of an evildoer and regards himself as a legitimate businessman. Yet in another powerful quote he complains about the way Antonio the Christian treated him:

> You called me misbeliever, cut throat dog, and spat upon my Jewish Gabardine (Act, 1 Scene 3, 24-25)

> He hath disgraced me and hindered me half a million, laughed at my losses mocked at my gains, scorned my nation, thwarted my bargains, cooked my friends, heated my enemies—and what is his reason? I am a Jew. (Act 3, Sc. 1, 52-55)

Shylock is actually pointing out that he is marginalized, becoming a laughing stock because he does not belong there. He is a victim of unprovoked prejudice. He has been termed as a 'dog,' a 'cur,' 'damned inexorable dog,' 'misbeliever' 'hound' having 'currish spirit,' 'his desires are wolfish, bloody, starved and ravenous' and an "alien." All through the play there is the cacophony of these racial insults being bandied about among all the Christian characters in the play. He is unmasking the unreasoning prejudice against the Jews and satirizing the Christian hypocrisy. By exposing the cruel treatment meted out to him, Shylock fortifies his stereotypical image of a "miser" and "mammon worshipper" and his practice of usury as a means of survival in the otherwise hostile world. Being expected to follow the rules of a "Christian," he behaves in a completely different manner, refusing to do as he is supposed to. He is angry at the slurs and he seeks to enhance his differences by being cruel. It can be seen that rather than being a result of his nature and personality, his actions are actually due to being disparaged—"The villainy you teach me I will execute, and it shall go hard but I will better the instruction. (3.1.55)

Deconstructing Christian Humanism

The response by Shylock to Jessica due to her actions portrays the fact that he is deeply human, which can be seen when Salerio and Salanio purposely mention Jessica's elopement. It is one of the most eloquent speeches in Shakespeare- humanizing Shylock and giving voice to his anguish and pain. He represents the entire race of Jews in particular and the marginalized in general.

> Hath not a Jew eyes? Hath not a Jew hands, organs, dimensions, senses, affections, passions? fed with the same food, hurt with the same weapons, subject to the same diseases , healed by the same means warmed and cooled by the same winter and summer, as a Christian is ? If you prick us, do we not bleed? If you tickle us, do we not die? Do we not laugh? If you poison us, we do not die? And if you wrong us, shall we not revenge? If we are like you in the rest,

> we will resemble you in that. If a Jew wrong a Christian what is his humility? Revenge. If a Christian wrong a Jew, what should his sufferance be by Christian example? Why, revenge. The villainy you teach me, I will execute, and it shall go hard but I will better the instruction.

With these words he begins arguing, expressing that he deserves to be given a respectable position, or at least be treated as an equal. Shylock's speech is no more than a wholesome desire firstly to be accepted as human being and secondly, to bring about a truly inclusive view of humanity which would include the "others" despite their differences. I find it pertinent to state that rather than reading this play as an evidence of the superiority of English culture, anti-colonial Indians quoted Shylock's speech in support of their right to freedom and equality. Echoing Shylock they asked whether Indians too were not human beings with right to freedom and equality. This speech of Shylock in this post Holocaust world has been recited with relish by Jewish actors. This has made *The Merchant of Venice* "the most popular play in Israel." Thus the play becomes a symbol of non-English/non-European/non-White/non-Christian people's heroic resistance to colonialism and its apparent civilizing mission.

Since Shylock exists within the Christian paradigm, his battle is a losing one and Mark Van Doren says Shylock, "is a man thrust into a world bound not to endure him, "yet he does not give up. Despite all the pleadings from Antonio's friend, Portia and the Duke, Shylock remains stubborn. He says: "by our holy Sabbath have I sworn to have the due and forfeit of my bond" (IV, 1, 36-38)

The intensity that can be seen in his speech, raises Shylock's character to that of being humanized. This is followed by a speech that can be regarded as greatly cogent and powerful, discerning his argument for his bond:

> What judgment shall I dread, doing no wrong? You have among you many a purchased slave, which like your asses and your dogs and

> mules, you use in abject and in slavish parts because you bought them . . . so do I answer you: the pound of flesh which I demand of him Is dearly bought; [tis] mine and I will have it. If you deny me, fie upon your law: there is no force in the decrees of Venice. Stand for judgment. Answer: shall I have it? (IV, 1, 90-104)

Shylock very shrewdly indicts the Christian hypocrisy of justifying the maltreatment of their own slaves because they have purchased them and denying him the bond, which he too bought dearly on the ground that he is making an inhuman demand. Portia in the courtroom defeats Shylock by a legal trick. Shylock is left destitute and compelled to convert. There can be seen no mercy for Jews in the play which Portia has proclaimed as being so glorious "that (it) falleth as the gentle rain"- which she had imposed upon Shylock to be shown for Antonio. Ironically by the end of the play Shylock the Jew is cast as an alien to Venice who will be aptly punished for instigating violence against "citizens" although earlier he has been acknowledged as a part of its wealth generating citizenry. Shylock in the end is defeated but at the same time is graceful and does not bow down to his victimizers. Shakespeare puts a mantle of dignity on him at the moment of defeat. He does not plead for mercy. He is not willing to become a Christian as he knows that this is not an invitation to assimilate but a way of asserting social power. Commenting on this ending a critic says, "the Christians are embarrassed and they know that the will not easily get rid of this Jew. . . . Shylock goes- but he will always come back." This is perhaps the truth as no society can ward off the 'foreigners' since the division between the self and its others has become blurred. Shylocks are members of society which has to come to terms with its prejudices.

Conclusion

Thus, Shakespeare exposes the Christians' false standard of friendship, love and so-called mercy. He is critical of the corrupt moral and ethical value system of his society. England of his time had embarked on the process of global explorations and expansions and he was critical of the anxieties and intolerance of his people toward the outsiders-blacks, Jews and others. Indeed, Shakespeare had made a remarkable statement by making Shylock what M.C. Bradbrook says, "fully human and symbolic or larger than human." In order to understand the importance of this, it is important to discern the historical and literary context, referring to the fact that the representation of Jews was done through negative guises. Ngugi wa Thiong'O expresses his views regarding Shakespeare saying that the ability to be critical of his own history along with culture shows his true greatness. According to Thiong'O, Shakespeare's most witty and effective arguments relate to the England during his time. Shakespeare is a great writer, not because he is 'one more English gift to the world alongside the Bible and the needle' but because he discerned to problems and issues pertaining to the time that he lived in and was able to effectively translate them in the form of literature, that still remains relevant in the present times. We today judging Shylock from post-colonial post-Holocaust perspective undoubtedly put more stress on the human side of Shylock than an Elizabethan audience did. The play today could not be read or presented without taking into consideration that there is more to Shylock than a mere comic villain.

Works Cited

Bailey, A. "Shylock and the slaves: owing and owning in *The Merchant of Venice*." *Shakespeare Quarterly,* vol. 5.66. (2011).

Barton, A. *The Merchant of Venice*. Boston: Houghton Mifflin, 1974.

Bradbrook, M.C. *Shakespeare and Elizabethan Poetry: A Study of His Earlier Work in Relation to the Poetry of the Time.* London: Chatto and Windus, 1951.

Charlton, H.B. *Shakespearean Comedy*. Oxfordshire: Routledge Kegan Paul, 1966.

Loomba, Ania. *Shakespeare, Race and Colonialism*. Oxford: Oxford University Press, 2002.

Marlowe, C. & T.W. In Craik. *The Jew of Malta*. London: Benn, 1966.

Pfister, M. *The Theory and Analysis of Drama*. Cambridge University Press, 1991.

Shakespeare, William. *The Merchant of Venice*. England: Longman, 1994.

Wertheim, A. "The Treatment of Shylock and thematic integrity in *The Merchant of Venice*." *Shakespeare Studies*, Vol. 6.75 (1970).

Yu, J. "A holistic defense for Shylock in *The Merchant of Venice*." *World Journal of Social Science*, 2.2 (2015). wjss.sciedupress.com

Postcolonial Feminist Poetry in India: A Pleasant Protest!

POONAM DWIVEDI
Panjab University Constituent College, Dharamkot, Punjab

The question has often been raised as to the stand of postmodernism towards postcolonialism. Going by their origin in history, we find that both saw the light of the day almost concurrently. Postcolonialism basically refuted the legitimacy of colonialism and wished to repair the damage done by the latter to native history and culture. To believe that postcolonialism only vitiates the aesthetic by politicizing it and postmodernism aestheticizes the political, as a critic (Bryden 137) opined is to misread the difference. The fact is that postmodernism winks at the politicization but so far as postcolonialism is concerned, it brings a sharper focus on the political. That, in fact, was its basic function and approach and that is why the postcolonialists went about re-writing history that was corrupted by the colonialists.

Now, when we debate the woman issue, we find a lot of difference. Postcolonialism stood for the suppressed native and later, it enlarged its vision to include the suppression of women in societies, whether colonized or not, and that was definitely a valid and desirable approach. Postmodernism, On the other hand, Postmodernism despite its theoretical debates about the construction of gender and seemingly taking a non-essentialist stand, has been practically more concerned about the LGBT communities and minorities on the bases of religion, caste, region, etc. That too is welcome, but the status of women has lost the criticality it had under postcolonialism.

One has to remind oneself of the actual position of women in the postmodern globalized (read corporatized) culture of the 21st century. It is still riveted to objectification of women. While discussing the emerging genre of corporate fiction in the first two decades of the present century—our postmodern age—a critic rightly observes: "So far as the women are concerned, they are still seen as objects of desire, what with stress on immaculate dressing in modern attire, acquiring latest gadgets and cars and going abroad without so much as a murmur on the advances of male bosses" (Batra 56). That is postmodernity, the practical aspect of postmodernism for you!

Predicament of Women in India

India is said to have got its independence by the tryst of destiny had half of its population comprising females i.e., young, old and children called progeny of the motherland. But independent India's fair sex poses a question "Am I independent even after the declaration of independence?" The quest for identity has been lit large after independence on the face of every women born in free India. To quote Simon de Beauvoir, a great French Feminist writer and author of *The Second Sex:* "One is not born, but rather becomes, a woman." You are a 'girl;' you have to follow do's and don'ts of the family and society. You have to remain in protective custody of the male members right from your birth till death. Kamla Das suffered this problem which has become a symbolic representation in our literature especially in the poem "An Introduction" she talks about her identity; she tries to find her true self:

> Dress in sarees, be girl
> Be wife, they said. Be embroiderer; be cook,
> Be a quarreler with servants. Fit in. Oh,
> Belong, cried the categorizers. Don't sit
> On walls or peep in through our lace-draped windows.
> Be Amy; or be Kamla. Or, better
> Still, be Madhavikutty. It is time to

> Choose a name, a role. Don't play pretending games.
> Don't play at schizophrenia or be a
> Nympho. Don't cry embarrassingly loud when
> Jilted in love . . . I met a man, loved him. Call
> Him not by any name, he is every man
> Who wants a woman, just as I am every
> Woman who seeks love. In him . . . the hungry haste
> Of rivers, in me . . . the oceans' tireless
> Waiting. (*Poemhunter* 14)

The thought of any society is fathomed from the turbulent sea of its emotions especially the fine-tuned, feeble voices, the suppressed and depressed meanings, the silent cravings as portrayed and picturized these days in a film *Lipstick under the Burqa*. If a hue and cry is raised in the name of a lipstick and attire in independent India, what more could we expect from postcolonial India's poetry. The emotions are mirrored of the contemporary poetry of a particular time in its poetics. Meera, the Hindi saint poet, portrays the contemporary times and the restrictions imposed on the princess (herself, when she was unmarried) and then on the queen (when she got married), how the princess and queen steered through all the odds of her times, is amply reflected in her poetry and devotional songs. The sentimental environment finds its mention in the poetry. Colonial poetry, whether during the Muslim rule or the British one, especially the female voices were of protest against the shackled Bharat Mata and the female conscience was revolting against the subjugated motherland. But Post-colonialism has left behind the poetic protest of Sarojini Naidu and the ilk behind to form its own caravan of fiery female poets like Kamla Das, Nandini Sahu, Toru Dutt and others who were more concerned with the inviolable human body especially of women. Sarojini Naidu was finding her contentment in "Awake!"

> Waken, O mother! Thy children implore thee,
> Who kneel in thy presence to serve and adore thee!

Reflective poetry shuttles between two worlds—the external and internal. If the poet reflects on her surroundings and wishes are expressed rhythmically, the poet dances to the tune of the surroundings and contemporary scenario. But if the poet finds inner to be too strong to mesmerize her soul and it is reflected in poetics, it is more or less an exercise in sublimity.

Liberty and Equality

Liberty and equality are the two edges of a sword with which the women fight their battle. But I will admit that this two-edged sword becomes the weapon of suppression and subjugation in the hands of female tormentors themselves. The man acts through the woman to subjugate the fair sex. The abortions are not done in vacuum and it is a harsh reality, sometimes forced and at other times coaxed by another female called mother-in law. Of course, sometimes it is voluntary. In any case, the infanticide is done by the woman herself. She is instrumental in infanticide, foeticide and female suicide.

Postcolonial poetry has a vast mass of poetry on foeticide which is a new phenomenon around the world. The problem of foeticide is found in our society only where the quest for male child leads us to abortions on a massive scale. Hence the poetry lodges its pleasant protest without hurting the murders and the conspirators. There is no denial of the fact that either the civilizations had governance patriarchy or matriarchy, but both the systems had their own shortcomings. We have seen matriarchy of the Pandavas and at the same time we have seen patriarchy of the Bhishmapitamaha, the grandsire, to get progeny from a Maharishi, Ved Vyas, out of the two queens and a slave-maid. The extremism in both the cases jolts the liberty and equality of womanhood because the victim is the woman; she is the instrument, she is the earth to produce a human crop- she is called *Pritha* from *prithvi*, i.e., earth.

When a woman outsmarts the persona of her times, the husbandry is looked down upon, to be considered a parasite, a second-rate citizen of an alien land. The spirit of authoritarianism, despotism and feudalism is lit large on the faces of the females of that times who wielded power- may be a queen in the palace or bandit queen in the Chambal hideout—both are armed with unquestionable command. History repeats itself and history never repeats itself also—a great paradox. The follies are repeated a hundred times, the virtues never find opportunities of being repeated! This debate would never end as history is often twisted and used to meet the parochial ends of justification.

But the female renaissance arrived only after independence to jolt the consciousness amongst the suppressed fair sex. The protest poetry writing is a new genre of our times. Whatever a woman feels, smells, speaks and writes becomes amplified in the books, social media and TV channel debates. The age-old social controls and sanctions are being loosened to have flight of fancy and fantasy irrespective of any gender discrimination. Sometimes, the imagination goes wild and the woman finds herself in wilderness. The divorce rate is increasing and it has become a routine in the society just to walk out of matrimony at the drop of a hat. The so-called sanctimonious marriage solemnized in heaven and performed on earth has been replaced with the marriage of convenience!

Fashion and make-up with descriptive beauty has lagged behind. The romantic dramas, encounters and tales of the romance have been buried in the pages of history. The intellectual exuberance and exercises of social reformation has taken birth in the thematic of postcolonial poetry. The quest for justice and gender dignity and economic empowerment has seen woman trooping out of the four walls of the houses and leaving behind hearth and needle of 18th century England and 19th century India. The demand for more and more representation in all sorts of avenues has the basic philosophy of liberation at its base. The economic empowerment has emboldened the womenfolk to manage their own affairs and to rear their offspring in their own style. The lineage has changed and men have no option except to accept, appreciate and to reluctantly guide the deluge of grouse let loose by the emotional outpour, which had been contained and suppressed for centuries.

The liberated and affluent families have produced authors like Nayantara Sahgal, who came to play the role of a guide, friend and philosopher to the aspiring multitudes in waiting. Conversely comes the case of persona of Kamla Das and her clan to outpour their sentiments. The diaspora comprising women of letters has its own tales of struggles and strives. But the writings of women writers, more or less, has protest against the gender discrimination and a challenge to the authority perpetuated over centuries in the name of patriarchy. The tell-tale signs of struggles, torture, depravity and all sorts of naked realities have their own flavour, but poetry penned by the feminists is aspirational, nostalgic and emotive-evocative as I say in my poem:

> Am I free from fear of survival?
> Am I not facing onslaughts of denial?
> Am I not customized to be a slave?
> Am I not domesticated to behave? ("Feminine Fragrance")

All segments of the society do protest in one way or the other. Children have their voices of protest registered through the feminist women only. The children literature is written mostly by the women in the postcolonial India. The old people have their own literature but their literature is authored by the time-tested poets of protest who either turned spiritual at the end of the struggle or gave way to the onslaughts of the labyrinth, that is life. The compartmentalized literature has now been abridged in journals of the genre especially devoted to these segments, but the specialized literature perishes after sometime as it is cloned and created to serve a purpose.

Conclusion

The only surviving and struggling literature with futuristic hopes and fantasies is feminine literature which craves for indulgence by all the sections of society—who want to have the support of the husband, laughter of the children and soothing advice of the old grandsires, a gossip of the neighborhood. A true amalgamation of the society living in peace, prosperity and piety may be the last chapter of my Feminine Fragrance- an anthology of poems which are smeared in protest, spearhead a revolution and evolve as humanistic being of universality. I shall conclude with the following lines from my poem which sum up the pent-up emotions of every woman:

> Should we, the women of the world
> let our wrath loose,
> On the half population
> Who proclaim to adore us
> Should we succumb to the
> lewd advances of hunt? ("Am I Independent")

The above stanza has a contrast to the poem 'Suicide' written by Kamla Das in her gush of emotions soaked in saddened and exhausted dilemma of body-soul conflict:

> Bereft of soul
> My body shall be bare.
> Bereft of the body
> My soul shall be bare.
> Which would you rather have
> O, kind sea?
> Which is the more dead
> Of the two? (Kamla Das, "Suicide")

The state of desperation and despondence has to be avoided with the women empowerment, and it is a continuous process with a feeling of well-being which is attained by gaining access to the recourses and autonomous authority. There are various abilities which empower a woman like taking one's own decisions which becomes a challenge. If Jane Austen was shy of writing a novel, if *Rape of the Lock* was written to portray the society of that time, similar conditions are prevalent in our postcolonial society. The instances of 'instant divorce' have rocked the postcolonial sentiments of womanhood in India. The domestic violence has to be recognized as a malady and the government has to pass several laws to curb gender discrimination. Education provides wings to the fancy and fantasy of a woman and she can assert herself, can have access to information and resources can explore options and gain confidence to bring in a change.

The process of liberation is as painful as the child birth. But it is a pain worth enduring because the test of freedom has life giving properties. Paulo Freire says, "Freedom is acquired by conquest, not by gift. It must be pursued constantly and responsibly. Freedom is not an ideal location outside of man; nor is it an idea which becomes myth. It is rather indispensable condition for the quest for human completion" (Freire). Let women of the world unite to 'partake' half of the pie, let us not 'overtake' the whole fiefdom of the patriarchy and die!

Works Cited

Batra, Jagdish. *Indian English Fiction (2001-2020): History and Reflections*. New Delhi: Atlantic, 2021.

Beauvoir, Simon de. The Second Sex. New York: Vintage eBooks, 1949. https://uberty.org>uploads>01/09

Brydon, Diana. *Postcolonialism: Critical Concepts in Literary and Cultural Studies.* London: Routledge, 2000.

Das, Kamla. "An Introduction." CV 12:46, p. 14. www.poem hunter.com

Naidu, Sarojini. "Awake." www.poetrynook.com> awake-9

Dwivedi, Poonam. "Feminine Fragrance," *Feminine Fragrance & Other Poems.*

Das, Kamla. "Suicide." https://www.poemhunter.com>

Freire, Paulo. "Pedagogy of the Oppressed: 30th Anniversary Edition." New York: Bloomsbury, 2000. www.goodreads.com>quotes

Postscript: A Note on Postmodernism from the Indian Perspective

JAGDISH BATRA
O.P. Jindal Global University, Sonipat

As is the norm in our universities, the contributors of this anthology have mostly gone by the principles and concepts of Postmodernism and other related western theories. There is a substantial corpus of Indian classical poetics and aesthetics that does not normally come into play but it should inform our understanding of literature—western or eastern. The Orientalist approach of the western litterateurs was evident during colonial times. The postcolonial critics flagged it rightly but the real postcolonial tendency would not stop at that. The postmodern message of centralizing the marginalized and providing an egalitarian platform to all ideas and epistemologies makes it mandatory for us not to overlook the ones which have been suppressed or ignored thus far.

The fact is that modernism or postmodernism are not totally alien to India. Talking about the physical conditions, although some scholars find the simultaneous existence of tradition, modernism and postmodernism here, yet these different categories can be subsumed under postmodernism because theoretically speaking, postmodernism does not brook any boundaries. For that matter, India can be called a "postmodern mélange—a kind of chaotic combination that the postmodernists would celebrate rather than be nervous about trying to find orderliness" (Batra 166). However, more than the material situation, the ideological background is important. In this context, we see that the Indian literature of yore, i.e., Vedic and classical Sanskrit texts have outlined philosophies comprehending all aspects of human existence.

Human mind dabbles in thoughts of all types. Over millennia, the corpus of Indian classical literature grew exponentially (according to one estimate, there are more than one lakh Sanskrit manuscripts extant presently), so it could not have forsaken all those stirrings of mind. We must remind ourselves that Saussure, the forebear of Structuralism that led to poststructuralism and became the foundation of postmodern thought, was teaching Sanskrit at Geneva and was fully conversant with the theory of language in Sanskrit texts. The various Orientalist scholars, viz., R.T.H. Griffith, Rudolph von Roth, Stevenson, Max Mueller et al, who translated various texts into European languages or produced lexicons did open up this treasure to the western world. Scholars admit that the concept of Structuralism was taken by Saussure from Panini's Sanskrit grammar text *Astadhyayi*. (Staal 357). Not only this, there are a number of Indian inventions that were appropriated by the West, re-named, re-packaged under their own brand name. Well-known Indologist Jeffrey Armstrong (Kavindra Rishi) points out that "Indian knowledge was appropriated and with minor changes declared its own by western scholars. ("Indian inventions").

Theoretically, the instability of sign informs poststructuralism and the negation of absolute truth is the cornerstone of postmodernism. The postmodern approach leads to so many "truths" and the resultant being unmanageable, uncipherable and incomprehensible according to the western epistemology is found to be chaotic. This chaos or disorder may trouble the western mind which is prone to thinking in linear and logical manner, and aspires to create order. But for Indians, chaos is something with which one has to live. If we cast our glance away from the manicured lawns and cities to nature, we find chaotic features in the form of jungles, planes, mountains, deserts, etc. with or without wild growth, but at the same time, there is great order in the rising of the sun and revolution of the earth and so on. Our ancient texts reflect this viewpoint. According to the renowned scholar Rajiv Malhotra, chaos is writ large and is actually entrenched in the Vedas, the Puranas and Hinduism in general for a reason and "its role is to counterbalance and dilute any absolutist tendencies as well as provide creative dynamism through ambiguity and uncertainty" (Malhotra 175). Absolutism is, thus, not favoured in Indian thought as in postmodernism.

And yet, the Indian viewpoint locates unity in this diversity because the differences are seen outside only; the innermost self being part of divinity that is same for everyone. Indian mind can comprehend contradictory concepts but it does not mean wallowing in disorder because the perfect order and equanimity too exist alongside. The dual nature of the universe cannot be wished away; this is how the world has been created with all its binaries as stipulated in the different variants of the philosophy of *Dvaitvaad* (dualism). The *devas* (gods) representing good and the *asuras* (demons) representing evil have to exist side by side. But it does not mean there is no conflict between them. In fact, conflict is always there and there is no final decimation of evil. Evil exists to give a fillip to the good which comes out victorious until evil rises again—a kind of dialectic process. The perennial conflict, thus, has a positive fallout. The beautiful parallel of deva-asura (gods-demons) cooperation in churning the ocean deserves mention here for its underlining of "cooperative rivalry" to attain bliss in human life, deva and asura being symbols of contrary tendencies within human mind: "Their mutual tension does not get resolved with one side defeating the other, and their stalemate produces all sorts of wondrous and beneficial objects before open conflict breaks out over questions of priority in partaking of the nectar of immortality. Significantly, nectar is produced only after a port of poison emerges from the ocean—demonstrating yet again the interdependence between good and bad" (Malhotra 184).

Coming to the play of postmodern tendencies in literature, we must admit that to make sense of this world and to transmute experience of it in a pleasant form in literature is the primary concern of every litterateur. For one, Indian poetics is riveted mainly to the aesthetic aspect and lays down the stylistic principles of literature in great detail. There is sizeable corpus available at present that deals with *dhwani, riti, alankar* etc. which enable the reader to enjoy literary *rasa* or aesthetic pleasure in an empathetic manner. Elements like irony, wit, parody, language use, etc. are well defined in Indian poetics. There is no doubt that in modern western literature, a lot of experimentation in respect of style and narratology has taken place and the modern Indian literature in various languages has gained from it. There has also been a gainful exchange between the Indian and western literature in some areas.

Style is like a garment as the general definition goes, but the content is what matters most. When we talk about the thematic part, we find the single most guiding star in Indian poetics is dharma which is the guide to lead life righteously in this world. It enjoins certain discipline; draws a certain *laxman rekha* besides showing the right path to an individual as also to society. The nature of dharma is two-fold: It can be malleable—it changes with *desh* (geographical location), *kaal* (time) and *patra* (person) even as there is also the *samanya* dharma or the general dharma that stands for righteousness and is to be observed by all. Interestingly, there is no single scripture or authority that lays down the minute contours of the path to be taken for the uplift of human spirit. All that these sources provide is to train the mind so that it can choose its own path towards enlightenment. The enlightened ones form their own dharma because they have transcended the worldly injunctions and discipline and are free from them. They live at a different—elevated, spiritual plane. They can very well interpret righteousness which for ordinary people is to be gleaned from different scriptures or leant from the gurus.

Dharma denotes duties of different people from a commoner to the king. It is a societal construct that lays down duties according to one's *asram* (stage of life—student, householder, ascetic or sanyasi), *varna* or *jati* which was originally profession-based but got clubbed with birth over time (Saraswati 77-78), etc. Dharma also provides bulwark and finetunes the actions of humans to attain various goals of life as denoted through the four *purusharthas*: *Dharmarth kaam mokshanaam.* The ultimate goal is *moksha* or liberation from the birth-death-birth cycle and attainment of affinity or oneness with the Supreme—depending on the interpretation of Vedas which one believes. The concept of moksha may not appeal to atheists who follow the Charvak philosophy, very much a part of Indian philosophical corpus. Their efforts cease with the first three *purusharthas*. Buddhists and Jains don't believe in God but they too believe in achieving a state of quintessential peaceful existence that is free from the sufferings of endless lives. The actions of litterateurs are also directed to help humans in this process of self-actualization, through helping the reader of the text or the viewer of the drama get trained in the dharmic way of life, and that will be possible when the litterateur rises above prejudices and follows the course of truth.

The very concept of dharma might look like postmodern chaos with contradictory constituents of the permanent and the temporal, of its varied applicability, of its validation by more than one source, etc. But there is a vital difference. While dharma helps man in a positive manner to choose the right path, the western postmodern viewpoint evokes negativity. An example of this negative approach can be found in the latest postmodern movement of Woke-ism which started as a call for Black activism in America but has now degenerated into the worst form of nihilism negating all norms—be it the familial hierarchy, marital allegiance, sexual difference, relationships, social equilibrium, political structures, cultural parameters and so on. Accepted notions of equality and democracy, motherhood and womanism are also under fire from this cult which believes in bullying and violence rather than cooperation and bonhomie. (Sharan).

Coming to some other postmodern tendencies viewed from the Indian lens, we find that like dharma, there are many concepts and philosophies which need to be understood differently from the western interpretation. If we view nation as taken up in the West, then India would appear to be a conglomerate of so many nationalities. Postmodernists lay stress on diversity of the external type and look for fragmented units. This postmodernist underlining of fragmentation has had a strong appeal for some Indian intellectuals immersed neck-deep in western academic ideologies. But the diversity of culture that is stressed is of external kind only located in food, dress, language, lifestyle, customs, etc. It is the intrinsic unity of culture based on commonality of roots in ancient history, philosophy of life and traditions that conjoins all Indians while the unity of the divine spirit present in all humans unites the entire mankind on this earth. Numberless narratives from our past emphasize this unity in diversity.

The epic Mahabharata is virtually a sea of stories. No wonder that the Indian English authors have taken full advantage of this rich repository and told the world many a story. Retellings have become a lucrative business. But there is a catch here. In order to sell more and make a fast buck, the writers bend over backward to contaminate the narratives and present to the vast readership in the West, corrupted and titillating tales dipped in exotic hues. This is something that smacks of Orientalist approach and has been noted by many scholars. Lau & Dwivedi, for example, have dubbed such a tendency as Re-Orientalism in their book *Re-orientalism and Indian Writing in English*. This approach, at best' is also submitting meekly to the postmodern dictum that "the past must be visited, but with irony" (Berry 88) that is taken as a commandment!

Some of the retellings have also been inspired by theories like feminism that holds a sway currently. Now, feminism all over the world need not and should not be stereotyped, particularly in a postmodern scenario. But the problem with these theories is also that these are applied in a straitjacketed and limited manner, without taking into account other factors that might be relevant. For example, questions are normally raised about the character of Ram for expelling Sita because one of his subjects—a washerman—had cast aspersions on Sita's character as she had been in Ravan's captivity. Feminists have therefore attacked Ram's image of a *maryadapurushottam* (Icon of just action). The entire episode needs to be viewed in a broader context, which will make us realize that Ram was riven between his duty towards his wife and his kingdom. As a king, he placed Raj Dharma (the dharma of the king/state) above personal or familial dharma. Nobody can dispute the fact that he loved his wife dearly. After sending his wife to the jungle, he did not marry—something that a king could very well do in those times; his own father had three wives. If Sita suffered as a dutiful wife, Ram too did not find solace in separation.

In the Indian scheme of things, the social is preferred to individual good which is diametrically opposite to the western bias towards individualism. The episode holds a lesson for the politicians of all ages, particularly of our time when the politicians do, whatever they can, to serve their own ends. All norms of public morality are thrown to the wind by them and public opinion is scoffed at, unlike Ram's reaction to a commoner's comment. He definitely did not believe in what the dhobi said, but going by the current moral discourse, he bowed to it. Though an avatar of lord Vishnu, he was in human form and underwent all that a human being is subjected to on this earth. That is why he is called *maryada purushottam*.

This is also a fact that sometimes we do injustice to historical characters by not applying historical criticism, and let us not forget that in the Indian tradition, Ramayana and Mahabharat are called *itihas*, though the message that these revered epics hold are timeless. That is because the ancient Indian hysterography laid stress on the moral lesson to be learnt from history. There are contemporary retellings which deal with the subject in a better way like the retellings of these myths by Devdutt Pattanaik, a mythologist of repute. In his retelling titled *Sita: An Illustrated Retelling of the Ramayana*, and also in a short book *The Ramayana: The Girl Who Chose,* Pattanaik presents Sita as a powerful woman who had a great role in making Ram a god, besides noting five choices made by Sita which show her sagacity and agency.

There is a lot in ancient culture that can make us understand the Indian notion of feminism, that is, providing equal status to women with men. The concept of *ardhnarishwar* underscores the complementarity of male and female. It is our colonial mindset that values an Amazon over Durga! The Indian family system with its signature sentimental attachment and with the woman at the core as the conveyor of culture cannot and need not be recast as per the tenets of western feminism which itself has failed to satisfy the womenfolk there. We must tackle the women question in our own way and progress, though slow, is happening. We tend to forget that in modern times, we saw a large number of women participating in the freedom struggle hand-in-hand with men, whether it was Gandhian Satyagraha or Subhash Bose's Indian National Army. Post-independence, politics has come to hold the key to all power and with the positive legislation in place, we see a large number of women occupying political positions starting from Gram Panchayat to the Parliament, and that shows women gaining power that could change their status in society in a big way.

The Postmodernists claim to stand for the marginalized; "claim" because the soft corner for the MNCs-led globalization and the imposition of western norms on lifestyles in the developing world does not support this assertion. However, taking the postmodern concern in the right spirit, we assert that moral indignation at the inhuman treatment of sections of Indian society is quite justified. The have-nots, destitute and the people tagged "Dalit" deserve a better deal. Casteism in Indian society is a big blot that needs to be effaced at the earliest. This is against the principle of equality which lies at the root of our spiritual thought.

The ancient text by sage Manu, called *Manusmriti* and Tulsidas's *Ramacharitmanas* have been attacked for the anti-women and anti-Sudra content. It is selective culling of a verse or two and so, the attempt becomes political rather than academic. Swami Dayanand Saraswati, founder of the Arya Samaj, opined in his scholarly work *Satyartha Prakash* that the *varna* system of the ancient time was basically profession-based and not birth-based which was a later aberration and in support of this assertion, he has quoted from the *Manusmriti* itself.[1] There is also a view that the *varna* system, to which the modern castes trace their origin, did not impute any hierarchy. This element was propagated during the British colonial rule. Lord Herbert Risley (1851-1911), a civil servant who held the charge of 1901 census, was behind inserting hierarchy in the caste structure which created discrimination. ("Did British").

In their brilliant book *Breaking India*, Rajiv Malhotra and Aravindan Neelakandan point out that while Max Mueller applied the term "Aryan" based on the Sanskrit word "arya" [meaning "noble"] to a group of languages and the people speaking it, later the colonial administrators cast it in the mould of race just as Risely turned jati and varna of Indian tradition into race—which is what the western mind was accustomed to in their culture. Further, the writers have also shown that the British rulers created "imaginary histories and racial myths" to propagate the Aryan-Dravid theory of antagonism in line with their policy of 'divide and rule.' Risley's funny theory based on measurement of nose to nominate a race was deservedly scoffed at by B.R. Ambedkar, the author of Indian constitution, in the following words:

> The measurements establish that the Brahmins and the Untouchables belong to the same race. From this it follows that if the Brahmins are Aryans, the Untouchables are also Aryans. If the Brahmins

> are Dravidians, the Untouchables are also Dravidians. If the Brahmins are Nagas, the Untouchables are also Nagas. Such being the facts, the theory . . . must be said to be based on a false foundation" (Malhotra and Neelakandan 60).

The DNA sampling procedure with its linkage to Risley's infamous 'nose-index' has been widely disputed as also the Aryan theory. (Malhotra & Neelakandan 425-30). The problem with regard to the Dalit movement in India is that vested foreign interests are encouraging fissiparous tendencies even now with a particular agenda which is not compassion for the downtrodden but an attempt to create divisions in society and seek balkanization of the country.

As for the *Ramcharitmanas* by Tulsidas, a few verses that show disrespect to women ought to be disapproved, being anachronistic for our times, but because of these lines, dumping the entire epic would be throwing baby with the bathwater. Tulsidas lived during the Mughal rule when Indians suffered humiliation, discrimination and oppression as also large-scale forcible conversions. *Ramcharitmanas* written at that time provided solace to the oppressed Hindus and kept them united; so did the entire Bhakti movement. The book is still revered as a holy text and recited in Hindu households because it relates the story of Lord Ram in a language that is widely understood in contrast with the Valmiki *Ramayana* written in Sanskrit, which however, is the most ancient, hallowed ur-text written by someone whose name proudly signifies a section of the Hindu community now. Indeed, *Ramcharitmanas* is a cultural icon and condemning lock, stock and barrel our spiritual texts on the basis of a minor part will be akin to asking a western postmodernist to shun Bible because it mentions that in the beginning, a male named Adam was created and then from one of his ribs, the female Eve was created (Holy Bible, Genesis 2.21-23).

The writing of history has been challenged in our times, and rightly so because the historians mingled fiction with it. Secondly, the postcolonialists rightly condemned the colonizers for corrupting the history of the colonized nations. Without taking up this backdrop in detail, we find that the fictionists of our time consider it their right to make a foray into history. Now, writing historical fiction in a truthful manner may appear paradoxical. It does serve good purpose when official history is found to be prejudiced or there are empty spaces to be filled up. From the Indian standpoint, truth is the highest value. While the postmodernists have declared these times as the 'post-truth' era because the search for truth is found to be problematic, Indian thought stipulates that one's conscience is the adjudicator in a situation when one faces dilemma and cannot get clear guidance from scriptures or gurus. But the conscience will guide only a person of *sattvik* (austere and noble) nature, not the one hankering after office or Mammon. So, when a litterateur ventures to re-write history, he has to bear in mind the great responsibility that comes with it, and serve the cause of truth only. We believe that truth always wins (*satyamev jayate*) and it is the touchstone for creativity or criticality in all domains—whether the litterateur or the critic wishes to explore the individual or the social, the inner desires of an individual or the collective problems of the world, like terror or environmental degradation. Herein lies the difference between western approach and the Indian one.

Another scenario that we see is the postmodern fear of the unknown. Science has developed much like Mary Shelley's Frankenstein developed the monster. So, our journeys into deep space bring specters of invasions by aliens which find depiction in the new age movies and even children's games, along with the ever-increasing dystopian literature with its own multiple tales of horror and nightmare. This can be taken as an admission of the failure of postmodernism to bring a semblance of assurance to humankind. Indian viewpoint supports cyclical order of creation and destruction and the immortality of soul as it keeps on changing body after each death. And in each lifespan, the soul achieves a better state as the result of noble karma or gets degraded due to evil actions. That, put simply, provides hope for the doers of good deeds and discourages doers of bad deeds—so much desirable for a happy and progressive society. It also provides stability and assurance to human mind as opposed to the western concept of linear development with death meaning end to the single life.

With this kind of writing on the wall, the individual feels lonely, what with the western insistence on individualism and the valorization of individual identity. Together, mankind may muster enough courage to face the uncertain catastrophes like the Corona virus epidemic. For this, we need to sublimate individual aspirations to common good. Sadly, the process of globalization stresses a commonality of culture based on external homogenization brought about by consumerism and propelled by the MNCs. India believes in homogenization achieved not through commercial globalization but through real sentiment of globalism based on the spiritual unity of mankind. And that will be possible only when the world is taken not as a market but as one family: *vasudhaiva kutumbukam*.

NOTES

[1]Swami Dayanand Saraswati refers to the verse from *Manusmriti* in his book *Satyartha Prakash:*

> *Shudro brahmantameti brahmanashcaiti shudrataam/*
> *Kshastriyajjatmevantu vidyadwaishyantthaiv cha*. (10.65)

Swami explains the meaning: "One who happens to be born in a shudra clan but has the attributes and is inclined to act like a brahmin, kshatriya or vaishya, he will verily become brahmin, Kshatriya or Vaishya. Similarly, one born in a Brahmin, Kshatriya or Vaishya clan who has attributes and proclivities of action like a shudra, he will become a shudra.

Again, one born in Kshatriya or Vaishya clan but has affinity with brahman/ brahmani or shudra, s/he will become a brahman or shudra. That is in the four varnas, whichever person (male or female) has affinity with whichever varna, s/he will be counted among that very varna." (77 trns. mine)

Works Cited

Armstrong, Jeffrey. "Indian inventions shaped the modern world; were stolen by the West" *Vedic Vidya*, 24 June 2021. www.youtube.com/watch?v=EoerErmL-3c

Batra, Jagdish. "Postmodernism and India: Exploring Indian English Fiction." *The Commonwealth Review*, Vol. 25.2 (2018), 157-68.

Berry, Peter. *Beginning Theory*. New Delhi: Viva Books, 2010, 2013.

"Did British Create the Indian Caste System? Rajiv Malhotra on Breaking India at Warwick" *Infinity Foundation*, n.d. www.youtube.com/watch?v=FrTUp2mKbWs&t=182s

Holy Bible. The New King James Version. Madras: India Bible Literature, 1982.

Lau, Lisa and Om Prakash Dwivedi. *Re-Orientalism and Indian Writing in English*. Hampshire, UK: Palgrave Macmillan, 2014.

Malhotra, Rajiv & Aravindan Neelakandan. *Breaking India: Western Interventions in Dravidian and Dalit Faultlines*. 2011; New Delhi: Amaryllis, 2020.

Malhotra, Rajiv. *Being Different*. 2011; Noida: Harper Collins, 2018.

Pattanaik, Devdutt. *Sita: An Illustrated Retelling of the Ramayana*. Gurgaon: Penguin, 2013.

___. *The Girl Who Chose*. 2016; Gurgaon: Penguin Random, 2021.

Sharan, Shankar. "Vichitra Prakriti wala Baudhik Pakhand" *Daily Jagran*. 18 Nov. 2021. https://epaper.jagran.com/epaper/18-Nov-2021-4-Delhi-City-edition-Delhi-City-page-12.html

Saraswati, Swami Dayanand. Satyartha Prakash. Delhi: Dehati Pustak Bhandar, 1960.

Staal, Frits. "The science of language," *Blackwell Companion to Hinduism*, ed. Gavin Flood. London: Blackwell, 357-58

The Four Vedas: (22 volumes), Trans. Swami Satya Prakash Saraswati and Satyakam Vidyalankar. Delhi: D.A.V. Pub. Division, 2011.

Contributors

Abigail Fracia Lapang Sunn is a research scholar at North-Eastern Hill University, Shillong. Her ongoing research focusses on the fiction of famed Japanese Author, Haruki Murakami. Her article titled, "Surrealism, Women and Haruki Murakami: A Study of Narrative Perspectives" was published in *Literaria.* She currently resides in Shillong with her family.

Abhinaba Chatterjee holds a Master's degree in English Literature and Translation Studies from Calcutta University and Annamalai University respectively, and an M.Phil. from Delhi University. He has published extensively on various fields of English literature including Shakespeare, Indian Writing in English and postcolonial theory. He has presented papers in many national and international seminars, both in India and abroad. He is presently pursuing doctoral research on Absurd Drama.

Aarti Duhan is a Ph.D. research scholar at SRM University, Delhi NCR. She completed her M.A. English and B.A. English (Hons.) from Tika Ram Girls College, Sonipat. She is a Gold Medalist at UG level. Currently, she is pursuing her Ph.D. on "Individual vs. Social in Mahesh Dattani's Plays."

Achebe S. is a doctoral research scholar at IIT Kharagpur. He completed his Master's degree in English Literature from Mahatma Gandhi University and M.Phil. from Amrita Vishwa Vidyapeetham. His areas of research concern gender and autobiography. Apart from this, he is interested in working on the intersection of various theories.

Antara Biswas completed her graduation and master's in English with a specialization in African and Caribbean Literature from Rabindra Bharati University, Kolkata. Currently, she is a doctoral student at Indian Institute of Technology, Roorkee. Her research areas include Gender Studies, Tattoo Culture and Feminist Criminology. Her research focuses on the representation of tattooed women in fiction.

Dr. Aparna Ajith did her Ph.D. from the Central University of Rajasthan. As a freelance journalist, she writes and translates articles for the Information and Public Relations Department, Government of Kerala. She has presented papers at national and international conferences and published in journals and edited anthologies and ezines. A winner of the Panorama Global Youth Literary Award 2020, she recently published a collection of poems entitled *Musings of Venus*.

Aparna Bhatt completed Masters in English Literature from Delhi University and also cleared NET LS. She worked as an Assistant Professor (Guest) at her alma mater and also taught at Maitreyi College, University of Delhi. She is a budding poet who uses both Hindi and English to give voice to her soul. She has self-published a collection of poems titled *Dil Ki Kalam Se* (2020) and is currently working on her next collection of verses.

Dr. Bimlesh K. Singh is Associate Professor & Head, Dept. of English, Mahatma Gandhi Central University of Bihar. He has special interest in Drama Studies, Comparative Literature and Postmodern Literature. He has supervised five Ph.D. and 50 M.Phil. dissertations, presented 25+ research papers at national and international conferences, published 20 research papers and five books.

Guhan Priyadharshan P. is a doctoral research scholar at the Indian Institute of Technology Kharagpur. He completed his Master's degree in English and Comparative Literature at Pondicherry University. His research interests include critical theory, continental philosophy, postcolonial, postmodern and queer studies.

Dr. Jagdish Batra, Professor of English and former Head, English Language Centre at O.P. Jindal Global University, is keenly interested in Indian English Fiction and Culture Studies. He has guided 50+ research scholars, published 60+ research papers, ten books besides presiding over conferences in India, Europe, and South-East Asia. A former Rotary International Scholar to USA, he has received many awards including the University Research Excellence Awards 2020 and 2021.

Jay Kumar is a Research Scholar at Mahatma Gandhi Central University, Mothihari. Twice he qualified NET in English. A poet and blogger, he has presented papers in seminars sponsored by UGC and National University of Educational Planning & Administration, New Delhi. He has also published poems in an anthology titled *The Flying Poetics*.

Lalthanzami is from Mizoram and currently a Research Scholar in University Institute of Liberal Arts and Humanities, Chandigarh University, Mohali. Her area of research is Cultural Studies.

Mahima Kashyap is pursuing her research from Mahatma Gandhi Central University, Motihari and is the editor of the departmental bimonthly newsletter, *Harmony*. Earlier, she served as a Guest Faculty in the Department of English and as an Editorial assistant for the University journal of social sciences. She takes keen interest in academic activities and creative writing and has published research papers and book chapters.

Dr. Mekhala Venkatesh is Head, English Department, Research Coordinator, School of Humanities & Social Sciences at Jain University, Bengaluru. She has teaching experience of 23 years. Dr. Venkatsh has many research publications to her credit and is a recipient of Kuvempu Bhasha Bharathi Puraskaara.

Dr. Neelam Yadav works at Delhi College of Arts & Commerce, University of Delhi. She did her Ph.D. on "On Going on an Indian Journey: Changing Perspectives in the Travelogues of Ajneya, William Dalrymple, Nirmal Verma and V.S. Naipaul." Her areas of interest include Travel Writing, Women Studies and African-American literature. She has published many articles and book chapters on themes like travel writing, Gender Sensitization etc.

Dr. Poonam Dwivedi teaches at Panjab University Constituent College, Dharamkot (Moga), Punjab. She is Associate editor of *Contemporary Vibes* and co-edits various research journals. She has presented papers at national and international conferences, published 35+ research papers and two collections of poems, viz., *The Confluence & Other Poems* and *Feminine Fragrance & Other Poems;* two books of criticism *A Critical Handbook of English Fiction* and *Modern Critical Thought: Aristotelian Méthodos*.

Pratibha Nehra is a Ph.D. scholar in the Department of English and Cultural studies at Panjab University, Chandigarh, specializing in Postcolonial theory, Cultural studies and Gender studies. She is also a member of the international non-profit organization *Students for Liberty*.

Dr. Prerna Srivastava is Assistant Professor, School of General Education, Bhartiya Skill Development University, Jaipur. Her Ph.D. is on "Negotiation of Contemporary Culture in the Selected Plays of Mahesh Dattani." She has published 13 research papers in journals and conference proceedings. She has more than ten years' experience, and has expertise in soft skills training, counselling and grooming students.

Dr. Priyanka Lamba is Associate Professor, Department of English, Dronacharya Govt. College, Gurugram. Besides, she is Dean, Student Welfare and professor-in-charge of Women Studies and Development Cell. She topped in graduate and postgraduate exams and has eighteen years of teaching experience. Her areas of interest are Women Studies, Postcolonial Studies and Folk Literature.

R. Jaya Pratha, Assistant Professor of English, V.V. Vanniaperumal College for Women, Virudhunagar, is also studying as a Research Scholar. She has qualified NTA NET . She has presented papers at international, national, state-level and institutional forums. She is also a soft-skills trainer, and has delivered talks.

Rajiv Malhotra is acclaimed author of several books on current affairs and cross-cultural encounters between the East and the West. He has worked as a senior corporate executive and a successful entrepreneur in the fields of information technology and media industries in USA for some 40 years. He founded The Infinity Foundation through which he has been fostering a better global understanding of Indian civilization.

Dr. Rashmi Gaur is Professor, Department of Humanities and Social Sciences, Indian Institute of Technology, Roorkee. She has authored multiple books and published papers in national and international journals. Her research work and publications address Professional Communication, Culture and Gender theories, and Feminism in Indian Writing.

Dr. S. Chitra is Assistant Professor of English, Yonphula Centenary College, Royal University of Bhutan. Earlier, she worked as H.O.D. in different colleges affiliated to Madras University. She has two decades of teaching experience. Her areas of interest include Culture Studies, Contemporary Literature, Gender Studies, Bhutanese Folklore. She has delivered keynote addresses and conducted workshops. She has presented 80+ research papers at international and national conference and published over 50 research articles.

S. Smruthi is doing M.A. English from Stella Maris College, University of Madras. A bronze medalist in her undergraduate program from Amity University, Noida, she also writes poems.

Dr. Sangeetha Noval teaches English and has worked with various Universities. She did her first M.A. in Rehabilitation Science for the Handicapped from Holy Cross College, Tiruchirappalli. Subsequently, she did M.A. and Ph. D. in English from Jaipur National University. She has 17 years of teaching experience and is Associate Professor and Head, School of General Education, Bhartiya Skill Development University, Jaipur.

Serir Lina studied at Tlemcen University in Algeria. She did M.A. in literature and civilization and defended a master thesis entitled "Dystopian Intertextuality in Zamyatin's *We* and Atwood's *The Handmaid's Tale*." She plans to do further research on the genre of dystopia in literature, cinema, and art.

Dr. Smarika Pareek, Associate Professor, University Institute of Liberal Arts and Humanities, Chandigarh University, received her Doctorate Degree from the University of Rajasthan. Her research interests include postcolonial studies and comparative literature.

Umesh Patra, Assistant Professor in English, Mahatma Gandhi Central University, Motihari, worked on a comparative study of the Odia Pala and Bertolt Brecht's epic theatre for his Ph.D. at

EFLU, Hyderabad. His research areas include Theatre and Performance Studies, Modern British Literature, and Queer Theory.

Vinita Nair has headed departments of English in various schools across Mumbai and Bangalore. She got back to the classroom teaching with the International Baccalaureate Diploma Programme to pursue research in Interactive fiction. Presently, she is pursuing doctoral research at Jain University.

Dr. Violetta Trofimova worked on Aphra Behn's prose writings for her Ph.D. from St. Petersburg State University, Russia. She has published a hundred articles in Russian, English and French and two monographs in Russian on early modern women writers. She is also a novelist.